Explaining English Grammar

Also published in
Oxford Handbooks for Language Teachers

Explaining English Grammar

George Yule

Oxford University Press

OXFORD
UNIVERSITY PRESS

Great Clarendon Street, Oxford OX2 6DP

Oxford University Press is a department of the University of Oxford.
It furthers the University's objective of excellence in research, scholarship,
and education by publishing worldwide in

Oxford New York

Auckland Cape Town Dar es Salaam Hong Kong Karachi
Kuala Lumpur Madrid Melbourne Mexico City Nairobi
New Delhi Shanghai Taipei Toronto

With offices in

Argentina Austria Brazil Chile Czech Republic France Greece
Guatemala Hungary Italy Japan South Korea Poland Portugal
Singapore Switzerland Thailand Turkey Ukraine Vietnam

OXFORD and OXFORD ENGLISH are registered trade marks of
Oxford University Press in the UK and in certain other countries

© Oxford University Press

The moral rights of the author have been asserted

Database right Oxford University Press (maker)

First published 1998

2019 2018 2017

20

ISBN: 978 0 19 437172 8

Set in Adobe Garamond
Typeset by Oxford University Press

Printed in China

This book is printed on paper from certified and well-managed sources.

for Mary

CONTENTS

ACKNOWLEDGMENTS

I would like to acknowledge the advice and constructive criticism of many students over the years who suffered through earlier versions of this material and whose cries of anguish forced me to try to write a better book. Special thanks, for their words of encouragement, go to Hugh Buckingham, Suzy Byrd, Hae-Young Kim, Doris Macdonald, Terrie Mathis, Robyn Najar, Michele Trufant, Kate Wolfe-Quintero, and Ann Yule-Millar. For detailed and extremely helpful reviews of earlier drafts of this work, I would like to thank Maryann Overstreet, Elaine Tarone, Henry Widdowson, and the editors, especially Anne Conybeare, at Oxford University Press.

The publishers and author thank the following for their kind permission to reproduce extracts and adaptations from works for which they hold the copyright:

Addison Wesley Longman Ltd. for an extract from C. Candlin, D. Larsen-Freeman, and M. Long: *An Introduction To Second Language Acquisition Research* (1991)

Bantam Doubleday Dell for an extract from: *The White House Transcripts* (1974) edited by G. Gold

Paul H. Forestell and Greg Kaufman for an extract from their *Hawaii's Humpback Whales* (1994) published by Island Heritage Press

Harcourt Brace & Company and Random House UK Limited for an extract from Katherine Anne Porter: 'Rope' from FLOWERING JUDAS AND OTHER STORIES, published by Jonathan Cape, copyright 1930 and renewed 1958 by Katherine Anne Porter

Heinle & Heinle Publishers for extracts from D. Larsen-Freeman and M. Celce-Murcia: *The Grammar Book* (1983)

Roy Hinks for an extract from his poem 'Articles' which first appeared in *Country Life* (1979)

The International Linguistic Association for an extract from Ziqiang Shi: 'On the inherent aspectual properties of NPs, verbs, sentences...' from *Word* 41 (1990)

Edward Klein for extracts from Edward Klein: *Trump Family Values*. This article originally appeared in *Vanity Fair*

Newsweek for extracts from 'The Letter Man' (3 February 1997) © 1997, Newsweek, Inc., all rights reserved, reprinted by permission

Newsweek for extracts from L. Reibstein: *Whose Right Is It?* (20 February 1997) © 1997, Newsweek, Inc., all rights reserved

Oxford University Press for extracts from: *The Spectator* (1965), edited by D. Bond

Oxford University Press for an extract from P. Green and K. Hecht: 'Implicit and explicit grammar: an empirical study' (1992) which appeared in *Applied Linguistics* 13

Prentice Hall Europe for extracts from D. Nunan: *Language Teaching Methodology* (1991)

Random House, Inc. for an extract from Ross Macdonald: *The Underground Man* (1971) published by Alfred A. Knopf Inc.

Rhoda Weyr Agency, New York and William Morrow & Co., Inc. for extracts from Deborah Tannen PhD: THAT'S NOT WHAT I MEANT Copyright © 1986 by Deborah Tannen, PhD

Sage Publications Inc., for extracts from R. Craig, and K. Tracy: *Conversational Coherence* (1983)

Teachers of English to Speakers of Other Languages, Inc. for extracts from K. Bardovi-Harlig and D.W. Reynolds: 'The role of lexical aspect in the acquisition of tense and grammatical aspect' (1995) *TESOL Quarterly* 29, 107–31. Copyright 1995 extracts from pp. 124 and 130 used with permission

Waveland Press, Inc. for extracts from David Yaukey: *Demography: The Study of Human Population Inc.*, 1985, reissued 1990, all rights reserved

PREFACE

This book has its origins in my attempts at responses, over the past fifteen years, to requests from learners and teachers of English for explanations concerning English grammar. The more I was required to explain, the more I found myself reading and thinking about the questions, and the more experienced I became at offering answers. This doesn't mean that the answers are necessarily or absolutely correct. They have turned out to be, for the most part, pedagogically useful answers. By this description, I mean that learners and teachers have been able to use the information offered in the following chapters as a way of thinking and talking about how the grammar of English works and what it is for. This approach provides answers to *why*-questions. The grammar is viewed as a set of constructions in which differences in form can be explained in terms of differences in conceptual meaning or interpretation in context. The framework of analysis is one in which form, meaning, and use are seen as interconnected aspects of what it is language users know when they know a grammatical construction.

The material reflects its pedagogical origins. The topics covered are those that give rise to the most *why*-questions. They are the most problematic areas of the grammar. Consequently, this isn't a comprehensive treatment of the type to be found in a standard reference grammar of English. It is a pedagogically oriented grammar. It is organized in such a way that the chapters can be read individually or in a different sequence from the one presented. The sequence presented is the one that I have come to use and reflects the fact that certain basic concepts seem to be more easily illustrated in the early chapters and some connections seem to flow better from one topic to another in the sequence presented here.

Each chapter begins with a description and exemplification of the basic forms and structures. In describing these forms and presenting information on the frequency of one form rather than another, I have benefited a great deal from the published results of many different corpus studies of contemporary English. These studies have provided a much clearer picture of where and how often a particular grammatical form is actually used in texts and hence how likely we are to encounter it. More information on those studies can be found in the references included in the Further reading section at the end of every chapter.

Following the description of basic forms, each chapter moves on to cover basic meaning distinctions conveyed by particular forms and structures. In this type of analysis, I have been helped by published research in semantics, the study of meaning. From a semantic perspective, each grammatical construction can be viewed as a regular and conventionally recognized means of expressing conceptual meaning. This discussion of conceptual meaning establishes connections between language structures and the representation of situations, with participants and actions, in the organization of experience. Additional information on this topic can also be found in the references in the Further reading sections.

After basic forms and basic meanings, each chapter includes a section on how meaning can be shaped by context and communicative purpose. In preparing this section of each chapter, I have included a lot of insights from studies in pragmatics and discourse analysis. For many people, pragmatics is the study of a speaker's (or writer's) meaning in context and that perspective is often invoked in the explanations of structures offered here. Work in discourse analysis has also helped us understand how structures are typically used in the presentation of information in text, both spoken and written. Throughout this book, the effects of information structure are often presented as a way of explaining choices of grammatical structures in texts. References to relevant studies in these areas are also included in the Further reading sections.

Within this general organization of each chapter, specific problem areas of different kinds are identified and explanations offered. After each major section, the main points are presented in summary boxes, followed by exercises on those points. Answers to these exercises are offered in an appendix. At the end of each chapter, there is one section containing discussion topics and projects for further investigation, and another section offering teaching ideas for classroom exercises, activities, and tasks. The Further reading section concludes each chapter.

Whether used as a coursebook, a self-study text, or supplementary reading, this material will, I hope, prove to have some value as a resource, or simply as a useful companion, for those learners and teachers who are prompted to ask why certain aspects of English grammar are the way they are. But mostly I hope they will realize that Explaining English Grammar isn't as difficult as it sounds.

1 INTRODUCTION

1 Which is correct: *Mary runs faster than I* or *Mary runs faster than me*?

2 We can say *a woman* and *her*, but what about **a her*? Why is it ungrammatical?

3 How can we explain why it's odd when learners say: *I am boring today*?

4 If *I shot the sheriff* is okay, what's wrong with **I smiled the sheriff*?

5 How do we explain the problems in **Lady go supermarket meet friend*?

'The greater part of this world's troubles are due to questions of grammar.'

The author of these words, Michel de Montaigne, was not an English language teacher, but he sounds like he's describing one of those difficult teaching days. While we will not solve any of the world's troubles in the chapters that follow, we will attempt to offer explanations for some of the major problem areas of English grammar. In this introductory chapter, we consider some basic terms and topics.

Overview

After briefly reviewing some basic grammatical terminology, such as NOUN, NOUN PHRASE, and PRONOUN, we try to define the nature of UNGRAMMATICAL English and contrast PRESCRIPTIVE with DESCRIPTIVE views of the language. We then look at some basic meaning distinctions, explaining the connection between terms such as SUBJECT, OBJECT, AGENT, THEME, SOURCE, and EXPERIENCER. The distinction between CORE and PERIPHERAL ELEMENTS of a message is illustrated, as is the relationship between LINGUISTIC DISTANCE and CONCEPTUAL DISTANCE in English. We then look at some distinctions associated with information structure, illustrating the role of GIVEN and NEW INFORMATION in accounting for the different expressions (e.g. *a woman, the woman, she*) used to talk about the same person. This first chapter has also been designed to exemplify the general type and sequence of topics that will be presented in the chapters that follow.

Basic forms

At the beginning of each chapter, there is a description of the basic forms being analyzed. In those descriptions, a general familiarity is assumed with many traditional terms for grammatical concepts. That is, terms such as SENTENCE (S), VERB (V), and NOUN (N), will be illustrated and used without technical discussion. There are, however, some terms that may need an introduction.

On terminology

A distinction is drawn between a NOUN (N) and a NOUN PHRASE (NP). Essentially, the term noun is reserved for single words. The forms shown in [1] are all nouns.

[1]   book, example, man, tradition, woman

In speaking or writing English, however, we rarely use nouns by themselves. We use them in phrases. When we add an ARTICLE (e.g. *a* or *the*) to the noun, we create a noun phrase. When ADJECTIVES (e.g. *good, old*) are included, we also have noun phrases. The forms in [2] are all noun phrases.

[2]   the book, some good examples, an old man, that tradition,
       a woman

Given this distinction, we can then see that a PRONOUN (e.g. *it, he, her, them*) is not a form that normally substitutes for a noun. We don't typically use the expressions in [3b] to refer to the same things in [3a].

[3]   a. In *the book*, there was *an old man* and *a woman*.
       b. *At the start of *the it*, *the old he* was helping *the her*.
       c. At the start of *it*, *he* was helping *her*.

As shown in [3c], we use the pronouns by themselves in place of the whole noun phrase. A pronoun in English is used in the same way as a noun phrase. Relative pronouns such as *who* and *which*, as we will see in Chapter 9, are also used as noun phrases. In discussing other important terms, such as subject and agent, we will be talking about the use of noun phrases rather than just nouns.

On being ungrammatical

The star symbol, or asterisk (*), which is placed in front of the sentence in [3b], is a conventional way of marking forms as UNGRAMMATICAL. (Such forms are sometimes described as 'starred'.) This symbol will be used in the following chapters to indicate that we are treating a form or structure, as used in that context, as not grammatically acceptable. In other contexts, these seemingly ungrammatical forms may be used in a meaningful way. The star symbol will only be used here to mean 'ungrammatical in the context indicated'. In this approach, a noun phrase such as *a her* is basically treated as an ungrammatical form in most contexts (such as [3b]) where the reference is equivalent to *a woman*, even though it is possible to hear someone say *When I heard the name Charlie, I was expecting a him and not a her* in one particular context.

To take another example, the basic form of the sentence presented in [4] would normally be treated as ungrammatical.

    [4]   *She is in stay.

If asked to explain why [4] is ungrammatical, we might say that, in terms of basic forms, *stay* is a verb, and here it has been put in a slot that is mostly reserved for nouns or noun phrases. That is, in the grammar of English, we normally have nouns, not verbs, in phrases after PREPOSITIONS (e.g. *in, on, at*). Putting a verb in a slot that is reserved for a noun or noun phrase will usually create an ungrammatical structure. The explanation, in terms of grammatical form, is relatively simple.

However, I have heard someone use the sentence shown in [4] and it sounded quite appropriate and meaningful in the context. My friend has a dog that is very well trained and, when told to *stay* in one place, the dog (*she*) will not move from that place. My friend can then say [4] to explain why her dog is sitting quietly. So, there is a state called *stay* that this dog can be *in*. We often represent states by using nouns after prepositions (e.g. *She is in love*) and that seems to be what one speaker is doing when using [4] to talk about her dog. We will have more to say about being *in love* in Chapter 6.

Notice that it is the function of the form (i.e. whether it is being used as a verb or as a noun) that determines whether the structure in [4] seems grammatical or ungrammatical. If one form is generally used as a verb (as in the case of *stay*), we will naturally think that it is ungrammatical when used as a noun. Thus, 'being ungrammatical' is using forms and structures in ways that they are not generally used, and for which no special context of use can be imagined. For many people, however, any discussion of what is grammatical or ungrammatical seems to lead to the issue of whether a structure is really 'good English' or not.

On good English

The issue of what is, and is not, 'good English' is rarely addressed in this book. There will be observations on what sounds more typical (in a context), what is more formal, more stuffy, more casual, or more frequent, but we will avoid the issue of what is better (or even *more better*). In language use, the concept of 'better' really depends on values unrelated to an understanding of grammatical structures. Consider the following common example where one version of a structure is sometimes claimed to be better than another.

For one English speaker (let's call him Bert), it may be extremely important that an example such as [5a] should be treated as the only acceptable form and that a version such as [5b] should be unacceptable as good English.

> [5]   a. Mary can run faster than I.
>   b. Mary can run faster than me.

The issue here is the correct form of the pronoun (*I* or *me*). Bert may insist that what is expressed in [5] is a version of *Mary can run faster than I can run.* This full version shows that the pronoun (*I*) is the subject of *can run* and that *me* would not be grammatical in the structure (i.e. *me can run). Therefore, says Bert, [5b] is ungrammatical and bad English.

Another speaker (let's call him Ernie) might respond that *me* sounds just fine in [5b] and seems to be the form that most people use in this structure. Bert is presenting a PRESCRIPTIVE argument (i.e. how it should be used) and Ernie is offering a DESCRIPTIVE argument (i.e. how it generally seems to be used). This type of discussion may be what is often associated with the topic of English grammar, but there will be very little of it in this book. In a case like this, we will be more concerned with explaining how both structures can be used in English.

In the particular case of example [5], it is possible to provide a reasonable explanation for both structures. To do so, we should consider a related structure that English speakers use, as shown in [6].

> [6]   Mary can run faster than ten miles per hour.

Looking at example [6], we can see that the basis of Bert's explanation (i.e. **Mary can run faster than ten miles per hour can run*) is not appropriate here. The expression *ten miles per hour* is not the subject of *can run*, but an object following *than*. The word *than* seems to be used in [6], and also in [5b], as a preposition. After prepositions, English tends to have object pronouns (*me, him*) rather than subject pronouns (*I, he*). For Ernie, preferring [5b], the word *than* can be used as a preposition. However, for Bert, preferring [5a], the word *than* is being used as a CONJUNCTION, that is, a form that connects two clauses, and the pronoun *I* is the subject of the second clause. From this perspective, both Ernie and Bert are right. Grammatically speaking, neither form is better English than the other.

In the preceding discussion, we introduced another two technical terms, SUBJECT and OBJECT, that will be used in some of the following chapters. English pronouns provide the clearest distinction between subject forms (*he, she, we, they*) and object forms (*him, her, us, them*). In the most typical cases, the subject (e.g. *the woman, she*) comes before the verb, and the object (e.g. *the books, them*) comes after the verb, as shown in [7].

[7]   a.   The woman wanted the books.
       b.   She took them.

We will have more to say on the role of subjects and objects in the discussion of indirect objects in Chapter 7 and relative clauses in Chapter 9. This initial description only deals with the forms and positions of subjects and objects in English sentences. That is, we have only considered what they look like and where they go in sentences. To describe these categories further, we have to move on, as we will do in every chapter, to talk about meaning as well as form.

Basic meanings

When we try to explain the meaning of grammatical structures, we tend to use different concepts from those found in the description of basic forms. We talk about the situations or events described by sentences. Instead of verbs, we consider the types of actions or states represented by the verbs. We are also interested in the kinds of entities and concepts represented by nouns and noun phrases. We try to describe the roles of the entities as participants in the actions performed within those events.

In this way, we move from a purely STRUCTURAL DESCRIPTION of basic forms as sentences, nouns, and verbs, to a more FUNCTIONAL DESCRIPTION of what a speaker or writer is doing with those forms, as in referring to events, participants, and actions. In a structural description, we are basically concerned with listing all the forms in a language and being able to say whether a particular form is correct or incorrect. In a functional description, we are more concerned with what meaning distinction is conveyed by the use of one form rather than another. For example, instead of just talking about the sentence, noun, and verb in [8], we can interpret the utterance as representing a specific type of event.

[8]   Someone stole my bag.

In this event, there is a central action (*stole*), plus one role involving the 'doer of the action', or the AGENT (*someone*), and another role involving the 'thing affected by the action', or the THEME (*my bag*). We will talk about agents and actions more specifically in connection with aspect in Chapter 3, modals in Chapter 4, infinitives in Chapter 8, and relative pronouns in Chapter 9.

We can also note that the most typical events we describe involve a human agent performing a physical action that affects a non-human theme (as in [8]). That is, the distinction between HUMAN and NON-HUMAN also becomes relevant. We can go further and distinguish between ANIMATE non-human entities (e.g. animals) and NON-ANIMATE non-human entities (e.g. objects, ideas). These meaning categories can be useful in explaining a number of grammatical features of English, including indirect objects in Chapter 7 and relative clauses in Chapter 9.

Returning to the roles of entities, we can describe actions by non-humans that affect humans, as in [9b], but there is simply an observed general pattern in which events are mostly described with human agents acting as the source or cause of actions, as in [9a].

[9]   a. The girl threw the ball.
       b. It hit the runner.

This connection between the agent as the source entity and the theme as the affected entity may provide a useful basis for explaining one distinction that seems difficult for many learners of English.

'*I am more interesting in English grammar*'

There is a distinction in English between pairs of adjectives such as *boring / bored, exciting / excited,* and *shocking / shocked.* These forms are normally used as in examples [10a, b, and c], but many learners produce versions of the type shown in [10d and e].

[10]   a. The lesson was interesting.
        b. The teacher was amusing.
        c. The students were interested and amused.
        d. I didn't like the lesson. I was boring.
        e. I am more interesting in English grammar.

In examples such as [10d and e], learners may use the *-ing* form of the adjective (*boring, interesting*) when they actually mean the *-ed* form (*bored, interested*). But why, they may ask, can't they say, *I am boring today*? The answer is, of course, that they certainly can say that (it's grammatically correct), but is it what they mean? The meaning distinction is not too difficult to explain.

These adjectives are derived from verbs that express emotions or feelings. When we talk about an emotion, we can focus on the SOURCE (i.e. who or what causes it) or on the EXPERIENCER (i.e. who or what is affected by it). When you are talking about the source, you use the *-ing* form. If a book (or a lesson or a person) causes the emotion, then it is *boring, interesting,* or *exciting.* When you are talking about the experiencer, you use the *-ed* form. If people experience the emotion, then they are *bored, interested,* or *excited.* The cause is *boring,* the experiencer is *bored.*

As we will do throughout this book, we can take these observations and summarize them, as shown in Box 1.1. We can also use this opportunity to include a list (as a teaching resource) of several adjectives that have this meaning distinction.

Summary Box 1.1 **Adjectives like** *boring* **and** *bored*

Source or cause is *-ing*	Experiencer or affected is *-ed*
Things or people are:	People (mostly) are:
amazing, amusing, annoying,	*amazed, amused, annoyed,*
astonishing, bewildering,	*astonished, bewildered,*
boring, confusing, depressing,	*bored, confused, depressed,*
disappointing, disgusting,	*disappointed, disgusted,*
embarrassing, exciting,	*embarrassed, excited,*
exhausting, fascinating,	*exhausted, fascinated,*
frightening, horrifying,	*frightened, horrified,*
interesting, intriguing,	*interested, intrigued,*
irritating, puzzling, satisfying,	*irritated, puzzled, satisfied,*
shocking, surprising,	*shocked, surprised,*
terrifying, tiring, worrying	*terrified, tired, worried*

When learners make mistakes in trying to use the forms in Box 1.1, they tend to do so by overusing the *-ing* form. That is, we mostly don't have to devote energy to helping them learn how to say that things are *boring*. Given an opportunity to teach or focus learners' attention on these forms, the teacher might be able to give greater emphasis to the *-ed* forms, providing or inviting examples in contexts where participants are affected (emotionally) by events. In this way, our learners might become more accurate when they decide to tell us how *bored* (or *interested*) they are in our classes.

As will often happen throughout the following chapters, an exercise will be offered, typically following a Summary Box, as exemplified in Exercise 1.A. Suggested answers for all these exercises are provided at the end of the book.

In many of these exercises, as well as in illustrative examples within the main discussion, the sentences or texts have been created specifically to focus attention on a particular grammatical feature. Most of the examples are actually recalled or slightly modified versions of sentences and texts that were heard or read in the process of analyzing natural discourse. In some cases, particularly in the discussion topics, the texts are presented in a way that is very close to their original form in print or as transcribed from recorded speech. It is hoped that the added difficulty sometimes experienced in dealing with genuine texts will be balanced by the benefits of becoming more familiar with actual examples of grammatical constructions as they are used in contemporary English.

Exercise 1.A

Read through the following text, underlining all the adjectives expressing emotions. Then, try to identify the 'sources' or the 'experiencers' for each adjective in the spaces provided.

Yesterday was a school holiday. Of course, it rained all day, so my kids were really <u>bored</u>. I wanted to do some work at home, but they interrupted me every five minutes and just became too annoying. I am amazed and astonished that their teachers are not constantly exhausted. I was irritated after only one morning with them and was really worried about the afternoon. So, I gave up my work and asked the little monsters if they would be interested in a movie. They were thrilled. Unfortunately, we chose to go to a really boring film. After about twenty minutes, they stopped being excited and fell asleep. I wasn't disappointed at all.

e.g.   (bored) kids

1   _____

2   _____

3   _____

4   _____

5   _____

6   _____

7   _____

8   _____

9   _____

10   _____

11   _____

Why can I say 'I shot the sheriff', but not *'I smiled the sheriff'?

In the discussion so far, we have concentrated on the central elements of structure (subject, verb, object), typically representing the main components of events (agent, action, theme). By focusing on these CORE elements, we can identify aspects of the grammar that indicate what happened, who or what caused it, and who or what was affected by it. There are, however, other elements that have a more PERIPHERAL role in the description of events. In English, these elements are typically found in preposition phrases.

Within a structure that is formed by a preposition plus a noun phrase, the entity represented by the noun phrase will have the form of an object (e.g. *with him, near them*), but that entity will not be directly affected by the action of the verb. In many cases, the preposition phrase will provide information about the circumstances of an event, such as when (*at five o'clock, on Saturday*), where (*in the room, beside the window*), or how (*with a ruler, by bus*).

In other cases, the use of a preposition will clearly mark that a participant was not directly affected by the action of the event. For example, there is a distinct contrast in meaning between the (i) and (ii) sentences presented in [11].

[11] a. (i) She kicked the dog. (ii) She kicked at the dog.
      b. (i) I shot the sheriff. (ii) I shot at the sheriff.
      c. (i) *We looked the report. (ii) We looked at the report.
      d. (i) *He smiled the boy. (ii) He smiled at the boy.

If it is grammatical to both *kick something* and *kick at something*, why can't we *look something* as well as *look at something*? The answer may be found by thinking about the differences in meaning between *kick* and *kick at*. When you *kick* something, there is a direct impact of the verb action on the affected object (ouch!). When you *kick at* something, there is the same physical action (*kick*), but there is no impact on the object (missed!). We normally interpret *kick at* or *shoot at* as meaning that the object didn't get hit. The preposition *at*, in these examples, indicates that the object is not directly affected by the action of the verb. In English, the actions represented by *look*, or *smile*, are clearly not considered to have any direct physical impact on the object. That is, you can *look at something*, because the something is not directly affected, but you can't *look something*, because it would imply that there was a direct impact of your look on the object.

Generally speaking, objects of prepositions are interpreted as not being directly affected by the verb action, as illustrated with other prepositions in [12].

[12] a. (i) Mark flew the plane. (ii) Mark flew in the plane.
      b. (i) Mika rode a horse. (ii) Mika rode on a horse.

In [12], we interpret the subjects (*Mark, Mika*) as having much more control over the objects (*plane, horse*) in the (i) examples.

These observations on the meaning of objects with and without prepositions are summarized in Box 1.2. It should be emphasized that the interpretations presented here, as throughout this book, are not being offered as the only or the complete analysis of the possible meanings of the forms under investigation. It is a common experience in the study of grammatical meaning that, as we find a way to explain one aspect of the relationship between form and meaning, we often discover other aspects that require further investigation. There are more detailed discussions of the role of prepositions in Chapters 6, 7, and 9, with the 'not directly affected' concept being explored more fully in connection with indirect objects in Chapter 7.

Summary Box 1.2 **Objects after *kick* and *kick at***

Structure: Subject + verb (= physical action) + object

Meaning: Object is directly affected by action of verb

Examples: *The man kicked the box.*
    *He looked the money.

Structure: Subject + verb (= physical action) + preposition + object

Meaning: Object of preposition is not directly affected by action of verb

Examples: *The man kicked at the box.*
    He looked at the money.

Linguistic distance

As will be noted on several occasions in the following chapters, there is a frequent relationship in English between LINGUISTIC DISTANCE and CONCEPTUAL DISTANCE. Linguistic distance can simply be measured by the amount of language (number of words or syllables) between one element and another. There is more linguistic distance between *shot* and *sheriff* in the sentence *I shot at the sheriff* than in the sentence *I shot the sheriff.* The word *at* creates more linguistic distance. It also creates more conceptual distance in the sense that the action of the verb *shot* is more separated from (i.e. has less impact on) the object *sheriff.*

The additional linguistic distance between *flew* and *plane* created by the presence of *in* (example [12a]) is interpreted as more conceptual distance (i.e. less control) between the action of the subject and the object. As a general observation, the more linguistic distance there is between any elements in English sentence structure, the more conceptual distance there will be in our interpretation of their relationship. This phenomenon will be discussed again in Chapters 7, 8, and (more briefly) 9. It's time for another exercise.

Exercise 1.B

Using the following verb + object combinations, create sentences with and without *at*, and indicate (with *) which forms are ungrammatical.

e.g.   punch / arm

He punched my arm.
He punched at my arm.

1   drink / milk

2   hit / ball

3   kill / bug

4   point / picture

5   smile / baby

6   swat / fly

7   yell / students

Photocopiable © Oxford University Press

Meanings in context

After looking at basic forms and basic meanings in each chapter, we will also include some observations on how meaning is shaped by context. In particular, we will consider how grammatical forms are used in the INFORMATION STRUCTURE of communicative messages. As language users, we do not simply spend our time trying to create grammatically correct sentences. We are usually trying to organize what we want to say (i.e. information) in a way that is suitable for our listeners or readers. We can assume that our listeners are already familiar with certain information, whereas other information will be new. That is, there is NEW INFORMATION and old, or GIVEN INFORMATION, in what we communicate. Different grammatical forms are associated with these different types of information.

When we noted earlier, in examples [2] and [3], that a noun phrase could consist of a pronoun (*him*) or an article plus noun (*a man*), or an article plus an adjective plus a noun (*the old man*), we said nothing about the preferred uses of one of these forms rather than another. Yet, there are preferences.

In example [13], the speaker is telling a story based on a set of drawings (presented later as Figure 1.1). All the noun phrases are in italics.

[13]   There's *a woman* in *a supermarket.*
She meets *a friend* with *a small child.*

> *They* stop and chat.
> Then *the child* takes *a bottle* from *the shelf*
> and puts *it* in *the first woman's bag*.

As each entity is introduced for the first time (i.e. new information), the speaker in [13] uses noun phrases with *a*, the INDEFINITE ARTICLE (e.g. *a woman, a supermarket, a friend, a small child, a bottle*). When an entity is mentioned again (i.e. given information), the speaker uses pronouns (e.g. *she, they, it*) or noun phrases with *the*, the DEFINITE ARTICLE (e.g. *the child, the first woman*). We should also note that the speaker can indicate an action without explicitly mentioning the agent, that is, by using a ZERO FORM (represented by ø). In [13], the two verbs *chat* and *puts* have no obvious subjects. Their subjects can be represented by ø as in [14].

[14]   a.   They stop and ø chat.
       b.   the child takes a bottle ... and ø puts it ...

This use of a zero form clearly represents given information, in the sense that the listener is assumed to know the subjects of these verbs. We can note that the zero form seems to be preferred when there are two actions in sequence and the subject is the same for both verbs. The subject of the second verb is assumed to be known. That is, the zero form is used when the referent (who or what we're talking about) is highly predictable.

When the referent is less predictable, but certainly given information, pronouns are used. Although they are brief forms, English pronouns remind us that the referent (among those we already know) is female (*she*) or plural (*they*) or neuter (*it*). That is, pronouns carry more grammatical information than zero forms, and tend to be used when an entity has become the main focus of attention.

Noun phrases with *the* (e.g. *the child*) carry even more information and are used to establish a known entity as the focus of attention. That is, after having the woman and her friend (*they*) as the focus of attention, the speaker in line 4 of extract [13] establishes a different focus of attention with *the child*. If there is a possibility of confusion among the known referents, then an adjective is often included, as in *the first woman*. If a referent can be inferred on the basis of assumed knowledge, then a noun phrase with *the*, exemplified by *the shelf* in [13], can be used. For this speaker, having mentioned *a supermarket*, there is no need to announce that 'supermarkets have shelves', as if it is new information. This is treated as inferrable given information, but clearly not so predictable that a pronoun could be used. We shall consider more examples of this phenomenon in Chapter 2, in the discussion of articles. Pronouns, as typically conveying given information, are also relevant to the analysis of certain phrasal verbs in Chapter 6 and relative clauses in Chapter 9.

From this brief description, we can see that speakers and writers organize the information structure of their messages on the basis of predicting how familiar the listener or reader will be, at any point, with what is the focus of attention. It is important to emphasize that this analysis reflects the speaker's or writer's perspective concerning information status and the focus of attention. We will return to the concept of speaker's perspective in the analysis of tense and aspect (Chapter 3), modals (Chapter 4), conditionals (Chapter 5), and reported speech (Chapter 10). Some basic clues to the speaker's perspective, as reflected in the choice of English noun phrases, are offered in Summary Box 1.3.

Summary Box 1.3 **Choosing *a woman, the woman, she,* or zero (ø): the speaker's perspective**

Least predictable information

New information

Indefinite article plus noun   *a woman*

Given information

(a) Establishing focus of attention
    (if more than one possibility)
    Definite article + adjective + noun   *the first woman*
    (if only one possibility)
    Definite article + noun   *the woman*

(b) Existing focus of attention
    Pronoun   *she*

(c) In sequence of actions
    Zero form   *stop and ø chat*

Most predictable information

Although a consideration of information structure was not traditionally part of grammar teaching, it does provide a useful way of thinking about certain features of English that are difficult for some learners. For example, in trying to describe the same drawings as the speaker of [13], one English language learner began his version as shown in [15].

> [15] Lady go supermarket meet friend and talk—
>   boy in cart taking bottle.

This learner clearly knows appropriate vocabulary, but is producing ungrammatical English. He might appreciate some help in recognizing, perhaps via naturally comparable examples such as [13], that markers of information structure are expected in English discourse. A first step might be some attention to the use of articles in English. That will be our topic in Chapter 2.

Exercise 1.C

The following description of the scenes in Figure 1.1 (on page 19) is by an adult English language learner from the Philippines. First, read over the description and underline the noun phrases. Then, answer the questions below.

the lady go to a supermarket

she want to buy something

she meet—met another lady with a little boy

they are talking—when they were talking

the two ladies they were talking

the little boy a juice maybe I don't know

the little boy put the bottle

which took from shelf into the bag of the lady

1   List the noun phrases with indefinite articles.

2   Would you say that these are appropriate grammatical uses in English? Yes or no?

3   Identify a noun phrase with a definite article that would be more appropriate with an indefinite article.

4   List the pronouns used to identify people.

5   Would you say that these are appropriate grammatical uses in English? Yes or no?

6   Find an example of a zero form used as subject of a verb.

7   Is this a typical grammatical slot for a zero form in English? Yes or no?

8   Find an example of a noun without an article.

9   Is this a typical grammatical slot to find a noun without an article in English? Yes or no?

10   What change might you suggest in the form of the final noun phrase (to help identify the appropriate referent)?

Discussion topics and projects

At the end of every chapter, there are some topics for discussion, or projects for research, that invite further investigation of the grammatical structures considered. These investigations may involve aspects of second language acquisition or the study of English for specific purposes. In many cases, these projects invite speculation or studies on issues that have no established solutions or answers.

1   The topic of grammatical rules, and how they should be stated, is one that continues to challenge almost everyone who tries to teach English grammar. Here is one opinion:

> Since there is no way of establishing a 'best' rule for any particular set of language phenomena, and our understanding of linguistic structure and of psycholinguistic processes is not such as to influence the formulation of pedagogical rules other than indirectly, there are sound reasons, both practical and theoretical, for learners and teachers to assume a cautious, if not skeptical, attitude towards any pedagogical treatment of language regularities. (Westney 1994: 72–73)

(a) Is this author suggesting that we should act as if there are no rules? Would you agree or disagree with that idea?

(b) Why do you think the author used the expression 'language regularities'? Is there a possible distinction to be made between 'regularities' and 'rules'?

(c) If possible, read the rest of Paul Westney's article and try to summarize the main points of this issue, along with your own reaction to the debate.

2   We can usually learn a lot about learners' use of grammatical structures by conducting some simple research projects. Here is one possibility. Ask one English language learner to look at the drawings in Figure 1.1 and then to tell the story of what happened (as an eyewitness), including an ending. Record the student's spoken version. Then, after chatting with the learner briefly about some other topic, ask him or her to perform a second task. This time ask the student to produce a written version of the same story.

After transcribing the spoken version, compare the use of noun phrases in both versions. What differences are noticeable? Is the learner more grammatical in one version? If possible, try to share your observations with the learner later.

Other options include a comparison between performances of the same task by a lower and a higher proficiency speaker, between the performance of one learner in English and (later) in his or her first language, or between one learner who gets a chance to prepare before speaking and another who does not. After completing any study of this type, try to think of the implications for our teaching practices.

Teaching ideas

At the end of every chapter, there are some ideas for teachers to help them think of exercises and activities for class. These are simply offered as a way of getting started and should be adapted or revised (or rejected) according to the needs of each local situation.

1 Sandy is now a woman

A traditional exercise for focusing on different forms of noun phrases involves changing the status of the main character(s) in a story. For example, a common change is from male to female in order to focus students' attention on different pronouns. (Students from a number of different first language backgrounds have a lot of trouble with *he* and *she*.) In the following example, the text is first read for comprehension. Then, students can be asked to revise it because Sandy is now known to be a woman.

> Police are looking for someone known only as Sandy. On Friday morning a man walked into a New York bank. He was wearing a black jacket and cap. Customers who saw him said he had a thin face and he looked about twenty. The man said he had a gun and demanded money. As he was running out, the alarm went off and surprised him and his cap fell off. Inside his cap, the name 'Sandy' was written.

2 The same old *boring* TV programs

With some groups of students, it will be possible to use an exercise on the *boring/bored* distinction like the one presented on pages 8–9 as Exercise 1.A. In most textbooks, however, this distinction is more typically presented in different kinds of fill-in-the-blank exercises. After a set of possible choices (see Box 1.1 on page 19) has been discussed, students can be asked to complete exercises of the type in (a) or (b).

(a) Choose only six of the following words to complete the text.

boring embarrassing satisfying surprising tiring worrying
bored embarrassed satisfied surprised tired worried

> The news was _____. Usually people are _____ with the same old _____ TV programs, but one man got so _____ of them that he threw his TV set out of a window. Obviously, he wasn't very _____ about his downstairs neighbors or even _____ about the loud crash.

(b) In each of the following sentences, use both the *-ing* and *-ed* forms of the word provided.

    (i) (*interest*) When the lesson is _____ , students will be _____ .

    (ii) (*bore*) But many students will be _____ if the teacher is _____ .

    (iii) (*excite*) Some movies are so _____ that kids can get very _____ .

    (iv) (*exhaust*) We got really _____ because the work was so _____ .

    (v) (*frighten*) The explosion was _____ . People were very _____ .

Note. After an exercise like this, it is helpful to focus students' attention back on the meaning distinction, with questions that essentially ask 'Who (or what) is the cause?' and 'Who (or what) is the experiencer?' for each example.

3 Don't shout *at* Superhero

As a way of raising students' awareness of the role of *at* in verbs like *look at*, the following exercise may be useful.

Step 1. Begin with some common mistakes such as:

    *He is looking us   *Don't shout me   *She's laughing you*

Some students may be able to volunteer, or the teacher may have to offer, better versions (including *at*) of these forms.

Step 2. Introduce the following short text about Superhero (with a local name perhaps) who is being attacked, as usual, by the bad guys. This text is for comprehension, either in spoken or written form.

    It's another tough day for Superhero.
    The bad guys shout at him.
    One of them kicks at him.
    Another stabs at him.
    Another punches at him.
    But none of them can hit Superhero.

(If the teacher doesn't want to, some students may be willing to demonstrate the meanings of the verbs here. But only the *at* versions!)

Step 3. Discussion point: Is there a mistake in the last line? Didn't they *kick*, *stab*, and *punch* Superhero, but they didn't *hit* him? How can that be? This discussion is directed towards establishing the distinction between *kick* and *kick at*.

Step 4. State (or restate) the distinction between uses of *kick* (= direct effect on object) and *kick at* (= no direct effect on object). Then ask students to decide if *at* is appropriate in any of these sentences:

(i)   He looked ___ the bottle of Pepsi.
(ii)   Then, he drank ___ it.
(iii) She laughed ___ the funny shape of the cookie.
(iv)   But she ate ___ it anyway.

Perhaps the students can explain their decisions.

Step 5. Ask students to create sentences to describe another day in the life of Superhero using the following verbs: *frown, scream, smile, wave, wink, yell.*

4 Eyewitness accounts

As noted in this chapter, the use of picture sequences, as shown in Figure 1.1, can help teachers and students identify appropriate grammatical forms for marking given and new information. The first few pictures of other sequences can obviously be used, but one teaching sequence can be illustrated with Figure 1.1.

Figure 1.1

Step 1. All students have copies of the four scenes in Figure 1.1. During a general discussion of how to start this story, the necessary vocabulary can be activated (e.g. *supermarket, shopping cart*). It helps to treat the situation as if the students are eyewitnesses to the events and will be asked to describe the events to someone who was not there. (This part is important because it forces students to think about what is given and what is new information for someone who cannot see the pictures.)

Step 2. Then, with the teacher's support, a story beginning is created, focusing on appropriate forms of the noun phrases. A written version can be created at this point.

Step 3. Having reached the problem stage of the events (as shown in the fourth drawing of Figure 1.1), students are encouraged to discuss versions of what happened next.

Step 4. After the discussion, students then have to write their versions of how the story continues and ends.

Step 5. Some versions of the rest of the story can be read out (by their authors) to the group.

Step 6. Some samples of the stories should be checked to see whether the markers of given and new information are being used effectively.

Note. This exercise can be completed by half of a group while the other half goes through the same procedure with part of another cartoon strip sequence. At Step 5, a representative from each group is given the task of giving the eyewitness account, and answering any questions. (See Yule 1997 for more examples and options.)

Further reading

General reference, with examples

Chalker, S. and E. Weiner. 1994. *The Oxford Dictionary of English Grammar*. Oxford: Oxford University Press.
Hurford, J. 1994. *Grammar: A Student's Guide*. Cambridge: Cambridge University Press.

More theoretical discussions

Huddleston, R. 1984. *Introduction to the Grammar of English*. Cambridge: Cambridge University Press.
Jacobs, R. 1995. *English Syntax*. Oxford: Oxford University Press.
Quirk, R., S. Greenbaum, G. Leech, and J. Svartvik. 1985. *A Comprehensive Grammar of the English Language*. London: Longman.

On boring *and* bored

Scovel, T. 1974. 'I am interesting in English.' *English Language Teaching Journal* 28: 305–12.

On kick *and* kick at

Dixon, R. 1991. *A New Approach to English Grammar, on Semantic Principles.* Chapter 8. Oxford: Clarendon Press.

On linguistic distance

Haiman, J. 1980. 'The iconicity of grammar.' *Language* 56: 515–40.

On focus of attention

Gundel, J., N. Hedberg, and R. Zacharski. 1993. 'Cognitive status and the form of referring expressions in discourse.' *Language* 69: 274–307.

Teaching issues

Batstone, R. 1994. *Grammar.* Oxford: Oxford University Press.
Odlin, T. (ed.) 1994. *Perspectives on Pedagogical Grammar.* Cambridge: Cambridge University Press.
Rutherford, W. 1987. *Second Language Grammar: Learning and Teaching.* London: Longman.

2 ARTICLES

1 Has any explanation been offered for the fact that both children and ESL learners are able to use *the* long before *a*?

2 Many ESL learners produce sentences of this type: *I am student* and *She wants to become doctor*. Why exactly is the indefinite article required here?

3 Isn't there a rule that proper nouns should be used without articles? Why do English speakers sometimes use expressions like *the John Park* and *a Calvin Klein*?

4 Why do people say *They go to school by bus*, with no articles? Why isn't it better to say *They go to the school by the bus*?

5 What does it mean when English speakers say I *was talking to this woman yesterday*? Shouldn't they say *a woman*?

'"*The*" *is the word*
that hammers
importance onto
rigid fact and
fixes to it
the burden of being
absolute.'

This is the beginning of a poem by Roy Hinks, first published in 1979, and quoted in Chesterman (1991). It is one attempt to explain the function of the articles in English. This chapter, though less poetic, will be another.

Overview

After a brief survey of the basic forms of the English DEFINITE and INDEFINITE ARTICLES, including the very important phenomenon known as ZERO ARTICLE, we will consider how an automatic article selection device—an 'article machine'—might work. In such a device, the concept of COUNTABLE versus NON-COUNTABLE (or MASS) is a key element and is discussed in the following section where the idea of a 'countable context' is offered in place of the traditional 'countable noun'. The more basic notion of INDIVIDUATION (or non-individuation) is then presented as a conceptual explanation for the distinction between the indefinite and zero article with singular nouns. The concepts of CLASSIFYING, for the indefinite, and IDENTIFYING, for the definite, are then explored as basic functions of the English articles. The absence of either of these articles in some common phrases is treated as significant for the interpretation, 'no differentiation required', of zero article. The pattern of article use in the INFORMATION STRUCTURE of a text is then illustrated in terms of GIVEN and NEW INFORMATION, along with the role of inference, and ANAPHORIC and CATAPHORIC uses of the definite article. Finally, the special function of a new article (*this*), replacing *a(n)* in some aspects of contemporary English, is described and illustrated.

Basic forms

Whenever word frequencies are reported for English, the articles account for almost ten per cent of most texts. It would seem to be hard to make sense of how English works without understanding the role of these common forms. In terms of basic form, there is a distinction between the INDEFINITE ARTICLE (*a* or *an*) and the DEFINITE ARTICLE (*the*). The form of the indefinite article depends on the pronunciation of the first sound (not letter) of the following word, with *a* preceding consonant sounds and *an* preceding vowel sounds. That is, you add an 'n' because of the spoken form, not because of the written form. There is also a high percentage of nouns occurring without any article, or with what is called ZERO ARTICLE (ø). In a description of the patterns presented in [1], the use of *a(n)* in the singular [1a] contrasts with zero article in the plural [1b], whereas the definite article is used in both singular and plural noun phrases, as in [1c].

[1]   a.   If there's *a* storm, you'll need *an* umbrella.
      b.   You'll probably need ø boots as well.
      c.   *The* boots will probably be more useful than *the* umbrella.

The nouns in [1] are all COMMON NOUNS used to refer to things that can be counted. A distinction is generally made between these COUNTABLE common nouns and two other types of nouns. The other types are PROPER NOUNS and NON-COUNTABLE common nouns. Proper nouns are easily recognized in writing because they begin with capital letters. They are mostly names of people, places, and special times, as in [2a], and are generally used with zero article. Also occurring with zero article are those common nouns that typically denote substances, as in [2b], or abstract concepts, as in [2c], which can be treated as non-countable.

[2] a. ø Santa Claus stays in ø Greenland until ø Christmas.
     b. ø Oil and ø water don't mix, but ø milk and ø sugar do.
     c. ø Money can't buy ø happiness or ø health.

These observations on the basic forms of articles in English are summarized in Box 2.1.

Summary Box 2.1 **Basic forms of articles and the types of noun that they precede**

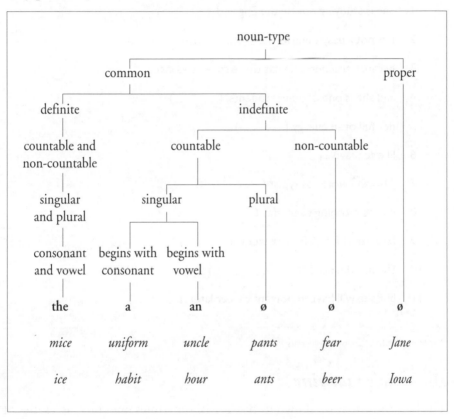

The different occurrences of *a(n)*, *the*, or ø (zero article) are easily observed in written English, but in spoken English these forms are much less distinct. In particular, the difference between unstressed *a(n)* and ø in speech may not be very noticeable at all. For both first and second language learners of English, the indefinite article may not even be heard in the beginning. If it's hard to hear, it's certainly going to be hard to learn. This would offer one simple explanation for the fact that *a(n)* is always acquired later than *the*.

Exercise 2.A

The following sentences illustrate many of the problems experienced by learners of English as a second language when they try to use articles. Using the information in Box 2.1, identify each of the points where a better choice of article (*a, an, the,* or *ø*) could have been made, then write that choice in the space provided.

    e.g.   My friend wants to be / dentist. (a_____)

    1   She is studying now in the England. (_____)

    2   It is not a easy thing for her, (_____)

    3   because teachers she has there speak too fast, (_____)

    4   and she is one of older students, (_____)

    5   not full of an energy (_____)

    6   like teenager. (_____)

    7   Also she works as typist (_____)

    8   during morning every day (_____)

    9   to earn a money for her study. (_____)

    10   She has the hard life now, (_____)

    11   but she will have important career later. (_____)

An article machine

The basic information shown in Box 2.1 is sometimes presented as a series of choices in the production of articles by what looks like a type of article machine. As illustrated in the diagram in Box 2.2, you can insert any noun into the article machine and, by making a number of choices, create a noun phrase containing the correct article.

If the machine has a reliable basis for identifying proper nouns (e.g. by an initial capital letter) and countable nouns (e.g. by plural *-s* endings), then it may be able to make a number of choices by itself. There is, however, a problem with identifying which nouns have 'unique referents'. We must assume that if there is only one instance of a type of referent, then it is 'unique'. This type of choice can only be made by a human who knows, or decides, what is unique in a particular context. Thus, the assumed use of the article machine is by a person in the process of creating a text and trying to decide which articles to include.

Summary Box 2.2 **An article machine**

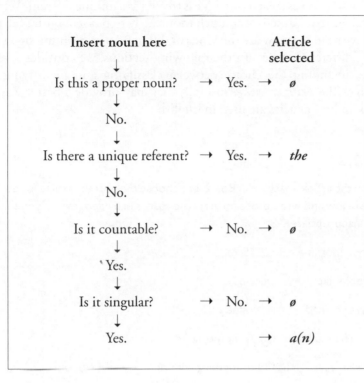

A number of problems do arise when comparing texts produced with the help of the type of article machine in Box 2.2 and those texts actually found in print. For example, following Box 2.2 (and Box 2.1), no proper nouns would ever occur with an article. This means that the grammatically acceptable sentences shown in [3], containing a proper noun with both the indefinite and the definite articles, would never be created.

[3]   a.   There was a John Park looking for you today.
      b.   Do you know if it's the John Park who was here before?

We need an analysis of article use that includes the sentences in [3] and explains the different functions of *a(n)*, *the*, and *ø* with proper nouns.

Other aspects of the article machine can be problematic. As we have already noted, the question about a 'unique referent' is not always easy to answer. The following two sentences [4a, b] appeared together in the instructions for replacing ink cartridges in one type of printer. If the articles are removed, can we use the article machine in Box 2.2 to identify the missing items?

[4]   a.   Dropping ___ print cartridge can cause structural damage resulting in ink leakage.
      b.   ___ damaged cartridge should not be used.

In the printed text, *the* was used in [4a] and *a* in [4b]. The article machine predicts *the* in both cases if each cartridge is treated as a unique referent. Yet the English speakers that I asked were much more likely to put *a* in both [4a] and [4b]. What we need to know are the kinds of differences in meaning signalled by choosing different articles. In the following sections, we consider several distinctions, including the choice between classifying and identifying an object (such as the *print cartridge* in [4a]), that may provide a better way of thinking about how articles are used in English.

Exercise 2.B

(a) Try to use the article machine in Box 2.2 to choose the correct article for each sentence below and write those forms in the spaces provided (even if you think they are inappropriate).

 1   Good morning, _____ Sam.

 2   It looks like _____ nice day.

 3   Have you had _____ coffee yet?

 4   No, I had to leave _____ home early.

 5   Here's _____ cup. Take anything with it?

 6   Just _____ sugar if you have one.

 7   There was _____ John or Jim Smith looking for you.

 8   Not _____ Jim Smith

 9   who writes all _____ bestsellers?

10   I'm not sure. _____ secretary talked to him.

(b) What problems did you find?

Photocopiable © Oxford University Press

Basic meanings

In order to talk about the meanings of the articles, we have to look at how they are used in combination with nouns to represent certain types of meaning choices. Some of the basic meaning choices can be described in terms of concepts like countable (or non-countable), singular (or plural), and individuation (or non-individuation).

Countability

The type of analytic framework presented in Box 2.2 depends on a recognition of nouns as countable (or non-countable) and singular (or plural). This may seem like a simple task with nouns like *bag* (countable, singular) and *apples* (countable, plural). Indeed, the expression *a bag of apples* could be remembered as a useful test phrase for COUNTABLE NOUNS because the indefinite article (with the first noun) and the plural form (of the second noun) are the traditional grammatical markers of countability in English. Other ways of identifying countability involve combination with words like *each* and *many*, italicized in [5a], as well as plural verb forms and plural pronouns, italicized in [5b].

> [5]   a.   How *many* apples are there in *each* bag?
>   b.   People *are* always asking strange questions, *aren't they*?

Traditional descriptions tend to treat countability (or non-countability) as a fixed property of English nouns that has to be learned as an inherent grammatical feature of each noun. This doesn't seem to be an accurate picture of how English nouns are used. Indeed, it may be very misleading to think of nouns as being fixed in terms of the properties, countable or non-countable. Nouns that are traditionally listed as countable will include words such as *apple* and *dog*, yet these words can easily be used in contexts that are associated with non-countable forms, as in [6].

> [6]   a.   She fed the baby a teaspoon of apple.
>   b.   He said that dog tastes best when it is cooked with ginger.

Notice that a change in the type of container from *bag* (of apples) to *teaspoon* (of apple) in [6a] can change the status of the noun (*apple*) from countable to non-countable. The entity seems to change from a thing to a substance. It is also a common observation that nouns usually listed as non-countable, such as *butter* and *sugar*, can be found in contexts that are clearly countable, as shown in [7].

> [7]   a.   There are several new butters being produced without milk.
>   b.   Can I have two sugars, please?

We can see that, in [7], two entities that are often treated as substances (*butter*, *sugar*) are actually being counted (*several butters, two sugars*).

Rather than say that nouns are either countable or non-countable, it may be more useful to note that the kind of thing being talked about changes in a countable context versus a non-countable context. We can then say that certain concepts are more often mentioned in one type of context rather than another. We shall return to this point.

Singular or plural?

With respect to the apparently simple choice between singular and plural, there are also potential problems. There are nouns that look plural (with *-s* endings), but are treated as singular [8a, b] and nouns that look singular, but can be treated as plural [8c, d].

[8]   a. Physics is fun and so is linguistics.
      b. The news is that measles isn't fun at all.
      c. The press were predicting problems.
      d. The public were ignoring them.

Those last two examples [8c, d] contain forms that are sometimes called COLLECTIVE NOUNS. Words like *class, club, committee, crowd, enemy, gang, government, staff, team,* and others that identify a *group* are also collective nouns. This type of label ('collective') is a recognition of the fact that it is the way in which an entity is perceived that determines its singular or plural status. In some cases, it is possible to find a group treated as both singular and plural in the same sentence. As illustrated in [9a, b], a group can be conceived as a single unit (with singular verbs, *was, has*) or as several individual members (with plural pronouns, *their, they*).

[9]   a. The audience *was* cheering and clapping *their* hands.
      b. Her family *has* decided that *they* can't afford a big wedding.

It is possible to continue listing a wide range of problems with recognizing different types of nouns in English. It is certainly important for teachers to recognize that some English nouns, normally used as non-countable (e.g. *advice, education, furniture, homework, information, leisure, violence*), have translation equivalents in other languages that are treated as countable. Yet, helping students to learn all the special characteristics of English nouns seems to be a large task and one that takes native speakers many years to accomplish. It would seem to be possible to make sense of the function of contrasting uses of the articles long before a large vocabulary of different types of nouns is acquired.

Individuation

Underlying concepts like countable or non-countable and singular or plural is the more general notion of whether an entity is being treated as a single unit or not. The process of classifying as a single unit, or INDIVIDUATION, is the key to the use of the indefinite article in English. The basic contrast is really between *a(n)* for individuation and *ø* for non-individuation.

The distinctive conceptual properties of an individual unit are that it has clear boundaries and that no part of the unit equals the whole. When you think of *a chair*, you tend to see a distinct individual entity, separate from other entities.

If you take that chair apart, you tend not to refer to each of the disconnected parts as *a chair*. In contrast, if you start with *water* and splash it in different places, each of the parts can still be called *water*. Notice that we're talking about *water*, with zero article. In a restaurant, you may hear a waiter mention *a water* (*Table 5 wants an iced tea and a water*). In this case, the indefinite article signals that an individual unit is being talked about.

In [10a], the noun *coffee* is being used to refer to an individual unit of some kind and in [10b] it is not.

> [10] a. I want to get a coffee.
>   b. I want to get coffee.

If the object is treated as an individual unit, then more than one individual of the same type will typically be possible (i.e. *two coffees*). Thus, the process of individuation predicts plural forms. Also notice that the boundaries of the entity in [10a] will be perceptually clear whereas there may be indistinct boundaries to the substance in [10b]. This type of conceptual difference is recognized in traditional grammars as a contrast between COUNTABLE and MASS. The substance in [10b] can be split into many different parts and each part can be described in the same way as the whole. If it's a bag of coffee and you spill it in the kitchen, there may be different parts of it on the table, on the chair, and on your shoe. But each part is still *coffee*. This is not true of the unit described in [10a]. If the unit is ever split or broken up, it can no longer be treated as a single unit. If you break what you have in [10a], you no longer have *a coffee*.

The tendency to treat concepts (and hence nouns) as either countable or mass is based on a frequency effect in experience. If an entity is mostly experienced as a distinct form (e.g. *a fork, a cup, a chair*), then it will be easily counted. However, if a certain type of entity is rarely experienced as any kind of individual unit, it will not normally be referred to as if it can be counted. In many grammar texts, this idea is presented in terms of a special class of mass nouns, or words exclusively for substances (e.g. *beer, bread, coffee, glass, gold, ice, oil, paper, soap, tea, water, wine*) and abstract concepts (e.g. *advice, courage, death, fear, help, hope, knowledge, progress, sincerity, suspicion*). It is useful to have this conceptual information about substances and abstractions, but it is misleading to suggest that they cannot be treated as individual units. When we need to talk about these substances and abstractions as single, separate instances, we use the indefinite article (e.g. *a beer, a coffee, a heavy oil, a cheap soap, a sudden death, a terrible fear*). The indefinite article is a signal that the following concept is being treated as a single instance of its kind. Some of these observations are summarized in Box 2.3.

Having used the concept of individuation to explain the difference between *a* and *ø* with singular nouns, we shall explore another crucial conceptual distinction, in the next section, to explain the difference between *a* and *the*.

Summary Box 2.3 **Countable versus non-countable contexts**

Properties of an entity in:	
Countable context	**Non-countable context**
a/an _____	*ø* _____
individuation	non-individuation
clear boundaries	indistinct boundaries
no part equals the whole	any part equals the whole
treated as discrete, separate	treated as substance-like, mass
often treated as concrete	often treated as abstract
can become plural	cannot become plural
co-occurs with *each, many*	co-occurs with *much*
Typical examples:	
car, house, boy	*drinking, waiting, luck,*
monkey, fault, way	*sincerity, education, music*

Exercise 2.C

(a) Look at the italicized words in the following sentences and decide in each case if the context is countable or non-countable.

   1   *Eating* is his favorite thing to do.

   2   Oh, yeah? What *food* does he like?

   3   Everything, even *vegetables*.

   4   How about a raw *onion*?

   5   Yes, and fresh *garlic*.

   6   Really? I guess he must like *beans*.

   7   Yeah, especially with *rice*.

   8   And *chocolate* of course.

   9   Of course, but surprisingly, he isn't fond of *cake*.

  10   What? I'd kill for a chocolate *cake*!

(b) Think about how the following nouns are typically used and, with the help of Box 2.3, try to decide if they appear in mostly countable contexts, mostly non-countable contexts, in both, or in neither.

cash	gang	satisfaction	cloth
garbage	scissors	enemy	government
steel	England	mathematics	ticket
equipment	patience	value	

Conceptual structure: classifying and identifying

As may have become clear in the preceding section, the indefinite article *a(n)* is closely connected, both historically and conceptually, to the number *one*. In many cases, the basic meaning of *a(n) X* is 'single instance of the X type of thing'. The definite article *the* is closely connected, historically and conceptually, to the demonstrative *that*. In many cases, the basic meaning of *the X* is 'that particular X'. At the core of the distinction between the two articles is a difference in how things are being treated by the speaker (writer). The articles are used to mark a broad distinction between CLASSIFYING and IDENTIFYING things.

Classifying is a process by which we name a thing (or things) as belonging to a class of objects. We talk about the thing as a member of a category. If you are asked to describe a new scene or picture, you typically classify or categorize the objects. Classifying objects, as illustrated in [11], is signaled by the indefinite article.

[11] there's *a* farmhouse with *a* horse, *a* dog and *an* old truck

If, however, you are trying to identify objects in a picture that a person can see or may remember, you use the definite article, as in [12].

[12] Can you see *the* farmhouse with *the* horse, *the* dog and *the* old truck?

Identifying is a process by which we refer to a thing (or things) as distinct from other members of the same category or class of objects. It has a distinguishing effect. Acts of reference (with *the*) are usually intended to pick out a specific thing or things. Indeed, the definite article mostly signals that the thing is to be treated as already identified. Classifying marks 'the kind of thing(s) I'm talking about' whereas identifying marks 'the specific thing(s) I'm talking about'. The same question, as in [13a], can be answered by classifying, as in [13b], or by identifying, as in [13c].

[13] a. What's making that noise?
      b. It's probably a dog outside.
      c. It's probably the dog next door.

Or we could say that the answer in [13b] is responding to the question 'How would you classify it?' and [13c] is in response to 'How would you identify it?'

Classifying, then identifying

From this basic distinction, there are a number of implications. The most powerful implication is that, in communicative terms, the definite article signals more than the indefinite article. Using the definite article implies that the classification has already been completed because the entity has already been identified. The indefinite article implies that the thing being classified has not already been identified. Using *a(n)* means that you are not in a position to use *the*. For example, if *an X* implies 'not yet identified' and *the X* implies 'already identified', there is an obvious sequence to the occurrence of these two forms. Classifying (*an X*) will most likely occur before identifying (*the X*), as in [14].

> [14] a. We watched *a* cartoon about *a* cat and *a* bird in *a* cage.
> b. *The* cat kept trying to get *the* bird out of *the* cage.

If the speaker has decided that the identifying function can be used, there is typically no need for classifying, as shown in [15].

> [15] Did you see *the* cartoon about *the* cat and *the* bird in *the* cage?

Occasionally, however, a speaker will treat an entity as already identified, discover that it was not, and have to present it afterwards in a classifying format. In [16], there is a change from *the cage* to *a cage*, demonstrating a different sequence from [14]. There is also a need to classify an entity already identified, as illustrated by the phrase *a parrot*.

> [16] A: Are you ready to go?
> B: Yes, but before I leave, I just have to check that Cindy is okay and *the cage* is closed.
> A: Pardon?
> B: Oh, I forgot, you haven't met Cindy. She's *a parrot* and I keep her in *a cage* when I go out.

Classifying (*a/an*)

Other common uses of the indefinite article can all be seen as following from its basic classifying function. Because it rules out a specific thing, the process of classifying will often imply *any* member of a class of objects. In [17a], the speaker is talking about *any* telephone. To classify is also a way to make a very general statement about a thing or person and so it is the process used in general categorization. Common examples are categorization by profession [17b] or by country [17c]. This is also the process used in typical definitions, as in [17d].

> [17] a. Is there a telephone near here?
> b. She's a doctor and her husband's a lawyer.
> c. He's an American.
> d. A bitch is a female dog.

This categorizing use of *a(n)*, especially in describing occupations or professions, is often not recognized by second language learners and results in ungrammatical forms such as **I am student* or **She wants to become doctor*. These learners need extra help in noticing that classifying a person as *a student* or *a doctor* always includes the indefinite article.

Many of these ways of classifying are also forms of labeling and could be paraphrased as 'one member of the class of objects with the label *a doctor* or the label *an American*'. This may help to explain the use of articles with proper nouns, as noted already in example [3]. The structure in *there was a John Park* signals that there was 'one member of the class of objects with the label (or name) *John Park* and that it hasn't been identified yet'. An attempt to identify the object is marked by the definite article and the descriptive phrase in *the John Park who was here before*. A similar process is evident in classifying objects by the name of the (probable) producer of the object, creating another context in which indefinite articles can appear with proper names, as in [18].

[18] a. I think that painting is a Picasso.
      b. Do you like my new watch? It's a Calvin Klein.

Already identified (*the*)

The use of an identifying signal as a means of specifying a thing or person implies that the thing or person can be treated as already identified. For English speakers, there seem to be many objects that can be mentioned as if already identified. Entities that are treated as the only members of their class, in physical terms [19a] or in sociocultural terms [19b], are referred to as if already identified. The concept of being the only member of a class naturally extends to special events (e.g. in history [19c]) or special phenomena (e.g. in geography [19d]).

[19] a. The moon goes round the earth which goes round the sun.
      b. The Pope, the President, and the Queen were all there.
      c. The Civil War was extremely destructive.
      d. The Pacific is bigger than the Atlantic.

Other entities can simply be treated as identified on the basis of information supplied by the speaker or writer. That is, some information (*who made this mess*) following a noun (*person*) is often enough to create an identified entity in a text, leading to use of the definite article, as shown in [20a]. This pattern is often found with general nouns (e.g. *person, place, fact*) and POST-MODIFYING phrases. These phrases come after (i.e. 'post-') the noun and restrict the general noun reference to a specific reference in the text, as illustrated in various ways in [20].

[20] a. I'd like to find *the* person who made this mess.
      b. *The* place I'm going to describe is where I grew up.

  c. He couldn't tell us *the* cost of all those repairs.
  d. He pointed to *the* fact that no lives were lost.
  e. We're not opposed to *the* concept of a land-for-peace deal.

Other entities are treated as definite because of PRE-MODIFYING expressions. These expressions come before (i.e. 'pre-') the noun and limit the reference in a specific way. Common examples are those expressions that indicate the end-point of a scale. Obvious end-points are *first, last, beginning, end, top,* and *bottom,* as in [21a, d]. Also treated as end-points of some scale are those entities described by the superlative forms of adjectives, as in [21b, c].

  [21] a. At *the* start, I thought I was *the* first person in her thoughts.
        b. I thought she was *the* most beautiful woman in the world.
        c. And I was *the* luckiest guy.
        d. But by the end, I found myself at *the* bottom of her list.

Clearly, the end-point of a scale is treated as an identifiable thing.

It may be examples of this type that lead to the common claim that the definite article has to be used for unique reference (as in Box 2.2). There are, however, many uses of the definite article where uniqueness is not a relevant property. For example, it is common to treat as 'already identified' many physically present entities, as in [22a], and entities that are recognized as part of an assumed shared life experience, as in [22b, c, d].

  [22] a. The glass on the table in the corner must be yours.
        b. The mail came while you were at the bank.
        c. She always takes the bus to the store.
        d. He likes to read the newspaper in the morning.

It is not necessary in any of these cases in [22] that there should only be one unique *table* and only one *corner* [22a], or one unique *bank, bus, store, newspaper,* or *morning* in the speaker's experience. Nor is it necessary that the bus or the store in [22c] should have to be 'known to the hearer' in any exact sense. The speaker can simply mark these entities as already sufficiently identified by the noun, almost as if they are to be treated as stereotypes in a shared social world.

No differentiation required

When this process is taken further and no differentiation of the entity is required at all, it is possible to use phrases that indicate 'not *a* bus' and 'not *the* bus', but just 'ø bus'. When a boy says he goes *to ø school by ø bus,* he is describing an event in which it is not relevant whether the entities *school* and *bus* are classified as a single unit or identified. They are marked as having no relevant individual existence or referential identity. This use of zero article, essentially signaling 'no differentiation required', is found in a number of expressions, some of which are included in [23].

[23] a. Who would want to be in ø prison?
      b. He'd rather stay at ø work than go to ø church.
      c. I'll be in ø town later and we can have ø lunch.
      d. Let's go to ø bed.

Rather than simply treat the expressions in [23] as idioms, with no explanation for the use of zero article, it would seem to be more useful to try to demonstrate how the functions of the articles *a(n)* and *the* are being significantly *not* marked in these cases. Zero article in these cases is a signal that it is not relevant for the entity to be classified as a unit or identified. Indeed, phrases such as *(go) to church* or *(be) at work* are used with a conventional implication that we're referring to kinds of activity rather than locations.

Some of these observations on the classifying and identifying functions of the articles are summarized in Box 2.4.

Summary Box 2.4 **Classifying and identifying functions of articles**

Classifying *(a/an)*	**Identifying** *(the)*
= describing	= distinguishing
There's a big ugly dog here.	*I've seen the dog, but not the cat.*
= introducing	= reintroducing
In a small village near a river …	*Meanwhile, back in the village …*
= a kind of thing	= the specific thing
Do you have a map?	*Where's the map?*
= not yet identified	= already identified
There's a policeman here.	*The policeman is here again.*
= unmodified	= post-modified
It's a fact.	*… I mean the fact that he's dead.*
= any member	= the only member
Is there a doctor in the crowd?	*She's the doctor in that area;*
a lucky guy; a president	*the luckiest guy; the President*
= labeling	= already labeled
I'm not an American.	*That's the American over there.*
= objects as category members	= objects in shared experience
a bank, a bus, a newspaper	*the bank, the bus, the newspaper*

The identifying function of the definite article is also found with plural nouns (*the dogs*). When plural nouns are used with zero article (*dogs*), a general classifying function seems to be signaled, with 'no differentiation required' between any members of the category. This distinction is fairly clear in an example such as [24] where the speaker uses zero article to talk about members of the category, then uses the definite article to refer to some identified members.

[24] I usually like dogs, but the dogs next door are too dangerous.

Exercise 2.D

In the following text, a beginning learner of English is describing a series of pictures to someone who cannot see them. (See Figure 1.1 on page 19 for the pictures.) Identify the points where better use of articles would improve the text. Write the articles you would add or change in the spaces provided.

e.g. There is / old woman (an____)

she is entering the store with the shopping cart. (1 _____ 2 _____)

She meets friend with the small child. (3 _____ 4 _____)

Small child is boy. (5 _____ 6 _____)

He is sitting in cart and woman is talking. (7 _____ 8 _____)

Boy is taking bottle (9 _____ 10 _____)

and putting in the bag old woman bag. (11 _____)

Then woman have problems for stealing the bottle. (12 _____)

But it was mistake. (13 _____)

Meanings in context

As noted already, the indefinite article is often used with the first reference to an entity, typically classifying it, and the definite article is used with second or later references to the same entity, as a way of identifying it. This pattern represents a common way in which information is structured in English text. NEW INFORMATION (i.e. information that the speaker presents as new to the hearer) is typically introduced with the indefinite article. As shown in [25], a news report can begin with the introduction of several new entities.

[25] a. This is *a* story of *a* picture that went for *a* spin.

   b. Last week *a* tornado ripped through *a* small town in Texas.

As the report continues, many of the entities can then be treated as already known or 'given'. GIVEN INFORMATION (i.e. information that the speaker treats as currently known to the hearer) can be presented with the definite article, as in [26].

[26] *The* tornado damaged many houses in *the* quiet little town.

Information that is treated as given will often be referred to by pronouns, as in [27] (where *it* is used instead of *the tornado*), but the definite article will be found in references to other entities that can be inferred. Once *a house*, for example, is mentioned, a large number of things about *the house* can be inferred and mentioned with the definite article. Thus, in [27a], *the roof* and *the windows* are inferrable entities. This type of given information is based on assumptions of shared background knowledge. Also part of that shared background knowledge will be a lot of information about what can happen if a tornado hits a house. For example, the fact that *things* in general will be blown away is treated as given in [27b], but one particular thing (*a photo*) is treated as new.

[27] a. It tore off *the* roof and blew out *the* windows of George
          Bober's house.

   b. Among *the* things that disappeared was *a* photo of George's
          dog Pooper.

In the story that continues in [28], we can see that *the next day, the garden*, and *the bushes* are treated as given, while *a piece of paper* is new in [28a]. Then, in [28b], *the paper* is given, but *a photograph* and *a dog* are presented as new.

[28] a. *The* next day, more than twenty miles away, Mary Sahrama
          was working in *the* garden of her small cottage when she
          noticed *a* piece of paper in *the* bushes.

   b. She picked up *the* paper and realized it was *a* photograph of *a*
          dog.

Notice that the new status of *a photograph* and *a dog* in [28b] suggests that these entities are different from the photo and the dog already mentioned in the text. In this sentence, the writer is presenting the entities as new from the perspective of the woman in the story. Of course, the reader immediately suspects that they are not actually new entities. This type of example should make us cautious about relying too much on the idea of first mention and second mention to describe the use of the articles in text structure. As already pointed out with example [16], it is not always the sequence of occurrence that determines the choice of the indefinite and definite articles. The choice is determined by the perspective taken on what is new (indefinite) and what is given (definite) at any point in the text.

Already given: anaphoric and cataphoric (the)

There is certainly a wide range of entities that, on first mention, can be treated as already given (with the definite article) in English text. On the basis of an assumption of shared knowledge, speakers and writers can treat many things as identifiable. Some inferred given information has already been noted in examples [27] and [28]. The process of inference behind the given status of *the handle* in [29a] follows from an inference of the type: if X is a cup, then X will have a handle. Inferences about the identifiability of entities can also follow from activities, as in [29c], where mention of *driving* implies a vehicle which then implies *the windshield*. Similarly in [29d], mention of *buy* leads to an assumption about *the price*. As further illustrated in [29e, f], many uses of the definite article can only be explained in terms of inferences based on assumed knowledge (i.e. that a snake is a reptile and that a surgeon is a doctor).

[29] a. I can give you *a* cup, but *the* handle is broken.
     b. We got *a* taxi and *the* driver was very helpful.
     c. I was driving along when suddenly *the* windshield shattered.
     d. I wanted to buy *a* watch, but *the* price was too high.
     e. A man bitten by *a* poisonous snake killed *the* reptile by biting off its head.
     f. There was *a* surgeon in addition to two nurses there, but no-one asked *the* doctor to help.

In all these examples, the definite articles are ANAPHORIC, that is, they are used to refer back to information already established. The listener or reader who is puzzled by the use of the definite article has to think back to what has already been said, written, or implied.

However, on some occasions, the definite article is used as a CATAPHORIC device, that is, to point forward. Sometimes at the beginning of a story, a writer will introduce a character or characters with the definite article, as in the examples in [30]. In such uses, the definite article is actually indicating that the status of 'already identified' will become clearer as the story proceeds. It is an invitation to read on to discover what is being treated as already known.

[30] a. *The* door opened and *the* killer walked in.
     b. *The* baby had been crying for twenty minutes before *the* girl got up and went into *the* kitchen.

A related storytelling device is illustrated in [31] where the use of definite articles at the start makes it seem as if we have joined a story already in progress. Extract [31] is the first sentence from a short story by Ernest Hemingway (see Hemingway 1987).

[31] *The* attack had gone across *the* field, been held up by machine-gun fire from *the* sunken road and from *the* group of farm houses, encountered no resistance in *the* town, and reached *the* bank of *the* river.

As noted earlier with the examples in [20] on page 35, the definite article is also used to introduce a general noun that is more specifically identified by a post-modifying phrase (e.g. *the person who made this mess*).

Clearly given (zero article)

Although it is not often noted, the clearest cases of given information are sometimes not actually marked by the definite article. They are marked by the absence of articles. This seems to be particularly common in texts providing instructions. If all the articles in a set of instructions are definite, then no meaningful choice between definite and indefinite has to be signaled. The presence of the definite articles may then be considered unnecessary. The result, as illustrated in extract [32] from some instructions on how to carve a turkey, is a text with no articles at all.

> [32] Grasp drumstick. Place knife between thigh and body; cut
> through skin to joint. Remove leg by pulling out and back.
> Separate thigh and drumstick at joint.

The grammatical point worth emphasizing here is that zero article in some texts is an indication that it is not relevant to distinguish the functions signaled by the definite and indefinite articles.

Some of these observations on the use of articles in information structure are summarized in Box 2.5.

Summary Box 2.5 **Articles in information structure**

New information: indefinite *a/an*	*This is a story of a picture. There's a woman with a child. …*
	A man has been arrested in connection with a crime. …
Given information: definite *the*	
(a) In experience	the *weather,* the *news,* the *law*
(b) Anaphoric	a *house* … the *house* a *car* … the *car*
(c) By inference	(a house) … the *roof,* the *garden* (buying) … the *price* (a snake) … the *reptile*
(d) Cataphoric	The *door opened and* the *killer walked in.*
Given information: zero article	*Remove ø lid before placing ø container in ø microwave.*

The absence of articles is very common in recipes. For example, there are no articles in the directions (Marsh 1963: 381) shown in [33].

> [33] In large skillet, heat oil and butter; add noodles, onions and garlic. Cook over medium heat.

It is also common practice in recipes to go one step further with given information and simply leave it out. Notice that, in [33], there is no explicit mention of where we have to *add noodles* (to what?), nor what exactly we have to *cook* (what?) *over medium heat.*

Exercise 2.E

In the following text, from a home repair manual, the articles have been removed. For each space, write down which article you think was removed plus any other article (including zero) you think would be acceptable in that space.

Plumbing emergencies. Toilet:

e.g. If the/ ø ____ water persists

1   in running into _____ tank,

2   remove _____ top

3   and jiggle _____ float

4   until _____ water stops.

5   If you are unsuccessful, stop _____ flow

6   of _____ water

7   by closing _____ valve

8   beneath _____ tank.

9   If _____ bowl fills and won't drain,

10 use _____ plumber's helper.

11 It should have _____ protruding narrow cup

12 at _____ end

13 designed for use in _____ toilets.

14 Press firmly into _____ drain hole

15 and work it up and down rapidly for _____ dozen thrusts.

A note on a new article

In contemporary English, there is one particular cataphoric device that seems to be functioning like an indefinite article. As illustrated in [34], indefinite *this* can be used to introduce new characters or entities in a text.

[34] a. There was *this* guy I met in my Japanese class …
       b. I was watching *this* TV show last week …
       c. Jimmy had *this* girlfriend in New Orleans …
       d. We were waiting for the bus when *this* car pulls up …
       e. There's *this* woman, she's a hurricane …

It is clear from the examples in [34] that the new article *this* has a first-mention, or introductory, role similar to *a(n)* and does not function like *the*. It appears at the beginning of stories and jokes where it seems to highlight someone or something that will be the topic of what follows. Generally, a character introduced as *this guy* (rather than *a guy*) will tend to be mentioned more often and be more focused in the story. While the indefinite article *a(n)* can be used to introduce many new entities, indefinite *this* seems to have developed in contemporary English as an article for highlighting a particular entity as the main focus of attention. It is an example of a grammatical innovation that is becoming extremely common in conversational English.

Discussion topics and projects

1   The following excerpts are from crime reports of the office of campus security at a college in the USA. Mark all the places where *a(n)*, *the*, and zero article occur in the reports. Then, with the categories of analysis presented in this chapter, try to explain the use of each form. Are there any problematic cases where the use is difficult to explain?

> March 10. A custodian reported that a vending machine in the College of Business Administration had been broken into the previous night.

> March 21. A female reported that a male had entered her dormitory room after midnight. The door was not locked. The intruder left when the woman screamed.

> March 23. A report of excessive noise in the men's restroom of George Hall was investigated. Security found clothing and empty beer bottles scattered on the floor, but the room was empty.

> March 24. A stolen green Dodge van was found in the Law School parking lot after a security officer became suspicious. The vehicle was reported stolen by the police department.

March 26. A caller to campus security reported that a drunk female was banging on a door of the N.H. dormitory. The suspect was detained by security officers after a brief scuffle.

March 28. A professor at the Institute of Geophysics reported being assaulted by a man in a Navy uniform. The man was angry because he had been denied entry into a geophysics graduate program. The suspect has been banned from the campus for one year. The case was handed over to the police department.

2   There is an interesting type of English phrase involving the indefinite article, exemplified by *have a look* and *have a drink*. In these examples, the noun after the indefinite article is formed from a verb, but not just any verb (i.e. we don't say **have an eat*). We can also *give the door a push*, but not **give the window a close*. We can also *take a walk*, but not **take a write*.

(a) First, try to list as many (grammatical) expressions of this type as you can.

(b) Among these expressions, can you think of an explanation for excluding **have an eat*, **give a speak*, and **take a think*?

(c) What difference is there between saying (i) *We talked last night* and (ii) *We had a talk last night*?

(d) What connection, if any, can you find between these expressions and the analysis of indefinite article functions presented in the chapter? (For some help with this topic, try Algeo (1995), Dixon (1991, Chapter 11), Stein (1991), or Wierzbicka (1982).)

3   We did not explore the range of place-names that occur with (and without) the definite article. Textbooks typically present lists of place-names under categories (e.g. countries, lakes, mountains), with exceptions, in an attempt to offer a regular pattern. A representative example for language teaching can be found in Frank (1993). One novel proposal by Horowitz (1989) suggests using the distinction of being *at ø home* versus *on the road* as a basis for thinking about zero article versus definite article in place-names. Zero article is to be associated with the state of being at home, while *the* with place-names is to be associated with traveling and away from home.

(a) Ask a number of people for their home address. Are all the names of streets, towns, and countries presented with zero article, as versions of being *at home*?

(b) Ask the same people about places they've traveled to and how they got there. Are all the names of highways, rivers, seas, oceans, and forests presented with the definite article, as versions of being *on the road*?

(c) Make a list of as many names as you can in the following categories: continents, countries, famous buildings, islands, lakes, mountains, oceans, rivers, states, and towns. Is there a noticeable difference between which names occur with *the* versus zero article?

(d) What patterns can you discover with the names of airports, churches, hotels, museums, pubs (bars), restaurants, and universities?

4   There was no specific discussion of generic uses of the articles in this chapter. As shown in the following examples, generic uses have a meaning like 'in general' or 'in most cases'.

> Dogs are domestic animals and easy to train.
> The dog is a domestic animal and easy to train.
> A dog is a domestic animal and easy to train.

(a) These generic uses may seem to remove the meaning distinctions between the articles (ø, *the*, *a*) that were presented in the chapter. Do you think that all three sentences above have the same meaning? Would they all be used in the same circumstances?

(b) It has been suggested (Chesterman 1991: 39) that a generic interpretation comes from the whole context of a noun phrase and not from the articles. It is worth considering in which contexts the generic uses of noun phrases are typically found. As an example of how awareness of generic uses of articles can be raised, read through the following text (Kaufman and Forestell 1994: 8) and underline the noun phrases that mention *whale(s)*. Then try to decide which are generic and why the article used (ø, *the*, *a*) seems appropriate in that context.

> In winter the Hawaiian Islands play host to a celebrity of sufficient distinction to have been designated the State Marine Mammal. While not anywhere near as numerous as the humans who come to Hawaii, the humpback whales' arrival nonetheless generates a great deal of excitement and interest. Most people who see the whales get a great deal of satisfaction and excitement from the experience, but it is clear that few really understand what a humpback whale is, and how it differs from other mammals, other inhabitants of the ocean, or other whales. In order to develop an accurate perception of the humpback whale, it is both interesting and informative to place it in the context of the general group of marine animals known as cetaceans.

Teaching ideas

1 Correct the spelling

As suggested by Roger Berry (1991), the following type of simple exercise is a way to have students practice the different articles and their pronunciation.

Make a list of familiar vocabulary items, with one obvious spelling mistake in each, and ask students to provide corrections. The following structure can be provided initially, to get students started.

> Pensil *The* s is wrong. It should be *a* c.
> Rular *The* a is wrong. It should be *an* e.

Note. The sentences produced during this exercise provide examples of *the N* being used for information that both speakers have (given information), whereas *a(n) N* is used to introduce something new each time. After the forms have been practiced, attention can be drawn to these functions.

2 Fill in the blanks

The most common exercise is to create sentences with articles missing and ask students to fill in the blanks. It can be _____ easy exercise if _____ students already know _____ vocabulary. It may be made more challenging by also removing the nouns and asking students to provide both articles and nouns in the blanks.

(a) In the earlier stages, it may be more supportive to provide a list of nouns, as here.

>   *Scotland, world, north, town, whisky, river*

> There's _____ small _____ beside _____ in _____ _____ of _____ that makes _____ best _____ in _____ _____ (so they say).

(b) For more advanced students, longer texts may be presented, minus articles, in a format known as a 'modified cloze' exercise. Short news items from newspapers, of the type shown below, are a good source of such texts.

> Near Amite, Louisiana, yesterday, _____ man riding _____ bicycle and carrying _____ gun in _____ small bag accidentally shot himself. According to _____ police spokesman, _____ man was riding _____ bicycle along _____ side of _____ busy road when he swerved and fell into _____ ditch. As he dropped _____ bag, _____ gun hit _____ ground and went off. He was wounded in _____ left buttock. _____ injured man was helped by _____ passing motorist.

Note. Some intermediate and advanced students might welcome some version of the article machine (Box 2.2) to use with these 'fill in the blanks' exercises. After completing the exercise, they may be able to reflect (i.e. to focus their attention and report) on how they made their decisions.

3 A tablespoon of apple

An interesting exercise was used in a study on countability, reported by Michael Akiyama and Nancy Williams (1996). They gave English native speakers and Japanese learners of English lists of food items, both smaller (*grape, strawberry*) and larger (*apple, onion*). They also provided terms for containers, both small (*spoon, glass*) and large (*bag, bowl*), as used in cooking. Participants had to create phrases consisting of a container and a food item, as shown here.

> a bag of onions
> a tablespoon of apple
> a glass of banana

This type of exercise can be used to practice articles in countable contexts. It may also help raise awareness that words like *apple* and *onion* can be used for things (single units) or for substances (not single units), depending on the size of the container. For lower level students, it may be necessary to first create vocabulary lists (with their help). One list will consist of terms for containers and common measuring utensils in the kitchen and the other will have terms for food and common cooking ingredients.

4 What's in your picture?

The classifying use of the indefinite article can be presented and practiced in a number of tasks using photographs or pictures. One student has a picture of the type shown in Figure 2.1 or 2.2 and has to describe all the objects. For familiar objects, some basic structures can be used:

> There's a(n) _____.
> I have a(n) _____.

For less familiar objects, it may be a good opportunity to provide these useful structures:

> It's like a(n) _____.
> It looks like a(n) _____.
> It's a(n) _____ or something like that.
> It's a kind of _____.

5 Spot the difference

A 'spot the difference' type of task can be used with students in pairs, requiring two photos/pictures that are similar, but contain a number of different objects (or similar objects with different properties). Figures 2.1 and 2.2 are examples. Each student takes a turn asking the other to discover differences between their pictures. Helpful structures to get students started are:

> Do you have a(n) _____ ?
> Is there a(n) _____ in your picture?

Figure 2.1   Figure 2.2

6 A carrot is a vegetable

The classifying function of *a(n)* is fairly easy to present in any type of category-defining exercise. There are many types.

(a) Start by providing (or eliciting) category labels such as *animal, flower, fruit* or *vegetable*. Then present (or elicit) different examples of each category (e.g. *banana, carrot, cat, daisy, horse, orange, rose, tomato*). The basic categorizing structures can then be elicited by asking about each example, in teacher–student(s) or student–student interaction:

> What's a(n) _____? It's a(n) _____.
> A(n) _____ is a(n) _____.

(b) Occupations are another type of category that can be listed (or elicited) and matched with brief descriptions or drawings. One structural pattern that will focus students on the need to include the indefinite article in such expressions is as follows:

> She designs buildings. She's _____ _____.
> She repairs cars. She's _____ _____.
> He cuts hair. He is _____ _____.
> He serves food in restaurants. He's _____ _____.

(c) As an alternative to (b) that can be more student-centered, give the students a chance to create their own business cards, each with a name and an occupation. (Encouraging them to choose unusual occupations could increase everyone's attention and entertainment.) Then, have one student introduce another by reading out the information on the card. Typical structures for this would be:

>   This is _____ . She's a(n) _____ .

(d) Provide (or elicit with pictures) a list of objects (e.g. *corkscrew, crash helmet, ruler, stapler, thermometer*) and a list of 'uses' of such objects. Scramble the sequences of both lists. Students then have to create sentences (written or spoken), matching object and use. Categorizing structures of the following type can be provided:

>   What's a(n) _____ for? It's used _____ .
>   A(n) _____ is used _____ .

7 Come out of the bank and go to the bookstore

The identifying function of *the* can be presented and practiced in a number of tasks where participants know the same things (i.e. already identified objects), but do not know how those things are arranged or connected. Assembly tasks, as described in (a) below, can be created with many different types of materials. Tasks that involve drawing or tracing a route, as in (b), are easy to create and can be used with very large groups. More examples of materials can be found in Yule (1997).

(a) One student has a number of objects (e.g. classroom items, Lego pieces) and another student has a picture of the objects in an arrangement or assembled form. The one with the picture has to instruct the other (or others) with the objects how to put them together. Typical structures:

>   Put the _____ on the _____ beside the
>   _____ .

(b) One student has a small map, as in Figure 2.3, with a delivery route marked to a number of locations (e.g. bank, bookstore, post office). He or she has to describe the delivery route to other students who have a similar map without the route. Typical structures:

>   Come out of the _____ and go to the _____ .

(c) A variation on the task in (b) can be designed with a small number of differences between the speaker's and the listener's maps. (Actually, for each speaker, there can be many listeners.) See Figures 2.3 and 2.4. For example, where one map has a *bookstore*, the other can have a *shoe store* in the same location. This difference can create discussions in which phrases with definite articles are answered by phrases with indefinite articles.

>   A Go to the bookstore.
>   B The bookstore? There isn't a bookstore.

Note. If some of these discussions can be recorded and later replayed, they can provide an opportunity to reflect on how the articles change in English as shared knowledge changes.

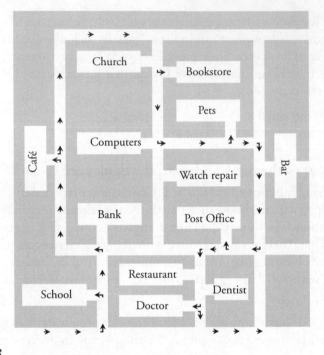

Figure 2.3

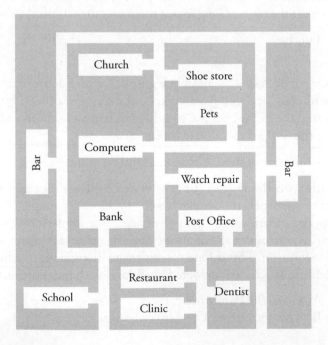

Figure 2.4

8 The information structuring role of the articles

(a) Take (or create) a short text, with several brief sentences, in which characters perform actions in sequence. Scramble the order of the sentences and ask students to recreate the original text (remembering the clues provided by the use of *a(n)* versus *the*). One simple example:

> The bird flew away.
> The dog ran towards the cat.
> I was watching a large dog in a garden.
> And the cat jumped down.
> The cat was trying to catch a bird.
> Suddenly a cat jumped on the fence.

Note. It's really useful to discuss this type of exercise with students after they complete it, to compare solutions and to get them to talk about why they chose certain sequences. They will inevitably use articles as they talk about the clues provided by articles in English.

(b) The inference-based uses of the definite article in English text can be illustrated by getting people to describe the inside of their homes (house or apartment). Native speakers or advanced proficiency non-native speakers can be recorded and those recordings played for students who have to identify the use of *a(n)* or *the* with first mention of words like *bathroom, bedroom, kitchen*, etc.

Alternatively, if students have, or are given, the necessary vocabulary, they can describe their homes (at present, or from their childhood) for others. This can be a written exercise, or spoken and recorded.

Further reading

General reference, with examples

Alexander, L. G. 1988. *Longman English Grammar*. Chapter 3. London: Longman.
Berry, R. 1993. *Articles*. Collins Cobuild English Guides 3. London: HarperCollins.

More theoretical discussions

Hawkins, J. 1978. *Definiteness and Indefiniteness*. London: Croom Helm.
Chesterman, A. 1991. *On Definiteness*. Cambridge: Cambridge University Press.
Christophersen, P. 1939. *The Articles: A Study of their Theory and Use in English*. Oxford: Oxford University Press.

An article machine

Huckin, T. and L. Olsen. 1991. *Technical writing and professional communication.* (2nd edn.) New York: McGraw-Hill.

On countability

Allan, K. 1980. 'Nouns and countability.' *Language* 56: 541–67.
Reid, W. 1991. *Verb and Noun Number in English: A Functional Explanation.* London: Longman.

On individuation

Wierzbicka, A. 1985. 'Oats and wheat: The fallacy of arbitrariness.' In J. Haiman (ed.): *Iconicity in syntax.* (pp. 311–42). Amsterdam: John Benjamins.

On information structure

Brown, G. and G. Yule. 1983a. *Discourse analysis.* Chapter 5. Cambridge: Cambridge University Press.

Anaphoric and cataphoric uses

Halliday, M. and R. Hasan. 1976. *Cohesion in English.* London: Longman.

On this as a new article

Wald, B. 1983. 'Referents and topic within and across discourse units: Observations from current vernacular English.' In F. Klein-Andreu (ed.): *Discourse Perspectives on Syntax.* (pp. 91–116) New York: Academic Press.

Language acquisition research on articles

Tarone, E. and B. Parrish. 1988. 'Task-related variation in interlanguage: The case of articles.' *Language Learning* 38: 21–44.
Thomas, M. 1989. 'The acquisition of English articles by first- and second-language learners.' *Applied Psycholinguistics* 10: 335–55.

Teaching issues

Berry, R. 1991. 'Re-articulating the articles.' *ELT Journal* 45: 252–59.
Master, P. 1990. 'Teaching the English articles as a binary system.' *TESOL Quarterly* 24: 461–78.

3 TENSE AND ASPECT

1 Why is it so common for learners to say *He is sleep and *He sleeping rather than He is sleeping?

2 If today is present, shouldn't it be used with present tense? Why is it okay to say, Today I slept late and missed my bus, with verbs in the past tense?

3 Why do English speakers say, If I was rich? It isn't about the past, it's about the future, so why don't they say, If I will be rich?

4 I just bought a car. Why can't I say, I'm having a car now?

5 Is there any difference implied by writing (a) rather than (b)?
(a) Scovel (1969) found that age was a factor in L2 learning.
(b) Age is a factor in L2 learning (Scovel 1969).

'Since one needs constant energy to "walk" but not so to "be a freckled redhead", the former is an Action and the latter a State.'

This apparently simple statement by Ziqiang Shi (1990: 53) is actually an elegant expression of a crucial distinction required in the study of English aspect. Conceptual distinctions of this type are the key to making sense of tense and aspect in English. Constant energy is also needed.

Overview

After a brief review of the basic forms of PRESENT and PAST TENSE, and PERFECT and PROGRESSIVE ASPECT in English, including a note on the role of MODAL VERBS, a basic structure for the English verb complex is presented. Some basic meaning distinctions between different tense forms are offered in terms of the REMOTE (or not) and FACTUAL (or not) status of perceived situations, including notes on the future, time expressions, and the HISTORICAL PRESENT. A distinction is made between LEXICAL ASPECT, concerned with inherent properties of verb meaning such as STATIVE, DYNAMIC, PUNCTUAL, and DURATIVE, and GRAMMATICAL ASPECT, concerned with an internal versus an external perspective on situations. The role of tense and aspect in marking BACKGROUND versus FOREGROUND elements of INFORMATION STRUCTURE in discourse is illustrated.

Basic forms

The most basic element in an English sentence is the verb. To describe the different forms of the verb, we need to talk about TENSE, which often has to do with the location of a situation in time, and ASPECT, which characterizes the way in which that situation is perceived or experienced. English has two distinct tense forms, PRESENT and PAST TENSE, and two distinct forms for aspect, PERFECT and PROGRESSIVE ASPECT, which are marked on the verb. (The progressive is also sometimes called the continuous.) In most descriptions, the use of the MODAL VERB *will* is included, typically as an indication of future reference. With this small set of technical terms, the range of English verb forms can be described, as in Box 3.1.

Summary Box 3.1 **Basic English verb forms**

Verb forms	Examples
Simple present	*I* love *your Mercedes.*
Present progressive	*You* are standing *too close to it.*
Simple past	*I* wanted *a car just like it.*
Past progressive	*You* were aiming *too high.*
Simple future	*I* will work *for it.*
Future progressive	*You* will be working *forever.*
Present perfect	*I* have worked *hard before.*
Present perfect progressive	*You* have been working *for nothing.*
Past perfect (pluperfect)	*I* had saved *my money.*
Past perfect progressive	*You* had been saving *pennies.*
Future perfect	*I* will have saved *enough.*
Future perfect progressive	*You* will have been saving *in vain.*

From the examples presented in Box 3.1, it is possible to describe a set of core elements needed to form verbs in English sentences. We always need a basic verb (e.g. *eat, love, sleep*) and a basic tense, either past or present. With a tense (e.g. past) and a verb (e.g. *eat*), we can create the simple verb structure in *I ate.*

Change the tense to present and we get *I eat.* These basic elements, tense and verb, are always required.

There are other elements, all of them optional, that can be added to create more complex verb forms. We can add a modal element (e.g. *will*) to get *I will eat.* We can also include elements that indicate aspect, either perfect or progressive. If we include perfect aspect (i.e. *have ... + -en*), we get the structure in *I have eaten.* It is simply conventional to analyze the verb ending in the perfect as + -en. Other verbs actually have different forms as endings, as in the perfect aspect versions of *I have loved* and *I have slept.* We can also choose progressive aspect (i.e. *be ... + -ing*), so that different forms of the verb *be* are included before the basic verb, ending with + -ing, as in *I am eating* or *he is sleeping.*

Exercise 3.A

After each of the sentences below, draw a circle round the correct description.

    1   I am hungry. present / past

    2   We have eaten. perfect / progressive

    3   I will eat soon. modal / perfect

    4   We wanted sandwiches. present / past

    5   But we were too late. present / past

    6   I'm waiting patiently. perfect / progressive

    7   They'll come soon. modal / perfect

    8   We've finished. perfect / progressive

The basic structure

There is a very regular pattern in the organization of all these elements used to create English verb forms. We can treat this underlying pattern, shown in Box 3.2, as the basic structure of all verbs found in the majority of English sentences. The forms in brackets are optional and, unlike the other required elements, are not used in every sentence.

Summary Box 3.2 **Basic structure of English verb forms**

Tense	(Modal)	(Perfect)	(Progressive)	Verb
PAST or PRESENT	(WILL)	(HAVE + -*EN*)	(BE + -*ING*)	VERB

1 The left-to-right order of components is fixed.
2 Each component influences the form of the component to its right.

The position of the modal element is illustrated in Box 3.2. A description of all the different modal verbs filling this position is presented later in Chapter 4. Also included in Box 3.2 are two observations on the ordering of the components. It is worth noting that, when both forms of aspect are included, the perfect always comes before the progressive. That is, as can be seen in example [1b], the *have* of the perfect comes before the *be* of the progressive. The particular forms found in example [1b] are explained by the second observation included in Box 3.2.

We can illustrate the second observation, that each component influences the form of the component to its right. From a sequence of elements, as shown in [1a], we can create the verb form shown in [1b].

> [1]   a. PRESENT TENSE, HAVE … + -EN, BE … + -ING, *sleep*
>   b. I have been sleeping.

The first element is created from the influence of PRESENT TENSE on HAVE (= *have*). The next element is created from the influence of + -EN on BE, attaching to the end to create BE + -EN (= *been*). The next element is formed by attaching + -ING to the verb *sleep*, once again at the end, to create SLEEP + -ING (= *sleeping*).

When we choose different elements, we get different verb forms, as shown in the connections between [2a] and [2b] or [3a] and [3b].

> [2]   a. PAST TENSE, HAVE … + -EN, *love*
>   b. I had loved.

In [2a], the effect of PAST TENSE on the HAVE element creates *had*. The influence of the + -EN element on the verb *love* results in *loved*, as in [2b]. Notice once again that the + -EN element actually becomes *-ed* at the end of most English verbs.

> [3]   a. PAST TENSE, BE … + -ING, *sleep*
>   b. I was sleeping.

In [3a], the PAST TENSE element combines with BE to create *was* and the + -ING element attaches to the verb *sleep* to yield *sleeping*, as in [3b].

In the beginning stages, learners seem not to realize that the aspectual forms consist of two parts. Instead of BE … + -ING, they will use only BE (**He is sleep*) or only + -ING (**He sleeping*). Instead of HAVE … + -EN, they may only use HAVE (** You have take it*). It is important for teachers to understand that a grammatical element that consists of two separate parts will always be very difficult to learn. It is quite natural to expect one form for one meaning (or function). The mistakes made by learners suggest that they are trying to use only one part of the aspect marker. Those learners need frequent and clear examples that allow them to notice and hear the distinct components of these complex verb forms.

Exercise 3.B

(a) In the space provided, identify the basic verb element, the tense (present or past), and the aspect (perfect or progressive, or both) in each structure.

		Tense		Aspect		Verb
e.g.	I was looking for you.	<u>past</u>	+	<u>progressive</u>	+	<u>look</u>
1	I have been sleeping.	___	+	___	+	___
2	You are sleeping a lot these days.	___	+	___	+	___
3	I work hard.	___	+	___	+	___
4	You have stayed out late too.	___	+	___	+	___
5	I stayed out late just one night.	___	+	___	+	___

(b) Using the components listed in 1 to 5 below, write out the verb forms which they describe.

e.g.	present+modal+*read*	<u>will read</u>
1	present+perfect+*fall*	_____
2	present+modal+progressive+*talk*	_____
3	past+progressive+*look*	_____
4	past+perfect+*have*	_____
5	past+perfect+progressive+*wait*	_____

Basic meanings

It is very tempting to think of each of the structures listed in Box 3.1 as having a specific meaning based on time reference. For example, the simple present form may be given a meaning such as 'actions habitual at present time' and illustrated with an expression of time like *every day*, as in [4]. The simple past form may be treated as denoting 'completed action in the past' and illustrated with expressions such as *last week* or *yesterday*, as in [5]. For the future perfect, a time expression such as *by next year*, as in [6], can provide support for a meaning like 'future action that will be completed prior to a specific future time'.

[4]   Toby eats three burgers every day.

[5]   He ate four burgers yesterday.

[6]   He will have eaten a thousand burgers by next year.

There is also a tendency to view the technical terms 'past', 'present', and 'future' as being three points on a simple time line which are similar to *yesterday, today,* and *tomorrow.* It is, of course, possible to find or create English sentences that appear to connect these time expressions directly with the tenses. However, there are many more English sentences that do not. As shown in [7] and [8], the present tense can be used when talking about past and future time and, as in [9], a present time adverb such as *today* can be used with a past tense verb.

[7]   Yesterday the landlord tells me my rent's going up.

[8]   Tomorrow I fly to London for a big meeting.

[9]   And today I woke with a splitting headache.

These observations suggest that the simple time-line view may not be the most helpful guide in making sense of tense and aspect in English. As may already be apparent, tense in English is not based on simple distinctions in time.

Tense

The basic tense distinction in English is marked by only two forms of the verb, the PAST TENSE (*I* lived *there then*) and the PRESENT TENSE (*I* live *here now*). Conceptually, the present tense form ties the situation described closely to the situation of utterance. The past tense form makes the situation described more remote from the situation of utterance. There is a very regular distinction in English which is marked by *then* versus *now, there* versus *here, that* versus *this,* and past tense versus present tense. In each of these examples, one is distant or remote from the speaker's situation and the other is not. In this analysis, past tense means 'remote' and present tense means 'non-remote'.

Situations in the future are treated differently. They are inherently non-factual, but can be considered as either relatively certain (i.e. perceived as close to happening) or relatively unlikely or even impossible (i.e. perceived as remote from happening). The verb form that is traditionally called 'the future tense' is actually expressed via a modal verb which indicates the relative possibility of an event. This modal also has two forms which convey the closeness (*I* will *live here*) or the remoteness (*I* would *live there*) of some situation being the case, viewed from the situation of utterance.

The key elements which vary in this account are being REMOTE or not, and being the case, that is, FACTUAL or not. The key constant is that those elements are viewed from the situation of utterance, that is, from the perspective adopted by the speaker or writer. Combinations of these elements can be used to describe some basic underlying conceptual distinctions between forms of the English verb, as shown in Summary Box 3.3.

Summary Box 3.3 **Meanings of the basic verb forms**

Concepts	Verb-forms
remote + factual	past (*lived*)
non-remote + factual	present (*live*)
non-remote + non-factual	future (*will live*)
remote + non-factual	hypothetical (*would live*)

According to Box 3.3, events described by the simple past tense form are presented as being facts and remote from the time of utterance. The simple present tense indicates that the events (also treated as facts or 'being the case') are non-remote.

The future

Future events are not treated as facts, hence are only possibilities. They are distinguished in terms of being non-remote possibilities versus remote possibilities. The forms of the verb used in statements about hypothetical (i.e. remote and non-factual) situations, such as [10], are usually described as past tense forms, but their reference is clearly not to past time.

> [10] If I was rich, I would change the world.

Just as remoteness in time from the situation of utterance is indicated by the past tense forms in English, so too is remoteness in possibility, as in [10].

This distinction between *will* and *would* in terms of remoteness of possibility (or likelihood of something being the case) is also found in other pairs of modal verbs, as shown in [11] and [12]. The b. forms represent the event as remote and hence less likely than the a. versions which are non-remote.

> [11] a. It may rain later.
>   b. It might rain later.
>
> [12] a. I can offer you some advice.
>   b. I could offer you some advice.

We will look at the different meanings of these forms in Chapter 4.

Reference to time

The widely recognized difference in time between situations referred to via the past and the present tense forms can be interpreted in terms of remoteness (or non-remoteness) in time from the time of utterance. Thus, the situation referred to by the speaker in [13a] is marked as remote in time from the utterance-time, whereas the situation in [13b] is not.

> [13] a. My parents worked in the fields all day.
>   b. And I work in the fields all day just like them.

The adverbial expression of remoteness in time (*then*) would naturally occur with [13a] and the non-remote expression (*now*) would more naturally be included in [13b].

Generally, adverbial expressions of time are used to establish time frames within which situations can be described. They do not determine how the speaker may choose to mark the relative remoteness of the event via tense. Thus, an expression like *today* can establish a time frame for talking about events that the speaker can describe as remote, via the past tense (e.g. *I slept late*), or non-remote, via the present tense (e.g. *I'm tired*).

The historical present

A very clear illustration of this point is the English HISTORICAL PRESENT, which is usually described as a way of making storytelling events more vivid. The impression of 'more vivid' may actually be another way of talking about something as less remote in experience despite its remoteness in time. For example, the extract (about a cat) shown in [14] has an adverbial of time (*last night*) establishing the time of the event in the past, while the actions are described in the present tense. The actual time of the event is remote from the time of utterance, but the actions described are presented as if they coincide with the time of utterance.

> [14] Last night Blackie comes in with this huge dead rat in her mouth
> and drops it right at my feet.

The speaker's *now*

These observations on tense in English would suggest that the widely used image of a timeline running from the past (*yesterday*) through the present (*today*) to the future (*tomorrow*) is not, in fact, the basis of the grammatical category of tense. Perhaps a better image would have the time of utterance (speaker's *now*) at the center and other referenced situations being viewed as extending in different dimensions of time or possibility away from that center. For any speaker or writer, the use of the present tense is an indication of what is currently treated as 'being the case', whether it is used in abstract generalizations, such as [15a], or simply personal comments, such as [15b].

> [15] a. Life is a beach.
>   b. My present life is like a nice day at the beach.

An attempt to illustrate the different perspectives is shown in Box 3.4.

Summary Box 3.4 **The speaker's perspective**

The time-line perspective

past time → present time → future time

The speaker's perspective

remote	←	non-remote	→	remote
(factual)				(non-factual)

The common use of the past tense in English to represent reported speech, as in [16b], would seem to fit a 'more remote' interpretation better than a 'past time' interpretation. The difference between the direct speech of [16a] and indirect speech of [16b] is not a matter of time, but of distance from the reporting situation.

> [16] a. She said, 'I am waiting here'.
>   b. She said that she was waiting there.

In [16a], we seem to be in the same situation as the speaker, hearing the exact words. In [16b], we are more distant from that situation. We shall consider this distinction in more detail in Chapter 10.

Exercise 3.C

Think of the situations described in the sentences below, relative to the situation of utterance. Try to decide whether they are presented as remote or non-remote, and factual or non-factual.

    e.g. I'm very happy here. (non-remote, factual)

    1   I'd rather be at the beach.

    2   I'll see you soon.

    3   I was asleep during the show.

    4   They may come this evening.

    5   He could run faster back then.

    6   We like what we see.

    7   I shall return!

Aspect

In discussing tense, we concentrated on the location of a situation. In order to talk about ASPECT, we have to look inside the situation. In terms of its internal dimensions, a situation may be represented as fixed or changing, it may be treated as lasting for only a moment or having duration, and it can be viewed as complete or as ongoing. These are aspectual distinctions.

Because aspect has to do with the kind of situation perceived or experienced, it can be expressed both lexically and grammatically. The grammatical expression of aspect is accomplished via the perfect and progressive forms of the verb. The use of these grammatical markers on the verb, however, is frequently connected to inherent properties of the verb's meaning, or lexical aspect. As illustrated in certain types of common problems (e.g. **I'm understanding English*), there may be difficulties with lexical aspect for many learners who can use the forms of grammatical aspect quite proficiently.

Lexical aspect

LEXICAL ASPECT can be discussed as a general vocabulary topic, but here we will focus on only verb meaning. The broadest conceptual distinction needed is between situations that can be treated as stative and others that can be treated as dynamic.

Stative or dynamic

Verbs commonly used with STATIVE meanings apply to situations that are relatively constant over time and describe cognitive (i.e. mental) states such as knowledge (*know, understand*), as in [17a, b], and emotion (*hate, like*), as in [17c, d], or relations (*be, have*), as in [17e, f].

> [17] a. We understand the questions.
>   b. And we know the answers.
>   c. We like our English class.
>   d. But we hate the tests.
>   e. We are intelligent people.
>   f. And we have opinions.

When these types of verbs are used, there is no action by an agent, nor is there any end to the state implied. They would sound odd in a direct answer to a question such as *What do you do?* where some action (a dynamic quality) is assumed.

Most verbs are not used with stative meanings, but have the concept of change as an essential characteristic and apply to DYNAMIC situations. Dynamic situations can be divided into those viewed as having almost no duration (non-durative) versus those having duration (durative).

Punctual or durative

Verbs used with non-durative meanings typically describe isolated acts (*kick, hit, smash*), as in [18].

> [18] a. She kicked the ball.
>   b. It hit the window.
>   c. And it smashed the glass.

Another term for non-durative is punctual aspect, related to the 'point in time' interpretation of expressions (*fire a gun, smash a window*) which do not extend through time.

In contrast, verbs with durative meanings describe situations that typically extend through time. DURATIVE aspect is an essential feature of verbs that denote activities (*run, eat*), as in [19a], and processes (*become, grow*), as in [19b].

> [19] a. We should run more and eat less.
>   b. We'll become more peaceful as we grow older.

This division of types of lexical aspect is summarized in Box 3.5.

Summary Box 3.5 **Types of lexical aspect**

Stative		Dynamic		
		Punctual	Durative	
Cognition	Relations	Acts	Activities	Processes
believe	*be*	*hit*	*eat*	*become*
hate	*belong*	*jump*	*run*	*change*
know	*contain*	*kick*	*swim*	*flow*
like	*have*	*stab*	*walk*	*grow*
understand	*own*	*strike*	*work*	*harden*
want	*resemble*	*throw*	*write*	*learn*

Those verbs that denote stative concepts in English tend not to be used with progressive forms. After buying a car, English speakers are not likely to tell people, *I'm having a car now*, because that would suggest a process (i.e. something happening) rather than a state (i.e. something fixed). It is important to emphasize that it is the concepts that are stative and not the verbs because, as will be noted later, many of those verbs can have more specific uses with progressive aspect.

Those verbs that are typically used with punctual aspect, describing momentary acts (*kick*, *cough*), take on a slightly different meaning when used in the progressive form. In most circumstances, sentences such as *He's kicking the box* or *Someone's coughing* will tend to be interpreted as repeated acts of *kick* and *cough* and not as single acts. The concept of repetition, which is sometimes described as the iterative aspect, can appear in other phrases (e.g. *again and again*, *over and over*), but it is notably absent from the meaning of verbs used statively.

Exercise 3.D

Using the conceptual categories (stative, punctual, durative) presented in Box 3.5, try to decide what kind of lexical aspect is involved in the basic uses of the following verbs.

e.g.	break (punctual)	4	enlarge	8	possess	12	smash
1	deserve	5	knock	9	prefer	13	sneeze
2	deteriorate	6	owe	10	rain	14	stroll
3	dislike	7	perceive	11	ripen	15	wish

Grammatical aspect

The basic GRAMMATICAL distinction in English ASPECT is marked by two forms of the verb. These are traditionally described as versions of the verb *be* with the present participle (Verb + -*ing*) for the progressive, as in [20a], and versions of *have* with the past participle (Verb + -*en/ed*) for the perfect, as in [20b].

> [20] a. I am/was eating.
>   b. I have/had eaten.

The conceptual distinction between these two forms involves two different perspectives. With the progressive, a situation is viewed from the inside as potentially ongoing at that point ('in progress'), relative to some other situation. With the perfect, a situation is viewed from the outside, typically in retrospect, relative to some other situation. The understanding of 'some other situation' in each case will depend on the tense assigned to *be* and *have*. These basic distinctions in grammatical aspect are summarized in Box 3.6.

Summary Box 3.6 **Grammatical aspect**

Grammatical aspect	Concept of situation
progressive	viewed from the inside, in progress
perfect	viewed from the outside, in retrospect

It is important to be aware of how the interaction of lexical and grammatical aspect is typically interpreted. In many cases the meaning that results from that interaction is implicated or inferred rather than stated. Such interpretations are justified most of the time, but they are not necessary meanings and can be cancelled. For example, uttering the sentence in [21a] might normally have the implication that the process is complete or finished. Such an implicated meaning is based on our typical experience, not on grammatical form. In fact, the initial interpretation can be amended if more information, such as the clause in [21b], is added.

> [21] a. Your plants have really grown.
>   b. Yeah, but they still have a long way to go.

Complete or incomplete

The most marked difference in implicated meaning associated with grammatical aspect is found when the verbs being used have dynamic lexical aspect. That is, verbs denoting acts, activities, and processes will be interpreted very differently when used with progressive as opposed to perfect aspect. Some examples are presented in [22] to [25].

[22] a. He is eating lunch.
　　　 b. He has eaten lunch.

[23] a. I am writing some notes.
　　　 b. I have written some notes.

[24] a. We are baking a cake.
　　　 b. We have baked a cake.

[25] a. She is learning karate.
　　　 b. She has learned karate.

In the a. examples, the implicated meaning is that the activity or process is ongoing and incomplete. In the b. examples, the implication is that those events are completed and some goal has been achieved. The potential for completion inherent in verbs describing activities and processes interacts with the external, retrospective view of the perfect to imply completion. This is what happens when a verb has dynamic lexical aspect.

When the inherent conceptual meaning of a verb is not dynamic and does contain a potential end-point, the external retrospective view of the perfect will not imply completion. As examples [26] and [27] suggest, when verbs with stative aspect are used in the perfect, there is no implicated meaning of completion.

[26] I have been ill.

[27] He has had the flu.

Even when adverbial expressions that suggest a period of time up to (and possibly ending at) the time of speaking are added to sentences containing statives, the perfect will not receive a 'completion' interpretation. Indeed, there is an implication in examples [28] to [31] that the pre-existing situations being described will continue.

[28] He has believed in Allah all his life.

[29] We have known Fred for many years.

[30] I have owned this car for two months.

[31] She has hated him since she first met him.

It is lexical aspect that seems to be the key in determining whether the use of the perfect implies that something is complete or not.

English verbs associated with stative meanings are mostly not found in the progressive. However, those that can be used with progressive aspect tend to imply that the state is being marked as not permanent, as in [32] and [33].

[32] You're being foolish.

[33] I'm having a terrible day.

In [32] and [33], the meaning of 'ongoing within a situation' associated with the progressive is certainly implicated, but the state is temporary, or, the state has the potential for ending or completion. These different implicated meanings associated with the interaction of lexical and grammatical aspect are summarized in Box 3.7.

Summary Box 3.7 **Combining lexical and grammatical aspect**

Grammatical aspect		Lexical aspect	Implicated meaning
perfect	+	dynamic	Completed activity, retrospectively viewed
perfect	+	stative	Pre-existing state, retrospectively viewed
progressive	+	dynamic	Ongoing activity, internally viewed
progressive	+	stative	Temporary state, internally viewed

From the preceding discussion, it is possible to view aspectual meaning in English as compositional. That is, each feature of lexical and grammatical aspect adds to the overall effect in implicated meaning. The tense of the verb will relate that implicated meaning to the situation of utterance. This is illustrated in Box 3.8 by looking at the complex aspectual forms in [34] and [35] and presenting a detailed analysis of their components.

[34] I have been working very hard.

[35] You had been learning a lot.

Summary Box 3.8 **Meaning components of verb forms**

I	PRESENT	HAVE + -*EN/ED*	BE + -*ING*	*work very hard.*
	time of utterance	external view in retrospect	internal view in progress	dynamic activity

(= at this time I look back at myself in an activity viewed internally as in progress.)

You	PAST	HAVE + -*EN/ED*	BE + -*ING*	*learn a lot.*
	remote from time of utterance	external view in retrospect	internal view in progress	dynamic process

(= at that time I looked back at you in a process viewed internally as in progress.)

The analyses offered in Box 3.8 show that both an external and an internal view can be presented within the same structure. They also make it clear that the internal view stands in a closer relationship to the activity (i.e. the verb) being described than does the external view. The external view is tied more closely to tense and the situation of utterance. It may be this feature, the connection between situation of utterance and marking a retrospective view of an event, that leads to the common observation that the present perfect in English often seems to describe 'a past event with current relevance'.

Exercise 3.E

Try to describe the components of conceptual meaning in these sentences. Follow the pattern presented in Box 3.8.

e.g.   I have been jogging.

(at this time I look back at myself in an activity viewed internally as in progress)

1   They had been swimming.

2   We were strolling in the park.

3   It has been raining.

4   She has saved a fortune.

Photocopiable © Oxford University Press

Meanings in context

The distinction in tense between remote (past) and non-remote (present) has a typical application in organizing information in discourse. Information that is treated as part of the BACKGROUND will tend to be expressed in the past tense. Information that is of current concern, in the FOREGROUND, will be expressed in the present tense. Background scene-setting, particularly in stories, is often expressed in the past progressive, and ongoing current situations are described in the present progressive. Viewing recent changes from the current situation is typically expressed by perfect aspect. The dominant contrast, however, is between background and foreground information.

In a magazine article

A rather clear example of how one writer uses different tense and aspect forms to indicate a change within one area of medical studies can be found in extract [36], from a magazine (*Scientific American*, November 1992). Look especially at the italicized verb forms.

[36] Drug resistance *was* mostly ignored in the U.S. until recently
because physicians *believed* they *had* access to all the antibiotics
they *might need.* They *were* wrong. Drug resistance *has been found*
in virtually every type of microbe that *has been fought* with
antibiotics. That *covers* everything from food-borne pathogens
such as Salmonella to sexually transmitted organisms such as
Neisseria gonorrhoeae. Surgical patients *are* now *dying* in U.S.
hospitals from wound infections caused by enterococcal bacteria
resistant to several different drugs.

The sequence of the writer's presentation in [36] can be traced through the
verb forms, from a remote factual situation (past tenses), through some
changes that are viewed retrospectively from the current situation (perfect
aspect), to a non-remote factual statement (present tense) of a general current
situation, to a specific result that is viewed as ongoing (progressive aspect) at
the time of writing. In this expository text, there is a pattern of using past tenses
for background information and present tense (with or without grammatical
aspect) for information that is in the foreground of the writer's focus.

In academic writing

A related observation can be made about academic writing where the results of
different research studies are being reviewed. There is a tendency to use past
tense forms to report on research that is identified as a finding, but not the type
of finding that the author uses as a generalization. Generalizations are
expressed in the present tense. In this way, some research results form a
background relative to which the foreground generalizations can be made.
Some extracts from one article on second language speech research (Leather
and James 1991) may serve to illustrate the pattern. Some specific results are
reported in the past tense, with the researchers (dates of publication in
brackets) as agents, as shown in [37a, b].

[37] a. Maidment (1976, 1983) and Ohala and Gilbert (1978) also
found that listeners can in some circumstances recognize
languages by their prosody alone.
b. In one of the experiments carried out by Cochrane (1980),
Japanese children *scored* higher than adults.

In contrast, generalizations by the current writer(s) are made in the present
tense, with researchers' names and publication dates in brackets, but not as
agents, as shown in [38a, b].

[38] a. There *are* often considerable differences in judgment
between one native judge and another (see de Bot 1979;
Strain 1963).

b. That some ontogenetic neurological change limits the ability
of adults to learn a new sound system *is* not proven (see, e.g.,
Flege 1988; Leather 1988).

This difference in the use of past as opposed to present tense may be made
clearer by comparing two potential ways, [39a] and [39b], of reporting the
same result.

[39] a. Scovel (1969) found that age was a factor in L2 learning.
      b. Age is a factor in L2 learning (Scovel 1969).

The choice of type of statement, and particularly its tense, has a clear influence
on the status of the information being presented. One specific result (past
tense, as in [39a]) may be different from possible others, but a current
statement of fact (present tense, as in [39b]) gives the information much more
authority.

In narratives

In less technical writing, a similar distinction can be maintained between
present tense for presenting general statements and past tense for specific
events. Notice how the author of extract [40] (James 1981: 49) uses tense shifts
to distinguish between general facts (present) and particular acts (past).

[40] It *is* remarkable how much damage a group of small boys *can* do
      to a building site if it *is* left unguarded. In loose moments I might
      pride myself on possessing a creative impulse but I don't have to
      do too much introspection before being forced to admit that a
      destructive impulse *is* in there somewhere as well. Under my
      supervision, dumps of mixed lime *were* well seeded with bricks. A
      brick dropped from high up into soft lime *makes* a very
      satisfactory glurp. Studded with bricks like ice-cream full of
      chipped chocolate, the lime quickly *became* unusable. We
      smashed tiles by the hundred. Porcelain lavatory bowls *were*
      reduced to their constituent molecules.

In narrative text, there can also be a general background versus foreground
effect associated with different tenses. Notice how there is a distinct shift of
tense, from past to present, in extract [41] when the author starts to describe
Dolly's fate. This is from a short story (Cheever 1982: 323).

[41] Donald Wryson, in his crusading zeal for upzoning, *was* out in all
      kinds of weather, and let's say that one night, when he *was*
      returning from a referendum in an ice storm, his car *skidded* down
      Hill Street, *struck* the big elm at the corner, and *was* demolished.
      Finis. His poor widow, either through love or dependence, *was*
      inconsolable. Getting out of bed one morning, a month or so

after the loss of her husband, she *got* her feet caught in the dust ruffle and *fell* and *broke* her hip. Weakened by a long convalescence, she *contracted* pneumonia and *departed* this life. This *leaves* us with Dolly to account for, and what a sad tale we *can* write for this little girl. During the months in which her parents' will *is* in probate, she *lives* first on the charity and then on the forebearance of her neighbors. Finally she *is* sent to live with her only relative, a cousin of her mother's, who *is* a schoolteacher in Los Angeles.

There is no obvious reason, in terms of narrating the events, why the fate of two people should be described in the past tense and that of another in the present tense, as found in [41]. One way to view the distinction is in terms of those events in the past tense being background for a consideration of Dolly's experience. The other events are depicted as remote. The events involving Dolly are described as if in present experience. It is Dolly who is, according to the tense used, in the foreground.

Within narratives that only use past tense, there is often a background role given to the past progressive and a foreground role for the simple past. In the opening paragraph of one detective novel (Macdonald 1971: 3), shown here as [42], the author creates a background effect with the past progressive while the events are presented in a simple past tense sequence.

[42]   A rattle of leaves *woke* me some time before dawn. A hot wind *was breathing in* at the bedroom window. I *got up* and *closed* the window and *lay* in bed and *listened* to the wind.

In a news report

In contrast to narrative accounts with a focus on past events, the typical news report is designed to focus on recent changes and the current situation. Headlines are inevitably in the present tense, as shown in [43].

[43]   Bankruptcy hits eateries
Pacific Food Services *has filed* for bankruptcy protection and *has closed* two of its restaurants. The company *grew* from a family business which *started* in the 1950s.

Also noticeable in [43] is the foregrounding of recent changes through the use of perfect aspect with present tense. These forms are sometimes called the 'hot news' perfects. The events described are actually in past time, but are treated as if they happened within the scope of present time. After the foregrounded news of the first sentence in [43], some background information is presented via past tense forms.

In spoken discourse

In spoken discourse, the foregrounding effect of the use of present tense within a narrative already established via past tense is often more dramatic. As shown in extract [44], from a recorded conversation, the speaker uses the past progressive for the initial background, or scene-setting, then shifts into the present tense to highlight the salient event in the story and her own internal reaction. She returns to the past tense for further background events, then shifts once again to the present for her foregrounded reaction.

[44]   I *was sitting* at the bus stop the other day and this woman *was sitting* across from me and I *see* this caterpillar drop behind her and *start* squiggling its way up to her and *I'm* just like, 'Should I tell her or should I not? Should I tell her?' I *sat* there for five minutes and *watched* it get up to her shoe and I *decided* I *can't* tell her. *I've* got to see what *happens*.

In a spoken account like [44], there is a clear dramatic function associated with the use of the present tense in contrast with the narrative past. This functional distinction between the use of different tense forms will be explored again later in Chapter 10.

A brief summary of these observations is presented in Box 3.9.

Summary Box 3.9 **Background and foreground information**

Background information	past tense
(specific acts, events, old focus, settings)	
Foreground information	present tense
(general statements, facts, new focus, changes)	

Discussion topics and projects

1   There appears to be a pattern in the use of present versus past tenses in different parts of a summary of research studies. Identify the tenses used in the following abstract of a research paper (Green and Hecht 1992).

Foreign language learners are commonly taught explicit rules of grammar, but often fail to apply them when confronted with communicative tasks. How well have they learnt the rules? Do they recognize where they are to be applied? Are they better at some rules than others? Above all, how is getting the language right related to explicit rule knowledge?

Twelve errors commonly committed by German pupils performing communicative tasks in English were put before 300 German learners of English at different levels. They were asked to state the rules they believed had been transgressed and to correct the errors. A peer group of 50 native speakers of English was given the same test. The learners' ability to state relevant rules and supply appropriate corrections for the errors is examined with reference to some of the assumptions and expectations that lie behind explicit grammar teaching.

(a) What patterns of tense choice are found in this text and what functions would you associate with those choices?

(b) Choose some other abstracts from the area of language studies and try to decide whether the observed patterns in the text above are widely used (or not).

(c) Choose some abstracts of articles from a totally unrelated field, identify the tenses used, and then compare the observed patterns of tense form and function to those found above.

2   Other types of lexical aspect are sometimes noted in terms of different perspectives on situations. Ingressive aspect expresses a focus on the onset of situations and is associated with verbs like *begin* and *start*. Egressive aspect expresses a focus on the end of situations, as in verbs like *stop* and *quit*. Continuative aspect is expressed by verbs like *continue, stay,* and *remain*. In each of the following examples, note that there are two verbs, but not two distinct actions. The second verb describes the action and the first verb focuses our perspective on an aspect of the action.

   (i)   We remained standing.
   (ii)   She burst out laughing.
  (iii)   He gave up smoking.
  (iv)   They kept on ignoring us.
   (v)   He came out swinging.
  (vi)   Quit complaining!
 (vii)   Leave off doing that!
(viii)   Don't go on asking for more!

(a) Try to decide whether the aspect in each case is ingressive, egressive, or continuative.

(b) What reason, in terms of aspect, would you offer for the preferred use of the + -*ing* form of the second verb in these examples?

(c) Would you associate the particles *out, up, on, off* with any specific types of aspect mentioned here?

3   The distinction between stative and dynamic aspect is clearly important in the grammatical description of verbs in English. With many examples, the distinction seems very straightforward. However, it is possible to find some 'stative verbs' used in sentences implying change and some verbs used with both stative and dynamic meanings. It may be that the category of 'stative' actually depends on a cluster of conceptual features, not all of which are expressed by the verb form alone. Some suggested features are:

constant over time
describing inherent properties
absence of an active agent in the event
cannot be expressed as an imperative
cannot be used with certain adverbs of manner (e.g. *deliberately*)
cannot be used with progressive aspect

Consider the following examples, and others you might think are relevant, and try to determine what are the key features that distinguish between stative and dynamic as conceptual categories.

Crime is increasing.
Be happy!
The knot is slipping.
Smell this rose.
Chocolate tastes great.
This garbage smells bad.
He intentionally ruined the party.
Imagine yourself in Hawaii!
Some people are very rich.
Love thy neighbor.
This bag weighs a lot.
He lives with his parents.
I'm thinking about her constantly.
Know yourself.
He's resembling his father more and more each year.
She is understanding her own problems better these days.

4   Another distinction in lexical aspect exists between actions which imply a result or goal (= telic aspect) and those which do not (= atelic aspect). A test for this type of distinction has been suggested by Brinton (1988) in terms of how the following question is answered:

If one was VERB + *-ING*, but was interrupted while VERB + *-ING*, has one VERB + *-ED/EN*?

Putting any verb in the VERB slot, a 'yes' answer will signify that the verb is atelic and a 'no' answer that it is telic.

(a) Try to apply this test to the following verbs (and any others you might choose) to discover which are telic or not.

arrive, chew, close, drown, land, open, sing, sing a song, succeed, swallow, swim, talk, try

(b) On the basis of this exercise, can you think of a better way to describe the concept of telic aspect in English? (For example, to a learner of English who thinks that the sentence *He has drowned and then we have saved him* is okay.)

Teaching ideas

1 Something's wrong here

Exercises that use incorrect sentences may provide the basis for introductory activities on the basic forms of the tenses and progressive aspect. One type can focus on errors of fact, as in (a), and another on errors of form, as in (b). An alternative, matching questions and answers, is exemplified in (c).

(a) A simple exercise that is based on the truth (or untruth) of statements can be used to help focus students' attention on basic verb forms. Within the vocabulary range of students, a number of inaccurate statements are created. The students' task is to say or write a corrected version. Here are some examples, using simple present and past tenses.

    (i) The sun rises in the west.
   (ii) The earth goes round the moon.
  (iii) Cats usually chase dogs.
  (iv) Water freezes at 10 degrees.
   (v) California is east of New York.
  (vi) Einstein was Swedish.
 (vii) Karl Marx was president of Russia.
(viii) Buddha was born in China.

Another version of this exercise can be designed with tag questions to focus on the negative forms of the tenses, as in these examples.

  (ix) Joan of Arc was English, wasn't she?
   (x) Confucius wrote in Korean, didn't he?

(b) Some very common types of mistakes of learners trying to use the present progressive can be incorporated into an exercise that also gives a sense of being 'inside' an event. In the following examples, students have to offer better versions of these utterances (following some introductory models, perhaps).

   (i) *Listen! Someone is shout.
  (ii) *Look! Snow is fall.

    (iii)   *Wait! I thinking about it.

    (iv)   *Stop! The light change to red.

    (v)   *Ouch! You're stand on my foot.

    (vi)   *Quick! The bus come.

    (vii)   *Just a minute! Somebody else using that.

    (viii)   *Hey! Move over! You're sit in my seat.

(c) For teachers who do not want to give their learners examples with incorrect forms, as in (b), it is possible to focus their attention on basic forms through another exercise type where questions and answers have to be matched. The simple instruction is: find the best answer for each question and draw a line to connect them. Examples:

    (i)   Did you see the TV news?   I don't know. He isn't here.

    (ii)   Why didn't you wait?   I'm trying to fix a flat tire.

    (iii)   Have you read any   Yeah, I've just read one of his
         Hemingway?   books.

    (iv)   Where's Fred?   No, I wasn't home last night.

    (v)   What are you doing?   We had to catch the last bus.

Note. If possible, after completing an exercise like this, students should be encouraged to talk about how they chose their answers. Then, in groups, they may also be willing to create a similar exercise for the other groups to complete.

2 What's Kula doing?

One exercise on the basic forms can combine a simple question–answer format (about a schedule) with notes on some common spelling patterns of the progressive forms.

Step 1. As a warm-up, the first question–answer activity can be about students' daily schedules. This may elicit verbs like *study, eat, write,* and *sit.*

Step 2. A basic structural frame can then be established:

    What is _____ doing at _____ o'clock? She's _____ing.

Step 3. As an option, some spelling notes can be made. Some examples are: Verbs ending in -e (e.g. *write*) drop the -e before adding -ing (e.g. *writing*). Verbs ending in consonant–verb–consonant (e.g. *sit,* but not *eat*) repeat the last consonant before adding -*ing* (e.g. *sitting,* but *eating*).

Step 4. A master schedule (prepared by the teacher initially, but later by individual students) is created. The following is just one possible format. (Students have blank versions of this schedule.)

    Kula's schedule
    7:00–7:30 run in park
    7:30–7:45 have a shower
    7:45–8:15 eat breakfast

8:15–8:30 ride bike to school
8:30–9:30 sit in language lab
9:30 –10:00 take a break
10:00–10:30 write notes or chat with friends
10:30–11:00 plan for afternoon class
11:00–11:30 swim or do aerobics
11:30–12:30 have lunch

Step 5. One by one, students have to ask questions, using the structural frame, and write the answers in their blank schedules. (After completing the spoken exercise, an opportunity should be given for students to go over and edit their written forms, to check their spelling, for example.)

As students become familiar with the format, other types of schedules, other spelling rules, and other structural frames can be incorporated.

3 True now?

To help students develop a feeling for the remote/non-remote and the factual/non-factual distinction, it is possible to create a judgment exercise in which they are asked to use the distinctions between now and another time, plus true and not true. For example:

Look at the following sentences and decide whether the speaker is referring to something that is 'true now', 'true at another time', or 'not true yet'.

  (i)   I could move faster when I was younger.
 (ii)   I'll be at the meeting if I can.
(iii)   I just love pineapples!
 (iv)   She said she had been ill.
  (v)   We are very happy here.
 (vi)   It's raining in Baltimore.
(vii)   The weather was awful during Spring.
(viii)   I wish I was there.
 (ix)   I might make it to Tahiti one day.
  (x)   Only love can break your heart.

4 *I learned* or *I have learned*?

The difference between using the simple past and the present perfect is difficult for a lot of students. The remoteness element of the past tense can be contrasted with the non-remote element of the present tense in the present perfect structure. That is, in a typical interpretation, *I learned English* sounds more remote from current experience than *I have learned English*.

Step 1. To bring out the contrast, ask students to complete a text with (a) all verbs in the simple past, then (b) those same verbs in the present perfect. A simple example is offered here.

My name is Dagmar. I'm from Germany.
(*live*) I _____ in America for two years.
(*be*) I _____ an exchange student.
(*be*) I _____ studying modern art.
(*see*) I _____ a lot of the country in that time.
(*help*) My host family _____ me travel all over.
(*enjoy*) I _____ my stay.
And I hope to return one day for another visit.

Step 2. After this exercise, discuss with students the different impressions of remoteness (past) versus retrospective recent view (present perfect), though not in such technical terms.

Step 3. Ask students to decide, in each sentence of another text, which forms of the verb are best in the spaces provided. One example might be:

When I (*be*) _____ in my own country, I (*think*) _____ that America (*be*) _____ full of rich people. Now that I (*stay*) _____ in Los Angeles for six months, I (*see*) _____ both rich and poor people. I (*be*) _____ studying medicine and I (*visit*) _____ some clinics in very poor areas. My picture of America (*change*) _____ a lot in this short time.

Step 4. Ask students to write a short text in which they make a contrast between an experience they *have just had* and an experience or opinion they *had* a long time ago (possibly as a child).

5   Have you ever ... ?

The forms *ever* ('at any time') in questions and *never* ('at no time') in answers concerning events viewed retrospectively ('up until now') are often used with present perfect forms. Structural frames would be:

Have you ever ... ? I have never ...

An introductory task might be for two students to be asked to perform (in front of the group or class) the deep voice and squeaky voice roles in the following interrogation.

Deep Good morning. I'd like to ask you a few questions.
Squeaky Okay.
Deep Have you ever been to France?
Squeaky No. I have never been to Europe.
Deep Have you ever studied French?
Squeaky No. I have never studied a foreign language.
Deep Have you ever smoked French cigarettes?
Squeaky No. I have never smoked.
Deep Have you ever drunk French wine?
Squeaky No. I have never done that. Well, maybe once. Or twice.

After discussing and identifying the structural frames, students (in groups, perhaps) have to create survey questions on a number of different topics, one per group (e.g. food, drinks, countries, beautiful places, scary things). Their task is to create a set of five questions for their topic (e.g. *Have you ever eaten frogs' legs?*; *Have you ever seen a ghost?*). When each question set is prepared, members of each group interview members of the other groups, collecting *Yes, I have* and *No, I've never …* responses. After all the noise and movement has subsided, the collected results (and any really interesting responses) can be discussed.

6 What on earth is (s)he doing?

A number of exercise types can be found to practice progressive aspect, with verbs that have both durative (a, b) and stative aspect (c).

(a) One format for focusing attention on progressive aspect is through a mime exercise. Each student is given a verb with dynamic aspect (e.g. *dance, eat, run, sing, swim, type*) to demonstrate. These verbs can simply be supplied by the teacher, on pieces of paper, to each student in turn. The student has to mime the action of the verb so that the others can identify which verb is meant. If it seems to work better, an alternative approach would have a brief introduction activating this kind of vocabulary, by getting students to talk about activities, sports, and types of work. Then each student writes an activity verb on a piece of paper. The papers are collected and mixed up in a box. As victims are selected to perform (taking a piece of paper from the box), the organizer instigates the performance with 'What on earth is (s)he doing?'

(b) *Why are they smiling?*

An alternative version can be developed around photographs or pictures from magazines. The moment of the photograph is treated as being 'inside' an event (in progress) and questions can be asked using progressive aspect (e.g. *What is she doing? Why are they running?*). Students can be encouraged to bring photos or pictures, accompanied by an appropriate question (or two). With the accompanying photograph here, we might have questions such as: *Why are they smiling? Where are they standing? What are they wearing round their necks?*

(c) *I'm having a bad hair day*

With a more advanced group of students, it may be possible to help them develop an awareness of the subtle meanings associated with the combination of stative verb plus progressive aspect. Their first task is to discuss and decide on a meaning for each of the (1) sentences below (with the teacher's support). Their second task is then to decide what the other (2) sentences might mean and why they might sound odd (most of the time). They can be encouraged to think of contexts that would be appropriate for these (2) sentences.

   (i)   (1) I'm having a bad hair day. (2) I'm having a car.
  (ii)   (1) He's being a jerk. (2) He's being a student.
 (iii)   (1) I'm hating this! (2) I'm hating fish!
 (iv)   (1) You're liking strange stuff today. (2) You're liking Canada.
  (v)   (1) I'm understanding her more. (2) I'm understanding English.
 (vi)   (1) She's not believing a word he says. (2) She's believing in God.

7 Once, more than once, or all the time?

There are many possible exercises to focus students' attention on lexical aspect. One type, as in (a), uses a connection with frequency expressions to distinguish meanings. Another, as in (b), attempts to connect grammatical tense and aspect with one kind of lexical aspect.

(a) One way to help students develop a sense of lexical aspect distinctions, such as stative versus punctual, is to help them make a connection with the 'number of occasions' implied by a structure. For example, students can be asked to read the following sentences and to discuss (or decide), with teacher support, which of the following expressions applies to each sentence: one time; more than one time; all the time.

   (i)   He suddenly jumped into the water.
  (ii)   Hae-Young understands Korean.
 (iii)   She is kicking the car tire right now.
 (iv)   My sister hates fish.
  (v)   Someone's coughing.
 (vi)   Something broke the window.
 (vii)   Bucky dropped the ball.
(viii)   Soo Yang has a car.

Note. After an exercise like this is completed, it may be a good opportunity to reflect on, and talk about, which features in the sentences provided the best clues to the interpretation.

(b) *I was walking one night*

The following exercise is from a study by Bardovi-Harlig and Reynolds (1995) that attempted to focus learners' attention on the use of past tense with activity verbs. It may work best with higher level (college English class) students. Students were asked to read a text and follow instructions like (i) and (ii) to identify specific forms.

(i) Find a sentence with only one verb in the simple past. Write it on the line below.

_____

(ii) Find a sentence with one simple past verb and one past progressive verb. Write it on the line below.

_____

Students were also asked to perform exercises like (iii), after reading the text, part of which is reproduced below.

(iii) Kerwin used the following verbs in the past progressive. He also used them in the simple past. Find the simple past forms, write them beside the past progressive and write the line where you found them. Look at the way the past progressive and the simple past are used. Can you tell a difference in meaning?

Past progressive	Simple past	Line
was walking	_____	____
was doing	_____	____

> Kerwin: I was walking one night. It was bitterly cold, around Christmas 1978, and I was walking. I think I was walking down to the river just to clear my head or to go for a walk. I love to walk. There was a man on the heating vent across the street from the State Department at 21st and E which was only a block from my apartment, and he called out to me. He said he wanted a buck to buy something to eat. I was very irritated with him for calling out after me. I didn't want to be bothered and I didn't believe him either. I thought, 'Well he just wants to get something to drink'; and I thought to myself, 'Well I'll fix him. I'll go and get him something to eat and that way he'll be frustrated and angry and didn't get what he wanted but at least I'll give him what he asked for.' So I went up to my apartment, got him a bowl of soup, got him a sandwich and a cup of tea, and brought it down. I set it down and walked away.

The rest of the text can be found in Bardovi-Harlig and Reynolds (1995: 130) who propose that class discussion of examples in context helps learners develop a better awareness of how grammatical and lexical aspect work in English.

8 Background and foreground

With advanced learners, it may also be possible to consider extended extracts from different texts (and text types) and identify how tense and aspect are used to put information into the background or foreground. Students can be encouraged to bring newspaper and magazine articles to class for study. As one example, here is an extract from a popular book on language and communication (Tannen 1986: 67–68). Students first have to identify the tenses used, then try to think of reasons (with teacher support) why certain chunks of the text are in different tenses.

> Anyone could get you what you want for your birthday if you told him what you want. In fact, you could get it for yourself, if it were the gift (the message) that mattered. What really matters is the metamessage: evidence that the person knows you well enough to figure out what you would like, and cares enough to spend time getting it.
>
> Nancy had mentioned her intention of buying a certain pair of work gloves, which were sold in the store in town. She felt cheated of a birthday present when, on her birthday, Thomas presented her with a pair of those gloves, which he had asked their neighbors to pick up when they drove into town. Nancy felt Thomas should have taken the trouble to figure out on his own something she would like, and pick out—and up—himself.
>
> Birthdays, like Christmas, can be setups for disappointment because so much seems to hang on the metamessages of gifts from those one is close to. But indirectness works very well in most situations, if people agree on how to use it.
>
> A Greek woman explained how she and her father (and later her husband) communicated. If she wanted to do something, like go to a dance, she had to ask her father for permission. He never said no. But she could tell from the way he said yes whether or not he meant it. If he said something like 'Yes, of course, go', then she knew he thought it was a good idea. If he said something like 'If you want, you can go', then she understood that he didn't think it was a good idea, and she wouldn't go. His tone of voice, facial expression, and all the elements of conversational style gave her clues as to how he felt about her going.
>
> Why didn't he just tell her that he didn't think she should go? Why wasn't he 'honest'? Well, he *did* tell her, in a way that was clear to both her and him. To the extent that we can even talk about honesty in communicative habits, any system that successfully gets meaning across is honest.

Further reading

General reference, with examples

Downing, P. and P. Locke. 1992. *A University Course in English Grammar.* Chapter 9. Englewood Cliffs, NJ: Prentice Hall.
Leech, G. 1987. *Meaning and the English Verb.* (2nd edn.) London: Longman.

More theoretical discussions

Bybee, J. 1985. *Morphology.* Amsterdam: John Benjamins.
Comrie, B. 1976. *Aspect.* Cambridge: Cambridge University Press.
Declerck, R. 1991. *Tense in English: Its Structure and Use in Discourse.* London: Routledge.
Dahl, Ö. 1985. *Tense and Aspect Systems.* Oxford: Blackwell.

On remote and non-remote

Fleischman, S. 1989. 'Temporal distance: A basic linguistic metaphor.' *Studies in Language* 13: 1–50.
Lewis, M. 1986. *The English Verb.* Hove, England: Language Teaching Publications
Lyons, J. 1977. *Semantics I and II.* Chapter 15. Cambridge: Cambridge University Press.

On the future

Huddleston, R. 1995. 'The case against a future tense in English.' *Studies in Language* 19: 399–466.

The historical present

Wolfson, N. 1982. *CHP: The Conversational Historical Present in American English Narrative.* Dordrecht: Foris.

Lexical aspect

Brinton, L. 1988. *The Development of English Aspectual Systems.* Cambridge: Cambridge University Press.
Vendler, Z. 1967. *Linguistics in Philosophy.* Ithaca, NY: Cornell University Press.

Grammatical aspect

Klein, W. 1992. 'The present perfect puzzle.' *Language* 68: 525–52.
Schwenter, S. 1994. '"Hot news" and the grammaticalization of perfects.' *Linguistics* 32: 995–1028.

Background and foreground

Bailey, N. 1989. 'Discourse conditioned tense variation: teacher implications.' in M. Eisenstein (ed.): *The Dynamic Interlanguage* (pp. 279–95) New York: Plenum Press.

Hopper, P. 1979. 'Aspect and foregrounding in discourse' in T. Givon (ed.): *Discourse and Syntax. Syntax and Semantics*, volume 12. (pp. 213–41). New York: Academic Press.

Schiffrin, D. 1981. 'Tense variation in narrative.' *Language* 57: 45–62.

In text analysis

Swales, J. 1990. *Genre Analysis*. Chapter 7. Cambridge: Cambridge University Press.

Trimble, L. 1985. *English for Science and Technology*. Chapter 8. Cambridge: Cambridge University Press.

Acquisition research

Andersen, R. 1991. 'Developmental sequences: the emergence of aspect marking in second language acquisition' in: T. Huebner and C. Ferguson (eds.): *Cross-currents in Second Language Acquisition*. (pp. 305–24). Amsterdam: John Benjamins.

Bardovi-Harlig, K. and D. Reynolds. 1995. 'The role of lexical aspect in the acquisition of tense and grammatical aspect.' *TESOL Quarterly* 29: 107–31.

Buczowska, E. and R. Weist. 1991. 'The effects of formal instruction on the second language acquisition of temporal location.' *Language Learning* 41: 535–54.

Robison, R. 1995. 'The aspect hypothesis revisited: a cross-sectional study of tense and aspect marking in interlanguage.' *Applied Linguistics* 16: 344–70.

Teaching suggestions

Aitken, R. 1992. *Teaching Tenses*. Walton-on-Thames, UK: Thomas Nelson.

Richards, J. 1985. *The Context of Language Teaching*. Chapters 11 and 12. Cambridge: Cambridge University Press.

Riddle, E. 1986. 'The meaning and discourse function of the past tense in English.' *TESOL Quarterly* 20: 267–86.

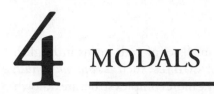

4 MODALS

1 In the beginning stages, many language learners produce structures such as: *I don't can play good. What exactly is ungrammatical about this sentence?

2 The modals are always presented as if they have lots of different meanings. Is it possible to describe one 'core' meaning for each modal?

3 Do the forms *can* and *be able to* mean the same thing? How about *may* and *be allowed to*? And *will* and *be going to*?

4 Why is *must* used in *We must get together for lunch sometime* when the speaker is being vague rather than certain?

5 How would I know when *you don't have to* is to be used as the opposite of *you must*, rather than *you mustn't*?

Child *Can I leave the table now?*
Parent *I'm sure you can, but you may not.*

This response by the parent has no doubt puzzled many children, leading them to wonder just what the difference is in English between *can* and *may*. These are both examples of modal verbs and their simple form disguises a fairly complex set of functions. We shall try to make sense of those functions, including an explanation of what the parent is trying to tell the child in this example.

Overview

After a brief review of the basic forms of the modals, including both the SIMPLE and PERIPHRASTIC MODAL VERBS, we consider their basic meanings in terms of EPISTEMIC and ROOT MODALITY. The core meanings of each simple modal (*can, may, must, will, should*) are then presented, along with the effects of different contexts on the interpretation of those core meanings. In each case, the distinct uses of related forms (*could, might, would, ought*) and periphrastic modals (*able to, allowed to, have (got) to, going to, supposed to*) are noted. A final section explains the different interpretations of INTERNAL and EXTERNAL NEGATION with modals.

Basic forms

As already noted in Chapter 3, there is a small set of verb forms in English which are described as modals. The SIMPLE MODALS, such as *can, may, must, will*, and *should* have single forms, whereas the more complex structures known as PERIPHRASTIC MODALS are formed with the verbs *be* and *have*, as in *be able to, be allowed to, be going to, be supposed to*, and *have to*. We can think of periphrastic modals as being 'phrase-like' in contrast to the single word forms of simple modals. Although the periphrastic modals do not function as direct equivalents of the simple modals in all their uses, it is possible to list the different forms in terms of related meanings, as in Box 4.1. Also listed in Box 4.1 are the historically related past tense forms of the simple modals.

Summary Box 4.1 **Simple and periphrastic modals**

Simple modals		Periphrastic modals
Present tense	Past tense	
can	*could*	*be able to*
may	*might*	*be allowed to*
must	—	*have (got) to*
shall	*should*	*be supposed to*
will	*would*	*be going to*

The basic set of modals shown in Box 4.1 does not contain *ought to* which, in terms of its form, would fall between the two types listed. It will be included in the discussion of *should*.

Exercise 4.A

With Box 4.1 as a guide, identify all the modal forms in the following text. Which are simple modals and which are periphrastic modals?

> Would you stop complaining about things? We're supposed to do our best and we should be able to finish this work before the boss has to start screaming at us again. If you could just concentrate on getting finished, we might be allowed to leave early this afternoon. You know he's not going to let us leave early if we can't get the work done.

There are some dialects in which combinations such as *I might could go* are used, but for most English speakers, the simple modals do not occur together. However, a simple modal can occur with a periphrastic modal, in that sequence only, as shown in [1].

[1] a. He may be able to help.
     b. They must be going to pay him.
     c. We will have to thank him.

The simple modals

The simple modals are normally characterized as a set on the basis of their distinct grammatical features in English. They are very different from main verbs. In some ways, they resemble the more common auxiliary verbs *be* and *have* because they do not occur with auxiliary *do* in questions or in negatives. However, the modals also have some quite special grammatical features. They do not have a distinct form for third person singular in the present tense, nor are they ever marked for progressive or perfect aspect. These distinguishing features are listed in Box 4.2, along with some potential errors that may be found in the English of beginners.

Summary Box 4.2 **Differences between modals and main verbs**

Category	Modal	Error	Main verb pattern
Third person present singular	*He may*	*He mays	(*He hopes*)
To infinitive	*He may leave*	*He may to leave	(*He hopes to leave*)
Progressive	—	*He is maying	(*He is hoping*)
Perfect	—	*He has mayed	(*He has hoped*)
Emphatic *do*	*He MAY leave*	*He DOES may	(*He DOES hope*)
Negative *do*	*He may not*	*He doesn't may	(*He doesn't hope*)
Question *do*	*May he ... ?*	*Does he may ... ?	(*Does he hope ... ?*)

The beginner who uses a form like *I don't can play* seems to be including *can* within a main verb negative structure (i.e. *I don't play*). If the learner's attention can be focused on phrases containing *can't* (i.e. *I can't play*), the *don't can* uses soon disappear.

Although there is no aspectual form of the simple modal, as shown by the two gaps in Box 4.2, the modal can be used with a following main verb marked for aspect, as shown for the progressive in [2a] and the perfect in [2b].

[2]   a. He may be leaving.
       b. She may have left.

In [2], the form of the modal (*may*) does not change while the *leave* action is marked as being viewed internally or in retrospect.

Exercise 4.B

Presented below are some ungrammatical forms of modals produced by beginning learners of English. Using the categories listed in Box 4.2, identify the most likely type of grammatical mistake found in each example.

e.g.   Do we must go? (Question *do* isn't used with a modal)

I   He cans swim.

2   It does can work.

3   Where does the book must go?

4   They are will going.

5   I don't can play good.

6   They have would done it.

7   You must to keep quiet.

Photocopiable © Oxford University Press

Basic meanings

English modals typically convey some indication of the speaker's perspective or attitude with respect to the situation or state of affairs being described. That perspective can be based on what is known or what is socially determined in the situation. The use of modals to indicate 'what is known' is called EPISTEMIC MODALITY. The use of modals to indicate 'what is socially determined' is described as ROOT (or sometimes 'deontic') MODALITY.

Epistemic modality

Epistemic uses often sound like deductions or conclusions made by the speaker. For example, given a referent (*Suzy*) and a description (*be ill*), speakers can express the relationship in a simple assertion, as in [3a]. However, they can also add some indication of their perspective on the likelihood of that relationship being the case, as in [3b] and [3c].

[3]   a. Suzy is ill.
     b. Suzy must be ill.
     c. Suzy may be ill.

The modal verbs indicate the speaker's assessment of whether the state of affairs is simply the case [3a], necessarily the case [3b], or possibly the case [3c]. That assessment is based on the speaker's deductions, from what is known. Modal forms used with this function are interpreted in terms of epistemic necessity [3b] or epistemic possibility [3c]. It is important to remember that it is the speaker's (or writer's) perspective that is being presented.

Root modality

Root modality is not based on the speaker's knowledge of facts, but on the speaker's awareness of what is socially determined. Root modals are typically used interpersonally and have to do with obligation and permission. Creating an obligation or giving permission are acts that are based on social power of some kind. For example, given another situation involving the referent (*Suzy*) and a description (*leave before noon*), speakers can express the relationship as a simple observation, as in [4a]. However, if the speaker has some socially-based power to control that relationship, then the speaker's perspective can be marked with modals to indicate the use of that power to determine the relationship, as in [4b] and [4c].

[4]   a. Suzy leaves before noon.
     b. Suzy must leave before noon.
     c. Suzy may leave before noon.

In [4], the modals indicate the speaker's perspective on whether the event simply occurs [4a], is required to occur [4b], or is permitted to occur [4c]. The speaker's social power is often based on some established social relationship (e.g. parent–child or boss–worker). Root uses of modals are common in polite requests and offers.

Necessary and possible

There is a clear parallel between the major distinctions made in both epistemic and root modality in English. That pattern is based on what is necessary and what is possible.

If I see someone buying a lot of milk at the store, I can come to the strong conclusion expressed in [5a] or the weaker conclusion in [5b].

[5]   a. He must drink a lot of milk. (= necessary)
     b. He may drink a lot of milk. (= possible)

These epistemic uses are knowledge-based and can be paraphrased as 'necessary that' (*must*) and 'possible that' (*may*).

If, in a different context, a parent wants a child to drink some milk, it can be expressed as a strong obligation, as in [6a]. Alternatively, if the parent is responding to a child's request for something to drink, it can be expressed without any strong obligation, as in [6b].

[6]   a. You must drink some milk. (= necessary)
        b. You may drink some milk. (= possible)

These root modality uses are socially-based, given the general social authority of parents in determining their child's behavior. In these examples, the modals can be paraphrased as 'necessary for' (*must*) and 'possible for' (*may*). These distinctions are summarized in Box 4.3.

Summary Box 4.3 **Epistemic and root modality**

Epistemic modality (= deductions from speaker/writer)

(a) Strong conclusion   *He must be crazy.*
    (necessity)   (= 'I say it is necessarily the case that he is crazy.')

(b) Weak conclusion   *He may be crazy.*
    (possibility)   (= 'I say it is possibly the case that he is crazy.')

Root modality (= requirements from the speaker/writer)

(a) Obligation   *You must leave.*
    (necessity)   (= 'I say it is necessary for you to leave.')

(b) Permission   *You may leave.*
    (possibility)   (= 'I say it's possible for you to leave.')

It is worth noting that when a simple modal and a periphrastic modal occur together in sequence, the simple modal will always come first, and it will normally have an epistemic meaning, as illustrated in [7].

[7]   a. You might have to work late.
        b. The others may be allowed to leave early.

Note that in [7b], the use of *may* has a 'possibly the case' meaning and that the speaker is not giving the others permission to be allowed!

In the sections that follow, we will use the distinction between epistemic and root modality to explore a consistent difference in the use of each modal. Individual modals have other distinct meanings and these too will be discussed and illustrated in context.

Exercise 4.C

Underline the simple modals in the following sentences and, using the distinctions in Box 4.3, decide whether they are best categorized as examples of epistemic or of root modality, and of necessity or possibility.

		Epistemic or root modality	Necessity or possibility
e.g.	I've got a lot to do so I <u>might</u> be late.	epistemic	possibility
1	Because of the rain, the roads will be dangerous.	_____	_____
2	All students must wear school uniforms.	_____	_____
3	Oh hello, you must be the new teacher!	_____	_____
4	Smoking may cause serious illness.	_____	_____
5	You will do what you are told, or else!	_____	_____
6	Your friend can come in and play with you.	_____	_____
7	Yes, you may smoke, but only over there.	_____	_____

Meanings in context

Having noted the basic meaning distinctions in the uses of modal verbs, we shall identify, in the following sections, the core meaning of each modal and then show how that core meaning is interpreted in different circumstances. In helping language learners to make sense of modals, it is important to encourage them to notice the context or circumstances in which those modal forms are used. The following examples, summaries, and exercises are designed to provide teachers with some resources to illustrate, for their learners, how the specific circumstances of use influence the interpretation of each modal verb.

The potential of can

Most grammar texts list three 'meanings' for the modal verb *can*. These are usually identified as 'ability', as in [8], 'permission', as in [9], and 'possibility', as in [10].

[8] a. Peter can swim.
　　 b. He can speak French.

[9] a. Can I borrow one of your pens?
　　 b. Sure, you can take any of them.

[10] a. It can sometimes get very cold here in winter.
　　 b. A visit to the dentist can be frightening.

The core concept which these three uses have in common is about 'potential'. The differences result from the way in which that 'potential' is perceived in different circumstances.

Ability

When the circumstances involve an animate agent, having the potential to perform actions or activities, there is typically an inference of ability, either natural or learned, for *can*. Most of the time, that animate agent is human and the action is physical, as in [11a, b], but the key elements are animate subject and dynamic verb, as in [11c].

[11] a. My son can play the piano.
　　 b. My daughter is only four and she can ride a bicycle.
　　 c. Hey, that's nothing. My dog can count to three.

It is important to recognize that it is the potential to perform the action that is being expressed in these sentences, not the actual performance.

Permission

The 'permission' meaning of *can* is tied to circumstances where social relationships, particularly social authority, are involved. It expresses root modality. In such cases, it is not the individual's potential for action that is being considered, but the potential for some social transaction to take place. The source of that potential is the social power of one individual relative to another. Of course, the social power may exist because the other person has something you want permission to use, for example, or borrow, or look at. In very clear cases, such as parent–child [12], or teacher–student [13], the potential for an event to take place is controlled by the one having social authority. Requests for permission are addressed to, and granted by, the one with social power at that moment.

[12] **Child**   Can I have another cookie?
　　 Parent No, but you can have an apple.

[13] **Student** Can we go now?
　　 Teacher You can leave as soon as you've tidied up.

Possibility

The 'possibility' interpretation of *can* occurs in circumstances where the potential for an event taking place has no specified source in terms of an animate agent or a social authority. The potential simply exists and is typically expressed without an agent as subject, as in [14] and [15].

[14] Things can get crazy around here sometimes.

[15] I'm sure these problems can be solved.

These types of constructions express epistemic modality. They will tend to be used when there is a desire to convey the potential for an event taking place, even when the speaker is not sure of how or when the potential will be realized.

Different interpretations of the potential of *can* are summarized in Box 4.4.

Summary Box 4.4 **The meanings of** *can*

Core concept: potential *can*		
Circumstances	**Interpretation**	**Examples**
Animate agent-subject as source Physical action, mental activity	ability	*Jim* can *speak Spanish.*
Social authority as source Social transaction (root)	permission	*The teacher says you* can *leave.*
Absence of agent-source Situationally specified (epistemic)	possibility	*Grammar* can *be fun!*

Could

As emphasized already, the relationship between *can* and its past tense form *could* is one of relative remoteness from the point of utterance. The combination of remoteness and potential in the conceptual meaning of *could* is interpreted differently according to the three types of circumstances shown in Box 4.4.

When the potential for an animate agent to perform an action is marked as more remote from the point of utterance, it can be interpreted as more remote in time, as in [16a], or as more remote in likelihood, as in [16b].

[16] a. I could run much faster when I was younger.
      b. With the right tools, I could fix it myself.

Remote potential in social terms creates an impression of less imposition and hence greater politeness, as in [17a]. It also marks less likelihood of social permission being given, as in [17b].

[17] a. Could I leave early today if we aren't too busy?
      b. Well, you could, but there's a lot of work to be done.

The 'remote potential' of some situationally specified events taking place also results in an interpretation of 'less likely', as in [18], with the source of that potential unexpressed.

> [18] a. The current plans could be revised.
>   b. Things could get worse.

Exercise 4.D

Look at each of the following examples and, using the distinctions shown in Box 4.4, try to decide whether the source of the potential for the event taking place is 'animate agent', 'social authority', or 'unexpressed'.

   1   Can your friend speak Arabic?

   2   People could get injured here.

   3   Sorry, but it can't be done today.

   4   Some kids can read at an early age.

   5   Can we go to the park?

   6   My father could fix anything.

   7   They said it couldn't get worse, but it did.

   8   Could I use your computer for a moment?

Be able to

In many grammar texts, *be able to* is often presented as a substitute for *can*, particularly where an 'ability' interpretation is clear. In fact, *be able to* is used to convey each of the different kinds of 'potential' shown in Box 4.4. However, *can* is used at least ten times more often than *be able to*. There is one very important difference in meaning, particularly in the past tense, as shown in [19].

> [19] a. We could repair the old car.
>   b. We were able to repair the old car.

When *could* is used, it is the potential that is implied. When *were able to* is used, as in [19b], the implication is that the actual event took place (i.e. they actually repaired the old car).

The possibility of may

The simple modal *may* has two main uses. One is socially-oriented (root) and has to do with permission. The other is knowledge-oriented (epistemic) and has to do with whether something will happen or not. A third use, to do with concession, is becoming more common. The core concept of *may* has to do with some event being possible (or not). The different interpretations of *may* result from the ways in which 'possibility' is perceived in different circumstances.

Permission

The socially-oriented (root) uses involve some social authority having the power to create or prevent the possibility of an event, hence the 'asking permission' interpretation of [20a] and the 'giving permission' interpretation of [20b].

> [20]   a.   May I take one of these?
>   b.   You may only register for two classes.

These types of socially-oriented uses are becoming much less common in everyday spoken English and tend to be associated with formal or official usage. In casual versions of the sentences in [20], *can* would be more frequent. Thus, in our very first example, the child tries to use *Can I leave?* with its newer permission meaning. The parent responds with an ability interpretation (*I'm sure you can*) and then insists on the older use of *may* for permission (*but you may not*).

Possibility

In its knowledge-oriented (epistemic) uses, *may* is interpreted as being equivalent to *may not*, indicating that an event is judged to have an equal possibility of occurring or not, as in [21a]. This equivalence is sometimes stated, as in [21b], and draws attention to the 'weak possibility' interpretation associated with epistemic *may*. There is also a tendency for epistemic *may* to receive stress in speech.

> [21]   a.   Our flight may be delayed.
>   b.   They may come later or they may not.

Concession

There is also a third interpretation of *may* which happens when the speaker wishes to acknowledge the possibility of some event or state of affairs being the case, but not necessarily relevant for the current discussion. This type of 'possibility' is interpreted as a concession, and is often followed by a *but* clause, as shown in [22]. It can usually be paraphrased by a clause beginning with *although*, as illustrated after [22b].

> [22]   a.   You may have good reasons, but that doesn't make it legal.
>   b.   He may be old, but he's still fit. (= Although he's old, he's still fit.)

These distinct interpretations of *may* are summarized in Box 4.5.

Summary Box 4.5 **The meanings of *may***

Circumstances	Interpretation	Examples
Core concept: possible *may*		
Source is human authority or social regulations (root)	permission	May *I come in?*
Source is speaker's knowledge Situationally specified Equals *may not* (epistemic)	weak possibility	*The bus* may *be late.*
Situation acknowledged, (+ *but*) not marked as relevant	concession	*I may be old, but I'm not crazy!*

Might

The difference between *may* and *might* is based on relative remoteness from the point of utterance. The remoteness of possibility interpretation of *might* results in a sense of 'uncertainty' about the likelihood of an event taking place, as in [23a], or a request being granted, as in [23b].

> [23] a. He's really busy now, but he might join us later.
>   b. Might I ask you a big favor?

When a possibility is marked as being remote, it can also receive a hypothetical or 'unreal' interpretation, as shown in [24].

> [24] a. His project is huge, but he might finish it one of these days.
>   b. Yes, and pigs might fly!

The remoteness associated with *might* also results in the concessive uses being marked as even less likely, or less relevant, in the speaker's view, as shown in [25].

> [25] a. That might happen, but we're not going to worry about it.
>   b. I might be mistaken, but I doubt it.

Exercise 4.E

Identify the uses of *may* and *might* in the following sentences in terms of 'permission', 'weak possibility (of occurrence)', or 'concession'.

1 I may be wrong, but that's what I think.

2 These pills may cause dizziness.

3 I'd like to take this chair, if I may.

4   We may be old-fashioned, but we believe in good manners.

5   Might I trouble you for a glass of water?

6   They might decide it isn't worth the effort.

7   Customers may smoke in designated areas only.

8   These exercises, as difficult as they may seem to be, are really good for
    you. Yeah, right!

Be allowed to

The periphrastic modal *be allowed to* can sometimes be used instead of *may*,
particularly in those root modality uses interpreted as 'permission'. This
interpretation is clearly appropriate when *be allowed to* occurs with other
simple modals, as in [26].

> [26] a. Will we be allowed to light the fire?
>   b. Oh, no. You won't be allowed to play with matches!

When *be allowed to* is used in the past tense, however, its interpretation differs
quite noticeably from *might*, as shown in [27].

> [27] a. They might have a break after lunch.
>   b. They were allowed to have a break after lunch.

With *might*, the interpretation is remote possibility, but with *were allowed to*,
the interpretation is remote fact. In [27b], the permission was granted.

The necessity of must

The distinction between the epistemic and root uses of English modals is very
clear in the case of *must*. The core concept in both meanings is 'necessity', with
socially-oriented (root) necessity being interpreted as an obligation, as in [28],
and knowledge-oriented (epistemic) necessity being interpreted as a conclusion,
as in [29].

> [28] a. You must wear a seat belt when driving.
>   b. You must concentrate on one thing at a time.
>
> [29] a. Look at that house! Those people must have a lot of money.
>   b. It must be hot in there with no air-conditioning.

Obligation

In socially-oriented (root) uses, there is a range of imposition from strong
obligation, which can be interpreted in terms of an order or even a legal

requirement, as in [28a], to weak obligation which comes simply from the speaker's sense of the importance of some action, as in [28b]. The weak obligation sense of 'necessity' allows speakers to express self-imposed obligations with first person subjects, as in [30].

[30] a. I must remember to feed the cat later.
      b. I must try harder next time.

Conceptually, the imposition of an obligation tends to apply to present and future actions (rather than states). It also involves animate subjects (typically humans) who are capable of performing those actions. The obligation meaning of *must* is often found in non-personal warnings and rules of the type shown in [31].

[31] a. Door must be closed when machine is in operation.
      b. Students must pay course fees before attending classes.

An interesting development in contemporary English is the use of *must* in statements that indicate a desire to meet some social obligation, but which are actually interpreted as vague arrangements rather than fixed events. As illustrated in [32], these expressions seem to carry the meaning that the social obligation is recognized as necessary, but the actual occurrence of the event that will fulfill the obligation is not to be fixed. The social obligation is being met by expressing awareness of the social obligation.

[32] a. You must come to see us one of these days.
      b. We must get together for lunch sometime.

English is not alone in having expressions of social obligation (without specific arrangements) and learners can quickly recognize the use of these types of expressions once they are explained or clearly illustrated.

Conclusion

In its knowledge-oriented (epistemic) uses, *must* indicates that some conclusion is necessary, given the speaker's assessment of what is known. That conclusion has the status of an inference and signals an assumption that no other explanation is available. Conceptually, that conclusion tends to be about past and present states, as well as actions. It can refer to non-animate subjects and can involve events viewed retrospectively (with perfect aspect) or internally (with progressive aspect), as shown in [33].

[33] a. Oh no, a traffic jam. There must have been an accident.
      b. The computer is on, so someone must be using it.

These observations are summarized in Box 4.6.

Summary Box 4.6 **The meanings of** *must*

Core concept: necessary *must*		
Circumstances	**Interpretation**	**Examples**
Present and future actions with animate subjects Aspect is rare Negation is common (root)	obligation	*You* must *wear a seatbelt.*
Past and present states and some actions Also with non-animate subjects Perfect and progressive aspect Negation is rare (epistemic)	conclusion	*It* must *be cold up there.*

As noted in Box 4.6, the negative form, *mustn't* or *must not*, is used to communicate an obligation, that is, with root meaning. It is not typically used with epistemic meaning. This point will be discussed later, in the section on negation (see pages 108–11).

Exercise 4.F

Identify the uses of *must* in the following sentences as conveying either an obligation or a conclusion.

   1   My watch has stopped. It must be broken.
   2   With that accent, you must be from Scotland.
   3   You must come up and see me sometime.
   4   No ifs or buts, you must wear a helmet.
   5   Wayne left. He must have been feeling ill.
   6   I mustn't forget to send him a Get Well card.
   7   Someone must have borrowed my dictionary.
   8   What goes up must come down.

Have (got) to

There is no past tense form of *must*. Expressions of past necessity are generally presented via the form *have to* for obligations, as in [34a], and conclusions, as in [34b].

[34] a. When I was in school, we had to wear school uniform.
     b. He was really big, he had to be over seven feet tall.

When *have to* is used in the present tense, it seems to provide an alternative to *must*, particularly in expressing the root meaning of obligation. As shown in [35], *have to* can be used in a wider range of constructions than *must*. (In casual spoken uses, it is often pronounced as if it was written as *hafta*.)

[35] a. Do we really have to go to this meeting?
     b. Yes, and we will have to present our report.

There is generally a preference for using *have to* when the obligation seems to come from some uncontrollable external source that compels an action, as in [36].

[36] a. Excuse me, but I have to sneeze.
     b. I'm really thirsty, I just have to get something to drink.

Another periphrastic modal form *have got to* is also used to convey 'necessity'. More typically found in informal speech, *have got to* is mostly used with the root meaning of obligation, as in [37a, b], but there are some common expressions, such as [37c], where the epistemic sense of a conclusion is clearly involved.

[37] a. They've got to try harder next time.
     b. If he gets a puppy, he's got to look after it.
     c. You've got to be joking!

Unlike *have to*, the form *have got to* does not occur with other modal forms. Both of these periphrastic modals differ quite significantly from *must* when they occur in the negative. As shown in [38], *mustn't* conveys an obligation *not* to do something [38a], whereas *don't have to* means that there is *not* an obligation to do something.

[38] a. You mustn't drink beer.
     b. You don't have to drink beer.

These and other distinctions involving negation will be considered in pages 108–11.

The likelihood of will

An important feature of modal *will* is the high frequency of abbreviated forms in positive (*'ll*) and negative statements (*won't*), as shown in [39].

[39] a. I'll be there at six. I won't be late.
     b. We'll carry those for you if he won't.
     c. Think it'll rain? I'm sure it won't.

A large number of different meanings are often associated with *will*, but three distinct interpretations can capture most uses of the form, with the examples in [39] illustrating 'intention' [39a], 'willingness' [39b], and 'prediction' [39c]. The core concept which these three uses have in common is 'likelihood'. Different interpretations result from the different ways in which the 'likelihood' concept is perceived in different circumstances.

Intention

When those circumstances clearly involve a future event that is planned, with the speaker as the one who is the reporting source for the likelihood being expressed, there is an implication of intention. In the most obvious cases, it is the speaker (first person) who has the intention, as in [40a], but the speaker can also report the intentions of others, as in [40b].

> [40] a. I will borrow some money and buy a car.
>   b. These competitors will try to win the grand prize.

One noticeable feature of *will* is the influence of the type of action described (in the main verb) on the preferred interpretation. With the 'intention' uses, a desirable action reported by the speaker tends to function like a promise, as in [41a]. An undesirable action tends to be interpreted as a threat, as in [41b]. When the speaker's intention is not clear in this respect, there is a joking response, shown in [41c], that makes explicit the two different interpretations.

> [41] a. I'll make dinner for tomorrow night.
>   b. I'll call the police if you don't leave.
>   c. **Jürgen** I'll talk to you about this later.
>   **Marian** Is that a threat or a promise?

Willingness

When the likelihood of future action is part of some social transaction, the commonly recognized interpretation of 'willingness' is normally present. As with other root functions, this 'willingness' typically involves animate agents and physical actions, as in [42].

> [42] a. Will you marry me? Of course I will!
>   b. We need some people who will work hard.
>   c. Cathy is crazy. She'll do anything for a laugh.

There are some cases where non-animate agents are treated metaphorically as exhibiting 'willingness' (or unwillingness), as if they had minds of their own. Speakers can complain, usually in the negative, about the 'willingness' of things such as doors and cars, as in [43].

> [43] a. The closet door won't open. Will you try it?
>   b. My car won't start. Will you give me a ride?

Also included in [43] are two question forms with *will* and second person pronouns (*you*) which rely on the willingness interpretation to make a request. In English, questioning someone's willingness in this form is a polite way of imposing the speaker's needs on someone else.

The focus of these socially-oriented uses of *will* is the current state of 'willingness' to perform some future action. Because it is the current state that is being considered, there is no implication of an event being viewed in progress or retrospectively. Hence there is no need to mark the structure with progressive or perfect aspect (i.e. we don't normally make a request by asking, *Will you be lending me ten dollars?*). When *will* occurs with verbs marked for aspect, it is usually conveying epistemic meaning.

Prediction

The epistemic interpretation of the likelihood of *will* involves 'prediction'. The act of predicting is, of course, done by the speaker, often about his or her own future actions, as in [44a], but the subjects of such predictions are frequently non-animate, third person forms, as in [44b, c].

[44] a. One of these days, I'll win the lottery.
b. The weather will be terrible on Sunday.
c. There will be lots to eat at the party.

The *will* that occurs in logical 'if A, then B' statements is clearly epistemic. Such uses are common in written, especially technical, texts, as exemplified in [45].

[45] a. If an external microphone is used, background noises will be recorded.
b. If the red light is on, the unit will be recording.

An important distinction exists between the uses of the negative form *won't* with epistemic and root functions. The focus of negation in epistemic uses is the following main verb, so that the pattern 'predict NOT come' underlies example [46a]. In root uses, the focus of negation is the modal, so that the pattern 'NOT willing to come' underlies example [46b].

[46] a. Paul won't come (because he's too busy).
b. Paul won't come (because he doesn't want to).

It is clear from the discussion of [46] that the same utterance under different circumstances can have different interpretations. The likelihood of an event can often be predicted because someone's intention or willingness is known by the speaker. In the normal course of informal conversation, however, that knowledge is not explicitly stated. These observations on the meaning of *will* are summarized in Box 4.7.

Summary Box 4.7 **The meanings of** *will*

Core concept: likely *will*

Circumstances	**Interpretation**	**Examples**
Speaker as source Planned future action Desirable (= promise) Undesirable (= threat)	intention	*I* will *call the police!*
Animate agent subject Physical action/activity Second person questions as requests Aspect rare Negation applies to modal Social transaction (root)	willingness	Will *you help me?*
Non-animate subjects common Third person, non-specific subjects Aspect common Logical statements (If A, then B.) Common in technical texts Negation applies to main verb (epistemic)	prediction	*The weather* will *be nice.*

Shall

Although *shall* is often presented as a first person substitute for *will*, this restriction is no longer common in contemporary English usage. There is often a general element of 'determination' on the speaker's part in first person uses of *shall*. It is possible to find *shall* used with each of the three interpretations of 'intention' [47a], 'willingness' [47b], and 'prediction' [47c], described earlier for *will*.

[47] a. We shall refer to this as the control condition.
      b. Shall we dance?
      c. I shall have finished this report by lunchtime.

There is a further root function of *shall* that is fairly common in legal (and related) texts. In examples such as [48a, b], there is a strong obligation interpretation associated with the use of *shall*.

[48] a. The license of a person who is arrested for driving while intoxicated shall be suspended.
      b. The Author shall prepare a manuscript which shall meet the following requirements.

There is, however, a general pattern of *will* becoming more frequently used for expressing all types of likelihood. Perhaps because of this, speakers often associate *shall* (and make use of this association for various effects) with an earlier period of the language. One common association is with older versions of the Bible from which quotations, as illustrated in [49], continue to be taken.

[49] Therefore shall a man leave his father and his mother, and shall cleave unto his wife: and they shall be one flesh.

Exercise 4.G

Identify the uses of *will* and *shall* in the following sentences as conveying 'intention', 'willingness', or 'prediction'.

1 I'll do what I can to help, I promise.

2 There will be blue birds over the white cliffs of Dover.

3 Give it to Mikey, he'll eat anything.

4 Don't call too early, I'll still be sleeping.

5 My pen won't write. Will you lend me yours?

6 I'll stop them making all that noise!

7 Her parents won't let her stay out late.

8 We shall concentrate today on modal verbs.

9 By now you will probably have heard enough about modal verbs.

10 Let's leave, shall we?

Would

The historical past tense form of *will* is *would*, often reduced in speech to *'d* after pronouns (*he'd*). The combination of remoteness and likelihood as the conceptual basis of *would* generally leads to an interpretation of some event as being distant in time or possibility from the moment of speaking. In many cases, remote likelihood is interpreted as not very likely at all (i.e. hypothetical).

The three interpretations of *will* presented in Box 4.7 can also be found with *would*. Quite often, the sense of remoteness comes from reported versions of what was said or thought. A reported intention is presented in [50a]. The root meaning of willingness is illustrated in [50b] and the epistemic meaning of prediction is contained in example [50c].

[50] a. They said they would be here by twelve o'clock.
      b. She hoped they would help her if she called them.

c. We wondered what would happen to us.

The most common socially-oriented (root) uses of *would* occur in question forms where the remoteness of likelihood interpretation is about the addressee's willingness to do something. This form of polite request is illustrated in [51].

[51] a. Would you do something for me?
b. Would you lend me some money?

This type of structure, beginning with *Would you* ..., has become almost formulaic in contemporary English for expressing requests and offers.

The remoteness element in *would*, combined with the epistemic interpretation of 'prediction', leads to two quite distinct uses. When remoteness in time (i.e. past) is combined with predictability of action, there is an interpretation of past habitual behavior, as in [52].

[52] a. When she was young, Anne would suck her thumb.
b. Every time I tried to talk to him, he would be too busy.

When remoteness in possibility is combined with 'prediction', there is an implication that the event has little likelihood of happening soon, as in [53].

[53] a. You would enjoy a vacation (if you took one).
b. They would do much better (if they studied more).

As indicated in [53], a prediction concerning remote possibility often involves some condition, either expressed or assumed in the context. This naturally leads to the frequent use of *would* in conditional sentences about hypothetical situations, as in [54].

[54] a. If I were you, I'd quit that job.
b. If they wanted to win, they would be fighting harder.

As shown in [54b], progressive aspect can be used with the main verb after *would* to refer to a hypothetical situation viewed as if in progress.

Be going to

Although it can often be used in place of *will* for expressing 'intention' and 'prediction', the form *be going to* is distinct in several ways. For example, *be going to* is not used to express the 'willingness' associated with *will*. Typically, *be going to* has an implication that the future action is related to the present and will occur relatively soon after the time of speaking. If a distinction between immediate future ('now') and more remote future ('later') is being made, then it will be done as in [55].

[55] a. I'm going to finish these exercises now.
b. And I'll get round to the others later.

This immediacy conveyed by *be going to*, as in [56], may be connected to the literal source of the expression, with progressive aspect, suggesting that the subject is currently on a path moving towards a goal. This sense of currently 'being on a path' can also create an implication that the action with *be going to* was already planned or decided.

[56] a. Close your eyes, I'm going to give you a surprise.
      b. Watch out! The monster's going to get you!

In these epistemic uses, the event is predicted to occur right after the time of speaking. The difference between [57a] and [57b], especially in the reduced form of casual speech shown in [57a], contrasts the immediacy of *be going to* with the type of conditional interpretation associated with *will*.

[57] a. I'm gonna be sick.
      b. I will be sick (if I eat any more of this ice cream).

Exercise 4.H

Identify the uses of the modal forms in the following sentences as indicating 'intention', 'willingness', or 'prediction'.

1   Would you sign this for me please?
2   He's going to be twenty-one tomorrow.
3   We were going to visit London, but it's too much.
4   You would love New Orleans.
5   He wouldn't have fallen if he hadn't been careless.
6   He thinks he's just gonna do whatever he wants.
7   They said they'd do anything we asked.
8   Wow, really? Well, that would be a change!

Photocopiable © Oxford University Press

The requirements of should

The core concept involved in the use of *should* has to do with 'requirements'. These are often socially-oriented (root) requirements, typically expressed in terms of appropriate behavior, as in [58].

[58] a. You should brush your teeth twice a day.
      b. We should call them before we go there.

Or they are knowledge-oriented required interpretations (epistemic), typically expressed in terms of what is most probably the case, as in [59].

[59] a. The journey should take two or three days.
      b. Your laundry should be ready for pick-up tomorrow.

Obligation

In socially-oriented uses, there is a weaker sense of obligation than is found with *must*, with the force of the speaker's utterance being interpreted as advice or a suggestion. One common occurrence of socially-oriented *should* is in a kind of *Why*-question which is used to question or deny the relevance of a social requirement, as in [60].

[60] a. Why should I go there when I'm quite happy here?
      b. Why should I do what everyone else does?

Probability

Epistemic uses of *should* are less common. They express the speaker's reasonable assumptions and are interpreted in terms of the probability of some event taking place, as in [61].

[61] a. He's the best runner, so he should win the race.
      b. It should be clear to everyone that he's a fake.

On many occasions, of course, speakers will base their assumptions about what is probable (epistemic) on what they know to be socially expected (root) in certain situations. In such cases, the use of *should* will imply both root and epistemic interpretations. The clearer cases will be distinguishable via the criteria in Box 4.8.

Summary Box 4.8 **The meanings of *should***

Core concept: required *should*		
Circumstances	**Interpretation**	**Examples**
Expressing appropriate behavior, correct ways of doing things, suggestions, advice (root)	weak obligation	*You* should *think of others.*
Expressing reasonable assumptions, probable occurrences (epistemic)	probability	*The work* should *soon be finished.*

Ought to

In the examples presented so far in this section, *should* could be replaced by *ought to*. Generally, *ought to* is more frequently found in speech than in writing, is most commonly found with socially-oriented meaning, and typically receives stress whereas *should* is mostly unstressed, as shown in [62].

[62] a. He ought to get a job instead of just sitting around.
      b. She doesn't care about money. Well, she *ought to*!

Perhaps because of its lack of distinct function, *ought to* is becoming less frequent in contemporary English.

Exercise 4.1

Identify the uses of *should* and *ought to* in the following sentences as conveying weak 'obligation' or 'probability' of occurrence.

1 Should I invite our neighbors to the wedding?
2 Dogs should be kept on a leash in public.
3 If they mailed it last week, it should be here by now.
4 Those who have studied should find the test quite easy.
5 Why should we always do what they say?
6 She ought to have said 'thank you' for the gift.
7 How long should it take to complete the task?
8 They say you should serve red wine with steak.

Be supposed to

The periphrastic modal *be supposed to* is used occasionally with a function similar to *should* in its root sense of weak obligation. There is an implication with *be supposed to* that the social requirement being mentioned is external to the speaker and may be one that the speaker feels is being ignored, as in [63].

[63] a. You're supposed to be studying, not watching TV.
      b. I'm not supposed to be laughing about it, but it's very funny.

The social obligations mentioned with *be supposed to* are generally treated as being weaker than those marked by *should*.

Negation and modals

The structural pattern of negation and modals is very consistent, with the full and reduced forms of the negative particle coming after the modal (*must not*, *can't*). In the analysis of the meaning of negation with a modal (e.g. *can*) and a main verb (e.g. *sing*), the relationship is clearer if we put the negative element (*NOT*) in front of the part it applies to (e.g. *NOT can sing*).

The effect of negation on the meaning of sentences containing modals is quite complex. Conceptually, there are two elements available for negation. The action or state (main verb) can be considered as negative or the modality (modal verb meaning) can be treated as negative. For some modals in knowledge-oriented (epistemic) functions, it is the action that is affected, as in [64].

> [64] a. Tom may come. = possible (Tom come)
>   b. But Ray may not come. = possible (Ray NOT come)

This pattern of modality–NOT–action is described as internal negation and indicates that the level of 'what is known' is not being negated, but the action is, as further illustrated in [65].

> [65] a. It won't rain. = predict (NOT rain)
>   b. It shouldn't last. = probable (NOT last)

In socially-oriented (root) functions, it is the modality that is affected by the negation much more, as in [66].

> [66] a. Your friend may leave. = permit (your friend leave)
>   b. But you may not leave. = NOT permit (you leave)

This pattern of NOT–modality–action is described as external negation and indicates that some parts of what is 'socially-determined' can be negated, while the nature of the action stays the same. More examples are shown in [67].

> [67] a. He won't help us. = NOT willing (help us)
>   b. He can't smoke here. = NOT permit (smoke here)

The patterns just described do not apply completely to *must* and *can*. There are some uses of *mustn't* that express the epistemic meaning of 'conclusion', as in [68a], but that meaning is much more commonly expressed by *can't*, as in [68b].

> [68] a. She mustn't have much money. = conclude (NOT have much money)
>   b. You can't be serious. = conclude (NOT serious)

The negative form *mustn't* is used much more frequently in its root (obligation) sense. Unlike other root modals, however, it involves a negation of the action, as in [69a]. When the obligation is negated, the form *don't have to* is used, as shown in [69b].

> [69] a. You mustn't do it. = oblige (NOT do it)
>   b. You don't have to do it. = NOT oblige (do it)

It is also worth noting that the two types of epistemic possibility, involving *may* and *can*, are negated rather differently. With *can't* or *cannot*, it is the modality that is negated, as in [70a]. With *may not*, it is the action that is negated, as in [70b].

> [70] a. It can't work. = NOT possible (work)
>   b. It may not work. = possible (NOT work)

In these examples, an interpretation that something is 'NOT possible' will have a stronger negative implication than an indication that something is 'possible NOT' to happen.

These distinctions are summarized in Box 4.9.

Summary Box 4.9 **Modals and negatives**

Modals	Interpretations with negative	Examples
can (= potential)	NOT able (action)	*I* can't *dance. We* couldn't *swim.*
	NOT permit (action)	*You* can't *go. They* couldn't *eat here.*
	NOT possible (action)	*It* can't *happen. It* couldn't *be done.*
may (= possibility)	NOT permit (action)	*You* may *not leave.*
	possible (NOT action)	*They* may *not come.*
	concede (NOT action)	*It* may *not be finished, but ...*
must (= necessity)	oblige (NOT action)	*You* mustn't *shout.*
	NOT oblige (action)	*You* don't have to *stay.*
	conclude (NOT action)	*She* must not *have much money* or *She* can't *have much money.*
will (= likelihood)	NOT intend (action)	*They* won't *do it.*
	NOT willing (action)	*She* won't *help. He* wouldn't *listen.*
	predict (NOT action)	*He* won't *win. You* wouldn't *like it.*
should (= requirement)	oblige (NOT action)	*You* shouldn't *smoke.*
	probable (NOT action)	*It* shouldn't *last long.*

Some periphrastic modals with negation follow the pattern of *don't have to*, with the modality negated, as in [71].

[71] a. He doesn't have to go. = NOT oblige (go)
      b. He isn't able to go. = NOT able (go)
      c. He isn't allowed to go. = NOT permit (go)

However, others are more typically interpreted with the action negated, as in [72].

[72] a. She isn't going to drive. = predict (NOT drive)
      b. She isn't supposed to drive. = oblige (NOT drive)

With such variation, it is hardly surprising that modals in English are problematic for learners. Teachers need to be very patient and supportive, and to provide lots of contextualized examples of these forms.

Exercise 4.J

Using Box 4.9 as a guide, try to identify the patterns of meaning in the following sentences, using the structure of the examples as an indication of where the 'not' element has to be placed.

e.g.	**A** Your horse won't win the race.	predict (NOT win)
	B Hey, my horse can't lose.	NOT possible (lose)
I	**A** He may not run fast enough.	
2	**B** You shouldn't bet on him then.	
3	**A** I don't have to listen to you.	
4	**B** You mustn't bet on a slow horse.	
5	**A** You can't tell me what to do.	
6	**B** I wouldn't tell anyone what to do.	
7	**A** I guess your horse can't be much good.	
8	**B** He may not be the best, but he's mine.	

Photocopiable © Oxford University Press

Discussion topics and projects

1   There is a lot of modality to be found in environmental print, some explicit and a lot more implicit.

(a) How would you interpret the type of modal meaning found in these examples in traffic signs (and any others you have noticed)?

(b) As a project, find a number of such street signs and try to express their 'message' by making the modality explicit. Some other examples are provided on page 115.

2 Modal verbs occur quite frequently in expository written discourse which presents a point of view and is designed to persuade. The following extracts are from a *Washington Post* article (June 13, 1993) by former senator Barry Goldwater. Identify all the modals and their most likely function in this context.

> After more than 50 years in the military and politics, I am still amazed to see how upset people can get over nothing. Lifting the ban on gays in the military isn't exactly nothing, but it's pretty damned close.
>
> Everyone knows that gays have served honorably in the military since at least the time of Julius Caesar. They'll still be serving long after we're all dead and buried. That should not surprise anyone.
>
> But most Americans should be shocked to know that while the country's economy is going down the tubes, the military has wasted a

half-billion dollars over the past decade chasing down gays and running them out of the armed services.

When the facts lead to one conclusion, I say it's time to act, not hide. The country and the military know that eventually the ban will be lifted. The only remaining questions are how much muck we will all be dragged through, and how many brave Americans will have their lives and careers destroyed in a senseless attempt to stall the inevitable.

Some in Congress think I'm wrong. They say we absolutely must continue to discriminate, or all hell will break loose. Who knows, they say, perhaps our soldiers may even take up arms against each other. Well, that's just stupid.

Nobody thought blacks or women could ever be integrated into the military. Many thought an all-volunteer force could never protect our national interest. Well, it has—and despite those who feared the worst, I among them, we are still the best.

What would undermine our readiness would be a compromise policy like 'Don't ask, don't tell.'

When you get down to it, no American able to serve should be allowed, much less given an excuse, not to serve his or her country. We need all our talent.

If I were in the Senate today, I would rise on the Senate floor in support of our commander in chief. He may be a Democrat, but he happens to be right on this question.

3   The types of meanings conveyed by modals in English can be expressed in a number of ways.

(a) There are adverbs (e.g. *certainly, maybe, perhaps, probably*) which are called modal adverbs. How many other modal adverbs can you think of? What type of modality (epistemic or root) is typically conveyed by those adverbs? Would you include words like *apparently, clearly, hopefully, likely, obviously, seemingly,* and *surely* in the class of modal forms?

(b) Modal meaning seems to be inherent in a number of English verbs. We used this fact when we proposed the interpretation 'predict [he NOT go]' for *he won't go*. We treated 'predict' as having modal meaning. How would you describe the type of modality that is associated with the following verbs?

advise	*forbid*	*permit*	*suppose*
assume	*guess*	*prohibit*	*think*
believe	*imagine*	*seem*	*want*
claim	*order*	*suggest*	*warn*

4   Modal verbs are often associated with politeness in English. There are two broad categories of politeness often discussed. Positive politeness describes the ways in which speakers try to accomplish their goals and desires by indicating that the hearers' goals and desires are similar because they are both members of the same social group. Negative politeness describes the ways in which speakers indicate that they are trying to avoid imposing on hearers' independence and freedom of action. Positive politeness focuses on connection, negative politeness focuses on independence. (For more discussion of these concepts, see Brown and Levinson 1987; Yule, 1996).

(a) Can you characterize the type of politeness most likely associated with each of the following sentences?

    (i)   It's a great movie, you'll love it. Let's go.
    (ii)   Would you like to go to a movie, if you're free?
    (iii) I'm sorry to interrupt you, but can I talk to you for a second?
    (iv)   You know the rules, you have to keep quiet here.
    (v)   We should get together for lunch.
    (vi)   You must be tired, so we ought to stop and rest.
    (vii) Excuse me, could you tell me what time it is?
    (viii) You wouldn't happen to have a pen I could borrow, would you?

(b) Can you think of other expressions involving modals that relate to politeness?

(c) Try to pay attention to what English speakers actually say when they doing things like making requests, offers, apologizing, refusing, seeking agreement, and other actions that involve modal verbs. What expressions (not just modals) are typically used to accomplish which acts?

Teaching ideas

1 It must be Yumiko

The basic epistemic uses of modals can be illustrated and practiced by using a simple scale: something is *probably* the case (90%), *possibly* the case (50%) or *not likely* to be the case (10%). Two exercises using this type of scale are offered in (a) and (b).

(a) For students who seem to learn best from written 'conversion' exercises, create a number of prompts, as shown below, and invite them to express the same information with modal verbs, following some examples.

    (i)   rain today (possibly) *It may rain.*
    (ii) picnic today (not likely) *We can't have a picnic.*
    (iii) plan to stay indoors (probably)
    (iv) movie (possibly)
    (v)   barbecue (not likely)

(b) An alternative version can focus on the 'conclusion' expressions that would go with the situations sketched below.

    (i)   phone rings (90% Yumiko) *That must be Yumiko.*
   (ii) knock at door (50% neighbor) *That may be my neighbor.*
 (iii) old photograph (10% Scott)
 (iv) Ray absent (50% ill)
  (v) Jan laughing (90% happy)

2 No skateboards

One way to help students become familiar with expressions of obligation (i.e. root uses of modals) is through the use of common street signs. Some examples are presented in the accompanying photographs. There are many different types of possible activities with such a theme. Here are two.

(a) As an out-of-class exercise, students are asked to find other examples (and draw them, perhaps) of the type of sign illustrated here. They have to bring them to class, as challenges for their classmates to explain. As structural frames for those explanations, the following expressions might be offered:

You must …
You have to …
You can't …
You mustn't …

(b) As an in-class exercise, students (in groups, perhaps) can be encouraged to write out short *must* and *must not* statements regarding their classroom rules and obligations. Then, on separate sheets, they have to create a sign to go with each statement. After the signs and statements are created, each group, in turn, holds up one of their signs and another group has to guess the correct statement. (This is based on a suggestion in Riggenbach and Samuda 1993: 96.)

3 The rules of the game

The modals of obligation and permission are often used in expressing the rules of games (e.g. chess, scrabble) and sports (e.g. baseball, cricket). First ask students to name some of their favorite games or sports. Then, ask them to state some of the basic rules, using structural frames such as: *You can/can't ... You must/mustn't ...*

(a) After this brief introduction, try to form groups with members who share an interest in some game or sport so that they can collaborate in writing out some of the special rules of that game or sport.

(b) Alternatively, create an out-of-class assignment in which each group has to find out, from a person or a book, some of the key rules of a game or sport that was listed in the first discussion. Those rules have to be brought to class, presented, and explained.

4 'Well, when I was young ...'

The focus of this exercise is the difference between what *could* or *had to* be done in the past versus the present. Students are asked to concentrate on the uses of *can/could, can't/couldn't*, plus versions of *be able to* and *have to*. Several different formats are possible.

(a) In small groups, students are asked to list what they *could/couldn't* do as children that they *can/can't* do now. They should distinguish between what they *are/were able to* do (or not) and *are/were allowed to* do (or not). Discussions before or after this exercise can focus on similarities and differences across cultures (if possible) in what children are typically allowed to do (or not).

(b) An alternative version can be designed on the theme of advantages versus disadvantages of being a particular age. One group might have 'being 16', another group 'being 60', or 'being 6'. Once again, students are encouraged to work on the *able to/allowed to* aspects of being these ages.

(c) As an out-of-class exercise, some students are assigned the task of interviewing (and recording) some more proficient (in English) and much older people on the topic of how things have changed since they were young. The interview questions can be discussed and designed in class beforehand, with a focus on what they were *able to/allowed to* do (or not) and restrictions/permissions. The recorded interviews can be replayed in class (with the interviewer in charge of explanations) and a recognition exercise used to focus on each type of expression that conveys an ability, a restriction, a permission, or an obligation.

5 Reforming Mr Rude

There are many ways to illustrate the politeness uses of English modals. A number of interesting ideas, and helpful lists of common phrases, are presented in Dörnyei and Thurrell (1992). One of their suggestions is to create some sample expressions of a speaker who is not being very polite. The students' task is to think of ways to change the form of what is said to make it much more polite. Here are some examples of Mr Rude talking to an office secretary.

   (i) You're not very busy. You can help me.
  (ii) Hey, listen. I want to say something.
 (iii) Give me a pen.
 (iv) I need a pencil sharpener. Where is it?
  (v) I don't have a lot of time. Hurry up.
 (vi) I don't think you understand English. Help me!
(vii) Tell me the time.
(viii) What is your name?
 (ix) I'm going to use your phone.
  (x) This office is open. I want help.

An alternative approach would be to create some samples of a speaker who is overusing expressions of politeness and ask students to revise them.

Note. This type of exercise provides a good opportunity for students to talk about their impressions of what is (and isn't) polite in the English-speaking environment they are (or will be) experiencing. It may also be helpful for them to discuss contrasts between cultures regarding what is (and isn't) considered polite talk.

6 You will meet a helpful stranger

There are a number of related tasks that can be used to help students become more familiar with *will* and *be going to*.

(a) In this task, students have to write, on a small piece of paper, one sentence that mentions a future event or state (preferably good). In the format of fortune cookie predictions, the sentence should have the structural frame: *You will ...* or *You are going to ...*

The pieces of paper are then collected in a box and mixed up. Each student then gets to reach in, take one piece of paper and read out the 'fortune'.

(b) As an alternative, provide students with a model of a horoscope, along the following lines:

> Your love of comfort will make you soft. You should look for a challenge, even a small one will do. No-one can do it for you. You won't regret the effort. You will meet a helpful stranger.

– Encourage students to express what they already know about horoscopes and what is typically in them.
– Draw attention to the use of modal verbs.
– Get students (in pairs or groups) to create a horoscope for a person they choose.
– Before the end of class time, have the groups read out their version for the class.

(c) Ask the students (in small groups, perhaps) to list between five and ten things that they think will be really different in the future. You may be able to use the image of a crystal ball that shows scenes from the future. Some topic areas: climate, diseases, energy sources, food, noise, pollution, population, traffic, wars, water quality.

7 Dear Abby

In most daily newspapers there is an advice column (sometimes called 'Dear Abby'). If possible, cut out some examples of letters to the column and bring them to class. Use one example to introduce the style, language, and a typical topic. Try to elicit suggestions from students on the type of advice they might offer. Draw their attention to the uses of *should, shouldn't, ought to, might, could,* and other modals. Here's one example (and some advice suggested by students):

> Dear Abby,
>
> I have been married for five years and I think my husband's interest in our love life has gone. He always says he is too tired. I still feel young and energetic, but I don't know how to get my husband interested. What should I do?
>
> From Frustrated in Fresno.
>
> Dear Frustrated,
>
> You should ask him in the morning.
>
> He might need to see a doctor.
>
> You should wear different clothes.
>
> You must make him a nice home-cooked meal.
>
> You should find somebody else.

Once the students understand the type of language involved, give them (in groups, perhaps) some other problems and ask them to write responses, with advice. Possible problems to use are:

(i)   My boyfriend spends all his money foolishly.
(ii)   My teenage son stays out too late every night.
(iii)   My husband's ex-wife is always telling him what to do.
(iv)   My father still treats me like a child.

8 That would be nice

With more advanced students, it may be possible to look at modals in extended discourse. Expository texts of the type presented in Discussion Topic 2 (pages 112–13) are possible source materials for a consideration of what kind of effect modals have on meaning. Students can be asked first to find the modals, then to remove them from the text, and to try to decide how the meaning has changed.

Alternatively, extracts from conversational discourse may provide a good source of modals being used in an informal way. A sample extract is provided here, adapted from Craig and Tracy (1983: 310). Students are asked first to identify the modals (including any periphrastic modals) and then to try to determine the meaning of each one by considering what changes in meaning occur when the modal is removed from the utterance.

(In this extract, two women students are talking about hot air ballooning.)

B Bright and pretty this time of year. Wouldn't you love to just sort of drift away?

K I don't know about this time of year I think it would be awfully cold up there coz you're not doing anything.

B I was thinking of an excuse to get away from exams and papers and stuff.

K Oh well that would be nice. I always thought California's supposed to have—when I first started getting interested in it—they had—they were one of the few places that had—places where you could go, and, someone would either take you up or learn—teach you how to do it and you could go. So that's what I want to do on my honeymoon. Go to California and—and balloon.

B (laugh) Hmm.

K But it would have to be someplace pretty.

B California would be interesting.

K I don't know.

B If you missed you'd either hit the mountains or the ocean.

Further reading

A note on terminology. The simple modals are also known as modal auxiliaries and modal operators. The periphrastic modals are also called quasi-modals and semi-auxiliaries.

General reference, with examples

Leech, G. 1987. *Meaning and the English Verb.* (2nd edn.) Chapter 5. London: Longman.

Palmer, F. 1988. *The English Verb.* (2nd edn.) Chapters 6 and 7. London: Longman.

More theoretical discussions

Bybee, J. and **S. Fleischman.** (eds.) 1995. *Modality in Grammar and Discourse.* Amsterdam: John Benjamins.

Coates, J. 1983. *The Semantics of the Modal Auxiliaries.* London: Croom Helm.

Palmer, F. 1990. *Modality and the English Modals.* (2nd edn.) London: Longman.

Perkins, M. 1983. *Modal Expressions in English.* London: Frances Pinter.

On epistemic and root modality

Hofmann, T. 1993. *Realms of Meaning.* Chapter 6. London: Longman.

Traugott, E. 1989. 'On the rise of epistemic meanings in English.' *Language* 65: 31–55.

On specific modals

Binnick, R. 1971. 'Will *and* be going to.' *Papers from the 7th Regional Meeting of the Chicago Linguistic Society.* (pp. 40–51). Chicago: Chicago Linguistic Society.

Bolinger, D. 1989. 'Extrinsic possibility and intrinsic potentiality: 7 on MAY and CAN + 1.' *Journal of Pragmatics* 13: 1–23.

Groefsema, M. 1995. '*Can, may, must,* and *should*: A relevance theoretic account.' *Journal of Linguistics* 31: 53–79.

Haegeman, L. 1989. '*Be going to* and *will*: a pragmatic account.' *Journal of Linguistics* 25: 291–317.

Tanaka, T. 1990. 'Semantic changes of *can* and *may*: differentiation and implication.' *Journal of Linguistics* 26: 89–123.

Tregidgo, P. 1982. '*Must* and *may*: demand and permission.' *Lingua* 56: 75–92.

Walton, A. 1991. 'The semantics and pragmatics of CAN.' *Linguistische Berichte* 135: 325–45.

Ziegeler, D. 1996. 'A synchronic perspective on the grammaticalization of *will* in hypothetical predicates.' *Studies in Language* 20: 411–42.

Negation and modality

Frawley, W. 1992. *Linguistic Semantics*. Chapter 9. Hillsdale, NJ: Lawrence Erlbaum.

Language acquisition research

Gibbs, D. 1990. 'Second language acquisition of the English modal auxiliaries *can, could, may*, and *might*.' *Applied Linguistics* 11: 297–314.

Haegeman, L. 1988. 'The categorial status of modals and L2 acquisition.' In S. Flynn and W. O'Neil (eds.): *Linguistic Theory and Second Language Acquisition*. (pp. 252–76) Dordrecht: Kluwer.

Teaching suggestions

DeCarrico, J. 1986. 'Tense, aspect and time in English modality.' *TESOL Quarterly* 20: 665–82.

Holmes, J. 1988. 'Doubt and certainty in ESL textbooks.' *Applied Linguistics* 9: 21–44.

5 CONDITIONALS

1 Some learners produce odd-sounding conditionals, such as *If I have money, everything would be better*. What is the problem here?

2 Is it better to include *then* in conditional sentences, as in *If I can't come, then I'll call you*, or leave it out, as in *If I can't come, I'll call you*?

3 Is there any difference when a conditional *if*-clause is put at the beginning of the sentence or at the end?

4 Does the *if*-clause in *He asked if he could leave* have any connection to a conditional *if*-clause?

5 Is there any difference between *only if* and *if only*? Does *unless* mean the same as *if … not*? And do *even if* and *even though* mean the same thing?

'If you are sitting in an exit row and you cannot understand this card, please tell a crew member.'

The sentence quoted here appeared on a United Airlines safety procedures card given to all passengers. It begins with a conditional *if*-clause. Here's another one: if I cannot understand the card, how can I do what it says? It seems that conditionals can be a source of problems in English. In this chapter, we shall attempt to explain how they are used and what they mean.

Overview

After a brief survey of the basic forms of *if*-clauses, noting the distinct features of REAL CONDITIONALS, expressing FACTUAL and PREDICTIVE relationships, and UNREAL CONDITIONALS, expressing HYPOTHETICAL and COUNTER-FACTUAL situations, we consider the basic meaning distinctions encoded by these forms and their typical contexts of use. Aspects of the INFORMATION STRUCTURE of CONDITIONALS are explored, focusing on their role in *restating*, including the use of TRUNCATED forms, *contrasting*, *listing alternatives*, and *giving examples*. The distinction between INITIAL and FINAL IF-CLAUSES is reviewed and the role of END-WEIGHT exemplified. The relationship between conditionals and the expression of *uncertainty* and *politeness* is considered. Finally, there is a consideration of EXCEPTIONAL CONDITIONALS (*only if, if only, unless*) and CONCESSIVE CONDITIONALS (*even if*), with a note on PARENTHETICAL CONDITIONALS.

Basic forms

In discussing modals in Chapter 4, we noted some uses that concerned possible events. Those possible events are often presented in terms of a conditional relationship. Structures known as CONDITIONALS present one event, typically in a clause beginning with *if,* as a condition for the occurrence of another event, expressed in a main clause. The *if*-clause is sometimes described as the ANTECEDENT and the main clause as the CONSEQUENT. There are different types of conditionals based on the degree of likely occurrence of the event in the main clause.

A broad distinction can be drawn between those conditionals that refer to situations presented as 'real' and those presented as 'unreal'. REAL CONDITIONALS can be divided into those that express some type of FACTUAL relationship and those that present a PREDICTIVE relationship. The UNREAL CONDITIONALS are used to express extremely unlikely or HYPOTHETICAL situations and also situations that are assumed to be contrary to known facts, or COUNTERFACTUAL.

Factual conditionals

FACTUAL CONDITIONALS are used to express a relationship between two events as generally happening or normally being true in the circumstances described. They can have both verbs in the past tense, as in [1a], or more usually, both verbs in the present tense, as in [1b, c]. They are also used to express generalizations, as in [1d].

> [1]   a.   In the past, if you wanted something, you saved up for it.
>   b.   Nowadays, if people want something, they just buy it.
>   c.   If they don't have any money, they use credit cards.
>   d.   But, if times are really tough, they just don't spend.

Predictive conditionals

PREDICTIVE CONDITIONALS present the main clause event as a possibility in the future which depends on the prior occurrence of the situation in the *if*-clause. That possibility, whether strong or weak, is typically expressed by a modal verb, especially *will,* in the main clause, as shown in [2].

[2] a. If you lend me some money, I'll pay you back tomorrow.
 b. But if you don't get paid, I may not get my money back.
 c. Trust me. If I make a promise, I will keep it.

Hypothetical conditionals

HYPOTHETICAL CONDITIONALS present the main clause event as unlikely, yet possible, given the situation expressed in the *if*-clause. The use of past tense forms in the *if*-clause is an indication of the remoteness of the possibility of the event. Modal forms associated with remoteness of possibility (*would, could, might*) are typically found in the main clause, as shown in [3].

[3] a. If you asked Jack, he might lend you the money.
 b. Yeah, but if he was broke, he couldn't help me.
 c. But if he did have enough money, he would give you some.

Those learners who produce sentences like *If I have money, everything would be better* are marking the hypothetical nature of the main clause, but not marking (i.e. not using *had*) the remoteness of possibility required in the *if*-clause.

Counterfactual conditionals

COUNTERFACTUAL CONDITIONALS present the main clause event within the context of an *if*-clause event that is known to be impossible. The presentation of actions or states that are impossible (in the current world) is marked by forms that indicate extreme remoteness, both in time and possibility, as illustrated in [4]. This is also one of the few constructions in English where a SUBJUNCTIVE continues to be found, as in the use of *were* in [4c].

[4] a. If I had called Jack earlier, he would have helped.
 b. So, if you hadn't waited so long, you could have avoided this problem.
 c. Yeah, and if I were rich, I wouldn't have this problem.

These distinctions are summarized in Box 5.1. In some grammar materials, the terms 'first conditional' (for predictive), 'second conditional' (for hypothetical), and 'third conditional' (for counterfactual) will be used.

Many of the sentences presented as examples in [1] to [4] could have *then* introducing the main clause, marking explicitly the ANTECEDENT–CONSEQUENT relationship as: *If* situation A, *then* situation C. However, the inclusion of *then* typically signals emphasis by explicitly marking the outcome in the consequent. It is not normally present in the majority of sentences containing *if*-clauses. Indeed, in conversation, the frequency of *then* following an *if*-clause is less than 1 in 10. Where it does occur, it tends to mark some kind of conclusion to a larger issue in the discourse beyond the immediately preceding *if*-clause. We shall return to the role of conditionals in discourse in pages 132–37.

Summary Box 5.1 **Basic types of conditionals**

Real	*If*-clause verb	Main clause verb	Situation
factual	present	present	generally true
factual	past	past	generally true
predictive	present	present modal	likely
Unreal			
hypothetical	past	past modal	unlikely
counterfactual	past perfect	past modal perfect	impossible
counterfactual	subjunctive	past modal	impossible

Exercise 5.A

The following sentences appeared in newspaper articles during a presidential election in the USA. Underline the conditional clauses in each one, then identify each type, using one of the four labels ('factual', 'predictive', 'hypothetical', and 'counterfactual') in Box 5.1.

e.g.   <u>If Americans want change</u>, they always vote for the challenger.   (factual)

1   If the President had a serious domestic policy, it
    remained a big secret throughout the campaign.(_____)

2   If the President wanted to make an impact, he
    would announce a highway rebuilding program. (_____)

3   If the new President doesn't fix the economy,
    he won't be popular for very long.   (_____)

4   If the Democrats took the opportunity to
    change things, they would push ahead with a
    national health policy.   (_____)

5   If the challenger had focused on the economy,
    he would have been more successful.   (_____)

6   If he hadn't relied on his past popularity, he
    would have been much more aggressive.   (_____)

7   If the new leader doesn't fulfill people's expectations,
    he won't be smiling this time next year.   (_____)

Basic meanings

Taking the basic categories of conditional structures presented in Box 5.1, we can look at their typical contexts of use and consider their meanings in terms of answers to these four basic questions: What happens?, What will happen?, What would happen?, and What would have happened?

What happens if … ?

Sentences containing FACTUAL CONDITIONALS are often found in academic texts. Factual conditionals seem to be favored when presenting information that is generally or habitually the case, or has the status of a rule. They tend to answer a question like *What happens if … ?* The examples in [5] are taken from textbooks on a. calculus, b. microeconomic theory, c. psychology, and d. research design.

[5]   a. If the radius *r* is 1, the circle is called the unit circle.
      b. If incomes, prices of related goods, or preferences change, the entire demand curve shifts.
      c. If you enter a dark room after being in sunlight, there are too few intact rhodopsin molecules for your eyes to respond immediately to dim light.
      d. If a task is difficult, fewer accurate responses are usually given.

In such constructions, it is normally possible to replace *if* with *when* or *whenever* to mark the relationship as temporal or as a definite correlation (i.e. whenever A happens, C happens). The structures found in factual conditionals, where both clauses have the same tense, can also be heard in informal spoken descriptions, as shown in [6].

[6]   a. If one of us cooks the meal, the other one washes the dishes.
      b. If the kids have homework, they do it right after school.

What will happen if … ?

PREDICTIVE CONDITIONALS are also found in informal conversation, especially when future plans are being discussed, as in [7a, b]. They can be treated as responses to the question, *What will happen if … ?* This may be the most familiar type of conditional heard by young children, as in [7c, d].

[7]   a. If the weather is okay, we'll have lunch outside.
      b. If you're feeling better, we can go for a walk later.
      c. If you don't finish your homework, there will be no TV.
      d. If you're good, we'll talk about it tonight.

In written text, predictive conditionals appear quite frequently as steps in the presentation of an argument, as in [8a, b], or as points in a procedure, where one event is a predictable consequence of another event taking place (or not), as in [8c, d].

[8]   a. If Reder's theory is correct, we shall find evidence of transfer in the data.
      b. If learners don't hear the sounds as distinct, they won't be able to produce them accurately.
      c. If one variable is known, the other can be calculated.
      d. If there is sufficient power at this stage, a green light will come on.

Although the main clause in real conditionals is frequently presented as a statement, it can also occur as a question, shown in [9], or as an instruction to do something, shown in [10].

[9]   a. If you aren't in your office, where will you be?
      b. If they have no blankets, how will they keep warm?

Conditionals followed by instructions or directives are extremely common in texts that are designed to give advice on how to do things or to explain procedures, as illustrated in [10].

[10] a. If you have a poor connection or are cut off on a long distance call, tell the operator and ask to be reconnected.
      b. If the mixture becomes too thick, add water.
      c. If a gift box is ordered, allow one additional day for delivery.
      d. If tuned to FM, extend the whip antenna for best reception.
      e. If the wood has knots or broken lines, don't buy it.
      f. If you witness illegal activity, call the police immediately.
      g. If you have any questions, please call our service representative at 557- 6500.

The examples in [10] are from a range of printed materials: a. telephone directory, b. cookbook, c. mail order catalogue, d. leaflet with radio, e. home repair manual, f. crime prevention booklet, and g. magazine advertisement.

What would happen if … ?

The most common contexts for unreal conditionals generally involve imaginary or fictional situations. The HYPOTHETICAL CONDITIONAL answers a question that begins *What would happen if … ?* and allows the expression of wishes and desires, as shown in [11].

[11] a. If I won the grand prize, I would buy a car.
      b. If we didn't have to study, we could have a lot more fun.

Hypothetical conditionals can also be found in discussions of potential outcomes when a number of alternatives are being considered. The examples in [12] are from discussions about the effect of different options for saving money during a financial crisis at a college.

[12] a. If we charged higher tuition, we wouldn't have to cut costs.
      b. Yes, but if we raised tuition, we would attract fewer students.
      c. If we reduced our photocopying, we could save a lot.
      d. And if we did that, we wouldn't be able to do our jobs.

The use of past tense forms in hypotheticals is an indication of the remoteness associated with the possibility being considered. In many of their uses, hypotheticals give an indication of the willingness of the speaker to do something despite his or her inability to actually do it. Some common ways in which this willingness is expressed are shown in [13].

[13] a. If we were free, we would love to go with you.
      b. If it wasn't for this awful flu, I'd be out there too.
      c. Believe me, if I could, I would.

Of course, such forms are also used in excuses for not doing something or not accepting an invitation.

What would have happened if … ?

COUNTERFACTUAL CONDITIONALS convey a negative implication with regard to what is expressed in the *if*-clause. They present a consideration of a situation that is assumed not to have taken place or not to be true. They tend to answer a question like *What would have happened if … ?* and allow the expression of imaginative versions of outcomes that are known to be otherwise. This aspect of their meaning may explain why they are used in excuses, as in [14a, b], in the expression of regrets, as in [14c, d], and sometimes in expressing relief, as in [14e], a newspaper quote from a survivor of an air crash.

[14] a. If the teacher hadn't made the test so hard, I could have passed.
      b. If my car hadn't broken down, I would have been on time.
      c. If I had studied more, I wouldn't have failed the exam.
      d. If we hadn't been so concerned with ourselves, we'd have noticed that he was in difficulty.
      e. We were going so fast that if we had hit the trees we would have been killed instantly.

The counterfactual structure is also used in reviewing historical events, typically to consider alternative scenarios. Those alternative scenarios are frequently used to highlight some specific aspect of the actual outcome being reviewed. The examples in [15] are of this type and are taken from university lectures.

[15] a. If you had been studying this topic in the Middle Ages, you would have been reading about it in Latin.

b. If our primitive ancestors hadn't decided to stand upright, we wouldn't have developed speech as we know it.

Because they allow a consideration of alternative (and often better) outcomes, counterfactuals occur in those arguments where blame is being assigned, as in [16].

[16] a. If you had remembered the map, we wouldn't have taken the wrong road.

b. Well, if you had stopped to ask someone for directions, we wouldn't have got lost.

A general summary of the meanings and uses associated with these four types of conditionals is presented in Box 5.2.

Summary Box 5.2 **Basic uses of conditionals**

Real	
Factual:	*What happens if … ?*
	For presenting habits, general truths, rules, typical patterns, correlations
Predictive:	*What will happen if … ?*
	For presenting future plans, real possibilities, postponing events, steps in an argument, points in a procedure, predictable consequences, instructions
Unreal	
Hypothetical:	*What would happen if … ?*
	For presenting wishes, imaginary future situations, alternative potential outcomes, remote possibilities, willingness
Counterfactual:	*What would have happened if … ?*
	For presenting the negative of what had happened, alternative past scenarios, excuses, regrets, and blame for past events

The use of the subjunctive in counterfactuals, as illustrated in [17], is another way of marking a situation as not actually being the case at the time of speaking.

[17] a. If I were you, I'd leave him.
b. If I were in your shoes, I wouldn't put up with it.
c. If that were to happen, he'd have to get out.
d. If that were me, I wouldn't stay with him.

Although sentences of the type shown in [17] continue to be used, there is increasing use of *was* instead of *were* in these types of sentences in contemporary spoken English.

Exercise 5.B

(a) These sentences are from an American university's guidelines for students attempting to register for classes by telephone. Try to decide whether each one mainly represents a typical pattern, a predictable consequence, a point in a procedure, an instruction, or a real possibility.

   1   If the line rings, but is not answered, the system is temporarily unavailable.

   2   If you get a busy signal, all lines are in use.

   3   If your enrollment is approved, the department will add the course to your schedule.

   4   If you are an international student, you must fill out an Immigration Status form.

   5   If you make an error, you can cancel the transaction by pressing the star (*) key.

   6   If you register for a course and do not meet all the prerequisites, your enrollment may be cancelled.

   7   If you are calling from a campus telephone, dial 4437.

   8   If the line is busy, call back a little later.

(b) The following sentences were taken from interviews with people after a weekly lottery had been introduced. Try to decide whether each one is best analyzed as an imaginary future situation or an alternative past situation.

   1   If people had voted for proper taxes, we wouldn't have needed all this gambling going on.

   2   If I weren't so unlucky, I might try it.

   3   If I won it, I'd quit my job.

   4   If I had been asked for my opinion, I wouldn't have agreed with it at all.

   5   If you bought a lot of tickets, you'd have a better chance.

   6   If somebody just picked any numbers, they could win it.

   7   If nobody picked the right numbers, the prize would just keep getting bigger each week.

   8   If we hadn't got this lottery thing, people would have found some other stupid way to waste their money.

Meanings in context

The presentation of two events in the relationship, *If situation A, (then) situation C,* indicates that situation A has to be assumed in order for situation C to be asserted. From this perspective, the function of the *if*-clause seems to be to establish a state of affairs which is to be assumed in order for the situation in the main clause to be considered. The *if*-clause creates a world of reference and the main clause presents one relevant outcome of the world being that way.

There are some clues in related structures that conditionals do have an information structuring function of this type. The information in the *if*-clause in [18a] can be expressed in a number of other ways that indicate an assumed state of affairs, as in [18b, c, d].

> [18] a. If   he's guilty, he'll go to prison.
>   b. Assuming …
>   c. Given that …
>   d. Provided that …

There are two things to note about all the conditional forms in [18]. First, they present some information (*he's guilty*) to be taken as shared knowledge between the speaker and hearer. Second, there is some uncertainty on the speaker's part about whether the information should be treated as definitely known or accurate. Both these observations can help to make sense of the form–function relationship of conditionals. In the next section, the uncertainty element will be explored. In this section, we will concentrate on the text structuring role of conditionals.

Restating

In many cases, the information presented in an *if*-clause has already been mentioned or suggested in the preceding discourse. In extract [19a], from a printer manual, the heading of the section of text is restated within the *if*-clause. In [19b], from the transcript of the famous 'White House tapes', then-president Nixon first mentions his topic, then restates it within an *if*-clause.

> [19] a. FUZZY PRINT *If your printout looks fuzzy,* try pressing the
>   PRIME key to try to restore print quality.
>   b. On the money, *if you need the money,* you could get that. You
>   could get a million dollars.

In extract [20], from a textbook (Hatch and Farhady 1982), notice how the *if*-clauses (in italics) assume shared knowledge between writer and reader that is derived from the sentences immediately before.

> [20] You have specified the topic in terms of syntactic elements
>   because you are fascinated by relative clauses. You want to know

more about how they are acquired. *If you are fascinated by relative clauses*, you probably have already read a good deal about them. *If not*, now is the time to start.

The first *if*-clause in [20] repeats material already mentioned in a previous sentence. The reduced, or TRUNCATED, conditional form *If not* can only be interpreted in terms of the immediately preceding main clause. Other truncated conditionals follow a similar pattern, typically dependent on the immediately preceding sentence, as in [21], even when that sentence is spoken by someone else, as in [21d].

[21]   a.   Some of you may have already completed the first part. *If so*, you can go on to section two.
   b.   You have to testify against him. *If you do*, we can put a stop to all this killing.
   c.   Walking around in bare feet like that you'll catch a cold and *if that happens*, you'll have no-one to blame but yourself.
   d.   **Jim**   That was a great dinner but I ate far too much.
        Anne *If that's the case*, you won't want any ice cream!

From the examples in [20] and [21], we can see that one function of real conditionals is to *restate* previously mentioned information as assumed or accepted before asserting some new information as a consequence.

Contrasting

Another function is exemplified by the truncated negative form, as already seen with *if not* in [20]. This type of *if*-clause indicates that a situation is being assumed which is opposite to, or in contrast with, the information in the immediately preceding discourse. This contrastive function of a conditional is sometimes indicated by other contrastive connectors (e.g. *but, however, conversely*), as illustrated by [22a] from casual conversation, and [22b] from a textbook (Kenworthy 1987).

[22]   a.   We'd like you to come, but *if you don't want to*, that's okay, we'll understand.
   b.   Sometimes learners will be able to imitate the new sound, but *if they can't* then the teacher needs to be able to give some hints.

It is important that the contrastive function of initial *if*-clauses should be recognized, particularly when there is no other connector signaling a contrast and some rather serious options are being presented. In the 'Miranda warning' (spoken by police officers in the USA, prior to an arrest), as shown in [23] (from Rush 1990), there is a distinct contrast between one action in the first sentence (*remain silent*) and another action (*talk*) in the *if*-clause. In a sense, knowing your legal rights depends on your ability to recognize a contrastive *if*-clause.

[23]   You have the right to remain silent. *If you talk to any police officer,*
       anything you say can and will be used against you in court.

These examples illustrate real conditionals, but unreal conditionals can also be
used to mark a contrast with something in the preceding discourse.

Listing alternatives

Related to the contrasting function, where essentially only one option is
contrasted with a preceding option, there is a use of the conditional which
presents a number of alternative ways of looking at an issue. In extract [24],
from a textbook (Levinson 1983), the issue being discussed is the analysis of
language and the three alternatives are each introduced by an *if*-clause (in
italics).

[24]   *If in an investigation explicit reference is made to the speaker, or to
       put it in more general terms, to the user of the language,* then we
       assign it to the field of pragmatics. *If we abstract from the user of the
       language and analyze only the expressions and their designata,* we are
       in the field of semantics. And, finally, *if we abstract from the
       designata also and analyze only the relations between the expressions,*
       we are in (logical) syntax.

This presentation of options may be preceded by a marker like *So* to indicate that the set of alternatives follows from an already established state of affairs, as in [25], from a parent talking to his two children.

[25]   Okay it's raining and we have to decide what we're doing this afternoon. So, *if you want to stay home*, that's fine, *if you want to play in your room*, okay, and I'll get on with my work, but *if you want to go to a movie*, we have to get moving soon.

Quite frequently, the listing of alternatives via *if*-clauses occurs where choices are presented one by one and each is followed by instructions to do something. Example [26] is from a recorded telephone answering system at a bank.

[26]   Premier Bank instant access. *If you have a balance inquiry*, enter request code 1. *If you have an automatic bill payment inquiry*, enter 2. *If you have a money mover inquiry*, enter 3.

Access to this type of information clearly depends on an ability to understand predictive conditionals.

Giving examples

A further type of information-structuring function of conditionals is their use in introducing examples to support a preceding statement. That function may be explicitly marked with introductory expressions such as *for instance* in [27a], from a textbook (Brown 1988) or *for example* in [27b], from a computer manual, and [27c], from another textbook (Hatch and Farhady 1982). However, the exemplifying *if*-clause may have no explicit marker indicating its function, as in [27d], from yet another textbook (Kenworthy 1987).

[27]   a.   Unlike a nominal scale, an ordinal scale is used to order, or rank, data. For instance, *if you were interested in ranking your students from best to worst* ... , you would be dealing with an ordinal scale.
         b.   You can specify the destination to which the source file is to be copied. For example, *if the destination is a drive name*, the source file will be copied to the current directory of the drive specified.
         c.   The researcher should consider which approach will be most efficient in giving answers to the research questions. For example, *if you decided to use a case study approach to investigate relative clauses*, you would most likely be disappointed.
         d.   Learners have a strong tendency to hear the sounds of English in terms of the sounds of their native language. *If you've never seen a lime before*, you may think it is an unripe lemon because that is the nearest equivalent of the fruits you are familiar with.

This information-structuring function is used with both real, [27b, d], and unreal, [27a, c], conditionals.

Sometimes a number of (typically three) *if*-clauses will be used in parallel sentences to exemplify and support a main point made earlier, as in extract [28] from a guide for international students (Barnes 1991).

[28]   Other visa officers give the same advice: Answer their questions frankly and honestly. *If you do not understand English very well,* you cannot pretend, to a native speaker, that you are fluent. *If some of your secondary school marks were low,* you cannot deny facts that appear on your school records. *If you did poorly on a standardized examination,* you cannot explain away the results.

The use of an *if*-clause for exemplification may also occur in a concluding sentence that illustrates how a series of previous statements can be understood via a single example. Extract [29], from a home repair manual (Philbin and Ettlinger 1988), has this type of structure.

[29]   Plywood stamped Grade A should have no blemishes. Grade B will have a few blemishes and repair plugs of knotholes. Grade C will have checks (splits) as well as small knots and knotholes. In Grade D large knotholes are permitted. So, for example, *if you buy Grade AC plywood,* one side will be perfect while the C side will have some knotholes.

A summary of these information-structuring functions of *if*-clauses is presented in Box 5.3.

Summary Box 5.3 **The information-structuring functions of conditionals**

Function	Situation A having been stated:
restate	If A, (then) C.
contrast	But if not A, (then) C.
list alternatives	So, if A-1, (then) C-1, if A-2, (then) C-2, if …
give example(s)	(For example), if A-1, (then) C-1.

Throughout the preceding discussion, there has been a focus on *if*-clauses in initial position. Though much less frequent (by a ratio of about one to four), sentence final *if*-clauses can occur in both written and spoken discourse. In final position, *if*-clauses seem to function mostly as afterthoughts, frequently acting as reminders of what is known, as illustrated in [30].

[30] a. There's no other choice, *if you still want to go there.*
b. I don't know why she goes out with him *if he's such a jerk.*

Final *if*-clauses can also function as qualifications on what has just been stated and, once again, convey the impression that they represent afterthoughts and are not the primary point of the message, as in [31]. These extracts are from business reports.

[31] a. the savings generated by the recent cost-cutting measures can be applied to future shortfalls in revenue, *if that should be necessary.*
b. the retail sector is slowly recovering and should start to show improved earnings *if current trends continue.*

End-weight

In contrast to the brief clauses found in [30] and [31], there are occasions when the *if*-clause is substantially longer than the main clause. English has a general tendency to move longer or 'heavier' chunks of information to the end of sentences. Known as END-WEIGHT, this process creates a strong motivation for putting lengthy *if*-clauses in final position. In extract [32], the speaker (in a radio interview) had already indicated his disagreement with government policy and uses the *if*-clause to draw attention to the effects of that policy. In this case the final *if*-clause functions almost like an appeal to change policy rather than simply as a statement of a condition.

[32] We have no other option *if the government continues to prevent relief supplies from being transported to the large numbers of people seeking humanitarian aid.*

A number of other examples of *if*-clauses in final position will be considered in the following section.

Exercise 5.C

The following extracts from a textbook on language teaching (Nunan 1991) contain a number of structures indicating conditions. Remember that, as illustrated in [18] on page 132, not all conditionals are introduced by *if*. First, underline all the conditional clauses. Then, try to identify the information-structuring function of each one, using the categories in Box 5.3.

I   While most native speakers of English would have little trouble in comprehending the sounds, words and clauses in this message, it is unlikely that they would be able to demonstrate comprehension by listening to the text and writing a precis or providing a verbal account. However, if they are provided with a context for making sense of the text then the task becomes relatively simple. For example, if the listener is told that text 1 is about 'washing clothes', then the individual constituents are much more readily interpretable, and the task of recalling the information in it is much easier.

_____

_____

2   The context in which language is used and the purpose to which it is put will play a large part in shaping language. Given this view, a logical place to start in our investigation of listening is to consider the different purposes for listening.

_____

3   This section consists of a set of exploration tasks which are designed to encourage you to experiment with and assess the ideas on listening contained in the body of the chapter. If you are currently teaching, you will have ready access to students with whom you might explore these ideas. If not, you should endeavour to get access to a small group of non-native students who may or may not be undertaking formal instruction. If this is not practicable, you can still create some of the listening tasks, and may be able to find one or two individual non-native speakers who will agree to take part in the activities.

_____

_____

4   It is something of a truism to suggest that communication involves the reduction of uncertainty through a process of negotiation. If language were totally predictable, communication would be unnecessary (i.e. if I know in advance exactly what you are going to say, then there is no point in my listening to you). If language were totally unpredictable, communication could probably not occur.

_____

_____

_____

Uncertainty and politeness

In the preceding section, we concentrated on the information-structuring function of *if*-clauses. However, they also serve an interpersonal function, marking the attitude of speakers and writers to their messages and their listeners. We will consider two related aspects of conditional structures in terms of uncertainty and politeness.

Uncertainty

One way to look at the function of some conditional structures in English (excluding factual conditionals) is as markers of uncertainty. In conditionals of the type shown in [33], the *if*-clause can be interpreted as an indication that the speaker does not accept one situation as certain prior to making the commitment in the main clause.

> [33]   a.   If you are going to the party, I'll go too.
>   b.   If I had known, I would have come sooner.

The meaning of the *if*-clause in [33a] can be treated as the equivalent of a 'yes/no' question (*Are you going to the party?*) which invites or assumes a positive answer before the statement in the main clause is to be accepted. Similarly, in [33b], the conditional can be treated as containing a question (*Had I known?*) and an assumed positive answer (*Yes*). This creates a situation (i.e. *I knew*) in which the action of the main clause would have occurred. The pattern just described is in fact a structure sometimes used in counterfactual conditionals, as shown in [34].

> [34]   a.   Had I known, I would have come sooner.
>   b.   Were he to do that, he'd be making a big mistake.

The existence of structures of this type provides some support for a view that conditionals may have something in common with questions. In conversational English, there is a pattern in which a speaker can pose a question and immediately follow it with a statement, as shown in [35]. This pattern clearly has a function similar to a conditional structure. That is, [35a] seems to convey a meaning very similar to *If you are ready, we can leave.*

> [35]   a.   Are you ready? Okay we can leave.
>   b.   You're not going? You'll regret it.

Another clue that there is a connection between conditionals and questions in marking uncertainty is in the way that questions and doubts are reported in English. After reporting verbs like *ask* and *wonder*, a very common structure is an *if*-clause, as shown in [36]. In these cases, the word *if* is not introducing a conditional clause, but it is marking uncertainty.

> [36]   a.   He asked if you were coming to the party.
>   b.   She was wondering if you were still angry with her.

In sentences such as [36a, b], the word *whether* is sometimes found instead of *if*. *Whether* is often used when the uncertainty involves a choice between two options (often between one idea and its opposite), as in [37].

[37] a. She asked whether you would wait or maybe come back later.
      b. I don't know whether they'll arrive today or tomorrow.

When two options are under consideration, both of them can be introduced by *whether*, as in extract [38], from academic writing (Nunan 1991).

[38] In terms of methodology, the debate, as we have seen, has been over the procedures through which learners attain mastery, *whether* and to what extent they should undertake exercises with a deliberate focus on form or *whether* they should pick up the grammar in the process of meaningful interaction.

However, in some of its conversational uses, the *whether … or* construction often marks the choice as having no influence or relevance for the situation expressed in the main clause, as in [39]. The contexts for such utterances typically involve an assumption that one of the conditional options was previously considered relevant.

[39] a. We are going whether he wants to or not.
      b. Whether you like it or you don't, I'm leaving.
      c. Whether it's hard or it's easy, I'm going to do it.

Politeness

The association of *if*-clauses with uncertainty on the part of the speaker may also help explain their role as politeness markers in English. The connection between politeness and modals was noted already on page 114. Basically, English speakers seem to be sensitive to a politeness rule that says, 'Don't impose'. When one speaker appears to be imposing upon another, there is a tendency to soften that act of imposition by mentioning willingness (*will* or *would*), potential (*can* or *could*), or possibility (*may* or *might*) within an *if*-clause, as in [40]. These *if*-clauses seem to be designed to mark the speaker's uncertainty, perhaps ritually, about his or her right to make an imposition on another.

[40] a. Ask him to wait a moment, if he would.
      b. Hold that open for me, if you can.
      c. I'd like to borrow one of your pens, if I may.

A number of other expressions are found in these 'polite conditionals', often conveying an unwillingness to assume that another person's time or schedule can be easily imposed on, as in [41].

[41] a. If you have time, could you photocopy this for me?
      b. If you're not too busy, would you help me with this?

c. If it's not too late, I'd like to get this finished before we leave.

The nature of the imposition can, of course, take many forms. There are *if*-clauses, such as those in [42], that seem to serve as general politeness markers for a variety of situations where some type of personal imposition might be perceived.

[42] a. I'm going to switch on the TV, if that's okay.
      b. If you wouldn't mind, I'd like to watch TV later.
      c. If you don't have any objections, we're going to watch the news.

Some of the indicators of uncertainty and politeness functions with *if*-clauses are summarized in Box 5.4.

Summary Box 5.4 **Conditionals in uncertainty and politeness**

Uncertainty	
If-clauses as:	yes/no questions
	inverted forms
	indirect questions
	reporting doubts
	options (*whether*)
Politeness	
If-clauses mentioning:	willingness (*will* or *would*)
	potential (*can* or *could*)
	possibility (*may* or *might*)
	time imposition
	personal imposition

It may be the politeness function that prompts the inclusion of a HEDGE on some reminders to pay bills or fees. Because there is a risk of offending customers by asking them to pay when they may already have paid, many companies include a conditional clause to cover that situation, as exemplified in [43a], from a journal subscription reminder, [43b] from a medical bill, and [43c] from Oxford University Press.

[43] a. It's time to renew your subscription, if you haven't done so already.

b. If you have already responded, we thank you for your prompt payment.
c. If this letter has crossed in the post with your payment, please accept our apologies.

Exercise 5.D

(a) You want some friends to help you move some heavy boxes. What different forms of *if*-clauses can you use as politeness markers when you ask for their help?

   e.g. willingness (*If you would ...*)

   1   ability

   2   time imposition

   3   personal imposition

(b) What ways of marking your uncertainty (with *if*-clauses) might also be used in your request for help?

   1   doubt

   2   options

   3   question

Photocopiable © Oxford University Press

Exceptional and concessive conditionals

In addition to the basic forms of *if*-clauses, there are several ways in which the conditional structure can be marked to indicate exceptional conditions. Exceptional conditions can be presented as exclusive, surprising, negative, or irrelevant. They can also indicate a type of concession.

Only if and *if only*

When a condition is emphasized as exclusive, the form *only if* (sometimes highlighted as *if and only if*) tends to be used, as illustrated in [44].

[44] a. We can use the emergency funds *only if* it is absolutely necessary.
       b. You can come, but *only if* you agree to behave.
       c. The state can raise taxes this year *only if* a special session of the legislature is convened.

The primary effect of an exclusive conditional like *only if* is to draw attention to the very exceptional circumstances required for the situation in the main clause to take place.

The form *only if* has to be kept quite distinct from the form *if only* which typically functions to intensify unreal conditionals expressing surprise, regret, or wishes. The expression *if only* will frequently occur without a main clause consequent stated, as shown in [45].

[45] a. **A** Yesterday was Bill's birthday.
      B Ah, *if only* I'd known earlier (I could have got him a card)!
   b. **A** We were looking for volunteers.
      B *If only* you'd told me sooner!
   c. *If only* I had known then what I know now!

Unless

When the exclusive condition is viewed as a negative, the form *unless* can sometimes be used. The meaning of *unless* is 'except under the following circumstances', as illustrated in [46].

[46] a. We'll manage *unless* some other disaster hits us.
   b. They won't come *unless* you ask them.
   c. Don't start *unless* you're sure you can finish.

In many of its uses, *unless* can be treated as a strong version of *if … not*. For example, [46c] can be paraphrased as *Don't start if you are not sure you can finish*. However, it can be very misleading for students to think of *unless* and *if … not* as the same. Whereas *if … not* can occur very generally, as in the examples in [47], *unless* cannot be used in counterfactuals [47a], or when the state described in the main clause is an outcome of something *not* happening or being the case in the conditional [47b], or when *then* is in the main clause [47c].

[47] a. If I weren't so broke, I'd help you out.
   b. If he didn't have such a big nose, he'd look okay.
   c. If you're not enjoying it, then I'll stop.

Even if

When the exceptional condition is presented as expressing a possibility that has no effect on the main clause, the form *even if* can be used, as in [48].

[48] a. I would enjoy working here *even if* they didn't pay me.
   b. He plans to drive *even if* there is a storm.
   c. *Even if* you feel better, you should stay in bed another day.
   d. I wouldn't go out with him *even if* he was the last living creature on the planet.

In some approaches, *even if* is described as a 'concessive conditional' because of its similarity in function to the expression *even though* (sometimes said and written as *even although*). While they are generally similar, there is a subtle difference between the uses of *even if* and *even though*. In a sentence like [49a], the effect of *even though* marks the difficulty as accepted and known, whereas in [49b] with *even if,* the difficulty can be presented as a possibility and hence perhaps not known yet.

[49] a. You should try it, even though it's difficult.
      b. You should try it, even if it's difficult.

Marking something as not necessarily accepted as true, but simply accepted for the sake of discussion is one text-organizing use of *even if.* In structuring their arguments, writers sometimes use *even if* to place disputed information beyond dispute temporarily in order to move their discussion forward with the main clause. This pattern is presented twice in extract [50], from a textbook on population studies (Yaukey 1985).

[50] But a cautionary note is appropriate. *Even if* the world's growth rate has peaked, the world's population size certainly has not. *Even if* the world's growth rate were cut almost in half—say, to 1 percent per year—the population of the globe still would double in 70 years.

More generally, the concessive use (meaning 'despite the fact that') of *even if* is to be found in PARENTHETICAL CONDITIONALS of the type shown in [51]. Parenthetical conditionals are those marked off in the middle of a sentence by commas or brackets.

[51] a. Drinking, *even if* it's just a glass of wine, is not permitted here.
      b. I'm telling you, *even if* he is your friend, that he isn't to be trusted with other people's money.
      c. He treated me kindly, *even if* rather coldly, while I was visiting.
      d. I'd like to send you my warmest (*even if* belated) wishes on your birthday.

A final, *even if* somewhat brief, summary of these ways of marking exceptional conditions is presented in Box 5.5.

Summary Box 5.5 **Exceptional conditions**

Exceptional conditions	Indication
Exclusive conditions	*only if*; *if and only if*
Intensifying unreal conditions	*if only*
Exceptional negative conditions	*unless*; *if . . . not*
Possible conditions that will have no effect	*even if*; *even though*; *even although*

Discussion topics and projects

1 There are a number of different ways in which textbook writers create possible worlds of reference (not the known world) in order to illustrate their points. Conditional *if*-clauses are often used, but a number of other conditional structures can also be found. It is usually possible to interpret those other constructions in terms of antecedents (the preconditions) and consequents (the outcomes). Try to identify the different forms used to establish conditions in the following extracts from a textbook on population studies (Yaukey 1985).

(i) Let us be optimistic and suppose, for a moment, that we have ideal death data for a country; that is, let us suppose that we not only have a complete count of deaths by year, but also that we know the age and sex of each person at death. Let us also assume that we have a good estimate of the total population by year as well as the age–sex breakdown of that total. If we had all this, then we would be in a position to compute not only the crude death rates but also the age–sex-specific death rates.

(ii) Wouldn't it be convenient if we had a measure of a population's mortality that avoided both of these limitations, that presented a single figure not influenced by the age–sex structure of the population? Life expectancy at birth is such a measure.

(iii) Let us make some simplifying assumptions about migration and fertility. Let us assume that there is no net migration for any of the cohorts during the five-year span from 1980 to 1985. Fertility changes between 1980 and 1985 could affect the size of only the youngest age category in 1985, that is, those aged zero to five in 1985.

(iv) Let us first suppose that mortality declined so as to improve life chances equally, across the board. For instance, try to imagine what would happen if age-specific death rates declined in such a way that survivorship between 1980 and 1985 doubled for every cohort. Each cohort would be larger in 1985 than it would have been under stable mortality conditions, larger in proportion to its original size.

(v) But what if survivorship does not change equally at all age levels? Then, indeed, mortality change can have an impact on age structure.

2 The following dialog was reported as a true story in a Chicago newspaper (see Akatsuka 1986).

Pope to telephone operator: I'm the Pope.
Operator: If you're the Pope, I'm the Empress of China!

The operator's response is of a type sometimes called an 'indicative counterfactual' (to distinguish these from other counterfactuals described earlier in the chapter). Such constructions are generally interpreted as meaning that the claim within the *if*-clause is not true or even absurd. In order for such structures to be interpreted correctly, a correspondence between the status of the claim in the main clause and the claim in the *if*-clause has to be recognized.

(a) How would you describe that correspondence, using the following expressions as examples?

> If he's rich, I'm Santa Claus.
> If he can run ten miles, pigs can fly.
> If your father is a famous opera singer, I'm the man in the moon.
> If you are Madonna's cousin, I'm the Sheik of Araby.
> If he passes that exam, I'll eat my hat.

(b) Can you think of other examples of this type? What seem to be the necessary ingredients in forming examples of this type?

(c) Why do you think a conditional structure is used to convey messages of this type (and not, for example, simply an expression like 'That's not true')?

(d) Why do you think these constructions are not expressed in the contrary-to-fact type of structures used in counterfactuals (e.g. *If he were rich, I would be Santa Claus*)?

3   Not all conditional messages employ *if*-clauses. Many stores and restaurants in the USA display notices like the following during the summer months: 'No shoes no service'.

To make sense of this notice, we have to understand that the first negative is a conditional, that is, if you are wearing no shoes, you will receive no service.

Rewrite the notices listed below (and any other similar notices or advertisements you have seen) to make explicit the relationship between the parts.

   (i)   No shoes. No shirt. No service.
  (ii)   No shirt. No service. No pets. No smoking.
 (iii)   No pain, no gain.
 (iv)   No pay, no play.
  (v)   No ticket. No nothing.
 (vi)   Garbage in, garbage out.
(vii)   Pick the numbers. Win a vacation for two.
(viii)   Keep smoking. Die young.

4   There seems to be a similarity in meaning between the conditional construction in (i) and the non-conditional forms in (ii) and (iii).

  (i)   If you do that again, I'll scream.
  (ii) Do that again and I'll scream.
  (iii) Don't do that again or I'll scream.

The structures might be represented as follows:

  (i)   If X, then Y.
  (ii) X, and Y.
  (iii) Not X, or Y.

(a) Can you think of other examples that follow these patterns?

(b) Obviously not just any two sentences can fill the X and Y positions in these constructions. What are the necessary elements in the meaning of X and Y in order for them to be used in structures (ii) and (iii) with the same function as (i)?

(c) What differences in the patterns occur when the *if*-clause contains a negative? (For example, *If you don't shut up, I'll scream.*) What changes in meaning do you notice between the (ii) and (iii) structures when the *if*-clause is positive versus negative?

Teaching ideas

1 Match the two parts

There is a traditional format for practicing any two-part structure which is often used with conditional sentences. The exercise provides recognition practice of the basic forms and can be used with all types of conditionals. The standard format is presented in (a) and a slightly different version (requiring more comprehension) is offered in (b).

(a) A set of sentences containing *if*-clauses is first created. Then, the *if*-clauses are listed (with numbers) in a column, and the main clauses (with letters) are randomly mixed in another column, as shown below. The students' task is to connect each *if*-clause to an appropriate main clause, either by drawing a connecting line, or by writing out the complete sentence.

  (i)   If we go by bus,   A. I would send a postcard.
  (ii) If I have time,   B. she wouldn't be rushing now.
  (iii) If I knew her address,   C. I'll help you later.
  (iv) If you keep interrupting, D. the trip won't be expensive.
  (v)   If she hadn't slept late, E. I won't be able to finish.

(b) Another version. Beginning in the same way as (a), create a set of sentences expressing events and conditions. However, when creating the two columns, do not include the word *if* and mix both types of clauses in each column, as shown below. The students' task is to create sentences, adding *if*, by connecting two clauses, one from each column.

(i)   I had lots of money   I'll go with you
(ii) you're going to a movie   it happened to you
(iii) you wouldn't say that   it's too expensive
(iv) I won't buy a new TV   you have to look for one
(v)   you want a job   I wouldn't work at all

2 Spend, now, nothing, later

A simple exercise for real conditionals can be created with some basic elements for both the *if*-clause and the main clause.

(a) In one version, two content elements for each clause are given. It is helpful to demonstrate the procedure with an example (*spend, now, nothing, later*) that is used to create a conditional sentence: *If you spend all your money now, you will have nothing later.* More examples:

(i)   mail, tomorrow, receive, Saturday
(ii) buy, this morning, eat, tonight
(iii) save, now, spend, summer
(iv) give, today, pay back, next week
(v)   record, TV program, watch, later
(vi) word hard, tonight, rest, tomorrow

(b) Another version. This exercise is based on expressions that are used when something is not immediately available. The prompts can be as simple as *phone number, call,* or more elaborate as *leave, phone number, call, later.* The process of forming sentences such as *If you leave your phone number, we'll call you later* should be demonstrated, allowing a range of possible (acceptable) versions. Other examples:

(i)   address, mail (application)
(ii) name, add (list)
(iii) book title, order (for you)
(iv) e-mail, send (information)
(v)   office number, deliver (boxes)
(vi) fax number, forward (copy)

3 If it's a girl …

In this exercise, we are anticipating a special event and planning alternatives. For example: *new baby, name, boy or girl.* The exercise is to think of possible names, including expressions such as *In my country*, and to express the information in real conditionals. Some examples:

> If it's a girl, we will call her Winifred.
> In my country, if it's a boy, the most popular name is Mohammed.

Other prompts:

  (i)   Win a prize, decide, new car or vacation for two
 (ii)   Visitors, give a tour, old or young people
(iii)   Long weekend, go somewhere, hot or cold weather
(iv)   Get a pet, buy supplies, dog or cat or …
 (v)   Make dinner, choose food, vegetarian or not

4 'If God had a name …'

There are many songs with titles or chorus lines that represent well-known (among English speakers) examples of conditional sentences.

One exercise might simply involve listening to these songs and interpreting them (as listening comprehension or dictation exercises). Examples of well-known titles are: 'If I had a hammer …'; 'If I were a rich man …'; 'If I ruled the world …'; 'If I loved you …'; 'If God had a name …'.

It is possible to use these songs as the basis of a karaoke-style activity or as a songwriting exercise where students create their own lyrics.

5 No pain, no gain

The following two exercises are based on common expressions or idioms in contemporary spoken English.

(a) There are a number of expressions that seem to have an inherent conditional relationship between the elements. For example, an explanation of the meaning of a saying such as *Nothing ventured, nothing gained* would typically involve a conditional as in *If you don't take risks, you won't gain anything*. An exercise can be created that helps students become familiar with these common formulaic expressions and also practice creating conditional clauses. Either in groups in class, or as an assignment out of class, students have to write out explanations of what they think (or discover) the following types of expressions mean. (Given a suitable context, students can take this list of expressions, and a cassette recorder, and record some native speakers' explanations of the meanings. Those recordings are played back in class.)

> Easy come, easy go.
> A stitch in time saves nine.
> You snooze, you lose.
> Spare the rod and spoil the child.
> No pain, no gain.
> Laugh and the world laughs with you.

(b) As noted by Ur (1988: 79), many superstitions can be expressed with initial *if*-clauses. Students can be provided with some of those *if*-clauses and given the task of completing the sentences (themselves, or by asking someone else). Some well-known English examples are provided here. Students should also be encouraged to express (via conditional sentences, of course) some other superstitions they have heard from other countries.

If a black cat crosses your path ...
If you walk under a ladder ...
If you break a mirror ...
If your ear is itchy ...
If you hear an owl in the night ...

6 If (only) you had locked the car door ...

There are many types of exercises for practicing unreal conditionals. Some can be closed, as in (a), or more open-ended, as in (b).

(a) In each example, two sentences are presented. Students have to create a sentence, either blaming themselves or someone else for what happened. The process of creating the first example should be demonstrated. (Notice that *if only* can also be used in these examples.)

The car door wasn't locked. The bag was stolen.
If you had locked the car door, the bag wouldn't have been stolen.

(i)   I wasn't paying attention. The food burned.
(ii) Mary fell asleep. The TV was left on all night.
(iii) We didn't look at the map. We took the wrong road.
(iv) The food wasn't covered. The ants were crawling all over it.

(b) Another version. The questions in this exercise are: *What would you do if you were ... ?* and *What would you have done if you had been ... ?*

To get them started, students can be given cards with one of the following descriptions on each. One student has to ask the question and another has to provide an answer. (This can be done in front of the whole class or in pairs.)

Dracula's neighbor
the first person on the moon
O.J. Simpson's lawyer
Michael Jordan's brother
The President of the United States
a friend of Michael Jackson
The Queen of England
the Dalai Lama

It may be more involving for students if they are the ones who choose the personalities (or descriptions). Each student can write one name or description on a card and put it in a box. Individuals, or pairs, have to take one card from the box and compose an answer.

7 Don't make promises unless …

As noted in the chapter, conditionals are sometimes used with imperatives. In exercise (a), we consider a project that elicits *if*-clauses with imperatives and, in (b), one that elicits imperatives with *unless* clauses.

(a) A large number of government offices, banks, and other institutions now have telephone answering systems that provide several options, all beginning with conditional clauses (*If … , press 1*). One project would be to ask students to call different institutions and write down some of the options (essentially an out-of-class dictation exercise). They bring their data to class and compare with what others found. An in-class project might be to create an answering system menu for anyone calling the class. Each person is assigned a number. Then each person has to have a skill or knowledge area that will be included in an *if*-clause, before the standard instruction. Examples:

> If you want to know about soccer, press 5.
> If you want to know about Chinese cooking, press 9.

This may work in small groups first, with the groups recording their messages when complete.

(b) Negative imperatives followed by an *unless* clause can be created by providing prompts such as *make promises (keep them)* and a structural frame like *Don't … unless … .* Some examples are offered to start with and students may be able to create their own versions, once they become familiar with the pattern:

make promises (keep them)
Don't make promises unless you can keep them.

  (i)   lie in the sun (sunscreen)
  (ii) order beer (over 21)
  (iii) start a project (finish it)
  (iv) ride a motorcycle (helmet)

8 For instance, but, so

With more proficient students, it should be possible to present many of the extended discourse extracts from this chapter, such as examples [20] to [29] and Exercise 5.C, as material for a consideration of how conditionals are used in information structure. Students can be asked not only to identify the form and type of conditionals, but also to note the other expressions (e.g. *for instance, but, so*) that accompany conditionals in texts, as clues to their function.

As an alternative, students can each be invited to bring in one photocopied page from a text they are reading (in another class, or at home), with the conditionals underlined. As each page is passed round (perhaps within groups of four or five), the types and frequencies of conditionals can be noted and some ideas developed on the ways academic and/or non-academic writers use conditionals in their texts.

Further reading

General reference, with examples

Azar, B. 1993. *Chartbook*. Chapters 9 and 10. Englewood Cliffs, NJ: Prentice Hall Regents.
Frank, M. 1993. *Modern English*. Chapter 13. Englewood Cliffs, NJ: Prentice Hall Regents.

More theoretical discussions

Akatsuka, N. 1985. 'Conditionals and the epistemic scale.' *Language* 61: 625–39.
Jackson, F. (ed.) 1991. *Conditionals*. Oxford: Oxford University Press.
Traugott, E., A. ter Meulen, J. Reilly and C. Ferguson (eds.) 1986. *On Conditionals*. Cambridge: Cambridge University Press.

Conditionals without if

Bolinger, D. 1977. *Meaning and Form*. Chapter 8. London: Longman.

Information structure

Ford, C. and S. Thompson. 1986. 'Conditionals in discourse: A text based approach.' In E. Traugott *et al.* (eds.): *On Conditionals*. (pp. 353–72) Cambridge: Cambridge University Press.

Conditionals in different text types

Horsella, M. and G. Sindermann. 1992. 'Aspects of scientific discourse: Conditional argumentation.' *English for Specific Purposes* 11: 129–39.
Mead, R. and W. Henderson. 1983. 'Conditional form and meaning in economics text.' *The ESP Journal* 2: 139–60.

On then, following if- clauses

Schiffrin, D. 1992. Anaphoric *then*: Aspectual, textual, and epistemic meaning. *Linguistics* 30: 753–92.

Uncertainty and questions

Haiman, J. 1978. 'Conditionals are topics.' *Language* 54: 565–89.

Politeness and conditionals

Brown, P. and S. Levinson. 1987. *Politeness*. Cambridge: Cambridge University Press.

Concessive conditionals

Konig, E. 1986. 'Conditionals, concessive conditionals and concessives: Areas of contrast, overlap and neutralization.' In E. Traugott *et al.* (eds.): *On Conditionals.* (pp. 229–246) Cambridge: Cambridge University Press.

Acquisition research

Bowerman, M. 1986. 'First steps in acquiring conditionals.' In E. Traugott *et al.* (eds.): *On Conditionals.* (pp. 285–307) Cambridge: Cambridge University Press.

Byrnes, J. 1991. 'Acquisition and development of *if* and *because*: Conceptual and linguistic aspects.' In S. Gelman and J. Byrnes (eds.): *Perspectives on Language and Thought.* (pp. 354–93) Cambridge: Cambridge University Press.

Teaching suggestions

Aitken, R. 1992. *Teaching Tenses.* (pp. 95–116). Walton-on-Thames: Nelson.

Ur, P. 1988. *Grammar Practice Activities.* Chapter 6. Cambridge: Cambridge University Press.

6 PREPOSITIONS AND PARTICLES

1 If learners can say (a), they also usually say (b). What exactly is wrong with (b)?
   (a) *He looked carefully at the picture.*
   (b) **He looked carefully up the word.*

2 Is there any reason why we say (a) and not (b)?
   (a) *at six o'clock in the morning on Monday*
   (b) **on six o'clock at the morning in Monday*

3 Is there any way of explaining why English speakers have to *fall in love* and not *on love* or *at love*?

4 Is there any core meaning to a particle such as *up* that would explain a connection between
   I filled it up, She woke up, and *He showed up?*

5 If we can say (a) and (b), why can't we also say (c)?
   (a) *We left it out.*
   (b) *We left out a lot of stuff.*
   (c) **We left out it.*

'*A host of childish combinations of this type are used in ordinary conversation, such as 'fill up', 'fill in', 'fix up', 'melt down', 'melt up' ... The fact that 'up' and 'down' can be used without changing the meaning indicates that the preposition has lost its significance; indeed, much of this is baby talk, entirely unsuited to technical matters; it should be shunned in serious writing.*'

Although this quotation comes from an older text (Rickard 1923: 145), it is still possible to hear negative opinions of this type being expressed. There are, however, a lot of 'serious' writers who don't seem to have paid much attention to this advice. Whether we like them or not, prepositions and particles cannot simply be 'shunned', because they have a crucial and very distinct role in the grammar of English.

Overview

After a brief survey of basic forms, distinguishing between PREPOSITIONS and PARTICLES, as they occur in PHRASAL VERBS, we consider the different types of prepositions (SIMPLE, COMPLEX, LEXICAL, and GRAMMATICAL) and their basic meanings in terms of *space, time,* and *metaphor.* The uses of particles, both SEPARABLE and NON-SEPARABLE, in four different types of phrasal verbs are illustrated and the conceptual meanings of some common particles (*up, down, off, on, out, away*) are explored. The different roles of prepositions and particles in INFORMATION STRUCTURE are presented, along with a brief note on the effect of END-WEIGHT on the use of phrasal verbs.

Basic forms

There is a fairly large set of forms in English which can function as either prepositions or particles. In structural terms, PREPOSITIONS are connected to the following noun phrase (containing a noun or pronoun) and form PREPOSITION PHRASES (*in the bed* or *on it*). PARTICLES are structurally connected to the preceding verb and, having more of an adverbial function, are sometimes described as 'prepositional adverbs' (*he gave up* or *she slept in*). When a particle is regularly combined with a particular verb, the resulting 'two-part' verb often has a distinct meaning and is categorized as a PHRASAL VERB.

Although a number of forms are used more often as prepositions (*at, from, of, to, with*) and a different set (*away, back, down, out, up*) are used more typically as particles, there are many more forms which can be used as both. In order to separate these uses, several distinguishing features can be noted. Generally speaking, particles are stressed in utterances whereas prepositions are not. When PRONOUNS (e.g. *him*) are OBJECTS, they will occur after a preposition, as shown in [1], but before a particle, if possible, as in [2].

[1]   They gathered *round him.*

[2]   Then they beat *him up.*

When adverbs (e.g. *quickly*) are used, they can occur between a verb and a preposition, as in [3]. Adverbs are not typically found between a verb and particle, occurring instead before the verb, as in [4].

[3]   They *searched quickly through* his briefcase.

[4]   Then they *savagely ripped up* his documents.

With questions and relative clauses, a preposition can be placed before the *wh-*form, as in [5a] and [5b].

[5]   a. '*From whom* are we stealing?' one asked politely.
       b. 'Just the guy *about whom* we were told!'

If particles, as in [6a, b], are placed before the *wh*-form, the sentences are ungrammatical (and sound very weird!).

[6]   a. * '*Up whom* are we sticking?' one asked ungrammatically.
      b. * 'Just the guy *out whom* we were told to knock!'

These basic distinctions are summarized in Box 6.1.

Summary Box 6.1 **Differences between prepositions and particles**

Verb + preposition	Verb + particle
Preposition is unstressed	Particle is stressed
Pronoun after preposition	Pronoun before particle
Adverb before preposition	Adverb not before particle
Preposition before *wh-* form	Particle not before *wh-* form
in questions, relative clauses	in questions, relative clauses

Learners are often given a lot of practice with simple verb + preposition sequences (as in *Look at the picture*) and learn that they can put an adverb between verb and preposition (c.g. *Look carefully at the picture*). Most learners have less experience with phrasal verbs. If they are not aware that adverbs are not usually placed between a verb (*look*) and a particle (*up*), as in *Look up the word*, then they will tend to follow the pattern they know best and produce ungrammatical sentences, such as * *He looked quickly up the word.*

One possible explanation for a number of the distinct properties of verb + particle combinations listed in Box 6.1 is that, as phrasal verbs, they function together conceptually as single units of meaning. They often have single lexical verb counterparts (e.g. *put back = return; put off = postpone; put out = extinguish*). Other reasons, mainly related to information structure, will be discussed on pages 174–76.

Exercise 6.A

Using the information in Box 6.1, identify each of the italicized forms in the following sentences as a preposition or a particle.

1   We're talking *about* a really big hurricane.

2   It came *across* the gulf.

3   and smashed *against* the coastline.

4   It just pushed *aside* everything in its path.

5   It must have blown *away* twenty trailers there.

6   People were using sandbags to hold *back* the water.

7   It had been so quiet *before* the storm.

8   'I had been working *beside* my old barn,' said Terri Mathis.

9   'The storm just knocked *down* that barn in two minutes.'

10   It blew *in* the glass windows

11   *of* several stores and office buildings.

12   It ripped *off* parts of roofs.

13   It pounded *on* everything in its path.

14   It knocked *out* the electricity

15   when it swept *over* the downtown area.

16   It went *past* some buildings without touching them.

17   It kept going *through* the outlying areas.

18   Finally it turned *to* the north.

19   Some people sought shelter *under* their beds.

20   It will take months to clean *up* the mess.

Prepositions

A distinction can be drawn in English between SIMPLE PREPOSITIONS and COMPLEX PREPOSITIONS. Complex prepositions such as *in accordance with, on account of, for the sake of,* and *in spite of,* contain nouns, whereas simple prepositions do not. A distinction is also sometimes drawn between the GRAMMATICAL uses and the LEXICAL uses of simple PREPOSITIONS. Basically, there is a set of one-syllable forms (e.g. *for, in, of, on, to*) which are not only the most frequently occurring, but also have very general conceptual meaning, and are treated as having a grammatical rather than a lexical function. Those simple prepositions which carry more specific conceptual meaning (e.g. *among, before, below, beside, toward(s)*) contribute directly to the meaning of the phrases in which they occur and are treated as having a lexical function. Most of them have two or more syllables. Replacing one preposition in its lexical function with another will result in a very noticeable change in meaning. These different categories are illustrated in Box 6.2.

Summary Box 6.2 **Simple and complex prepositions**

Simple prepositions		Complex prepositions
Grammatical	Lexical	(Prep) + NP + prep
at	*above*	*in accordance with*
by	*among*	*on account of*
for	*before*	*in addition to*
from	*behind*	*on behalf of*
in	*below*	*in case of*
of	*despite*	*by means of*
off	*during*	*for the purpose of*
on	*opposite*	*with reference to*
to	*toward(s)*	*for the sake of*
with	*under*	*in spite of*

In the sections that follow, there will be a concentration on the function of those forms which have primarily grammatical uses. The lexical and complex prepositions are largely explained by their general dictionary entries.

Exercise 6.B

In the following sentences (from the package label of a common pain medicine, often used for grammar headaches), circle the prepositions, and identify the different types using the three categories ('grammatical', 'lexical', and 'complex') presented in Box 6.2.

                                                             Type

1 For the relief   _____

2 of minor aches and pains   _____

3 associated with the common cold   _____

4 and for the reduction   _____

5 of fever.   _____

6 Take with food or milk.   _____

7 Do not give this product to children _____

8   under 12.   _____

9   In case of accidental overdose,   _____

10   seek the professional assistance of a doctor.   _____

11   Do not use during pregnancy.   _____

12   Store at room temperature.   _____

Basic meanings: prepositions

Prepositions in English mark a relationship between a following noun phrase and a preceding noun phrase, verb, or adjective. The basic one-syllable forms seem to be used to indicate an extremely wide range of different kinds of relationships, suggesting a multitude of different meanings for each preposition. Despite the tendency in some grammar texts to attribute 'meanings' to these prepositions, their grammatical uses are actually tied to the conceptual meaning of the noun phrases which come after them. The key to understanding the uses of these basic prepositions is to be found in the number of regular distinctions made in English between different types of concepts. These distinctions appear to have their origins in the way in which entities are located in space and, more specifically, how spatial locations are perceived.

Location in space

Locations can be *points* in space and treated as having no relevant dimension. We are often *at* a point in space. Locations can be lines or *surfaces* and treated as having one or two dimensions. We may be *on* a line or *on* a surface. Locations can be *areas* or interior spaces with volume and treated as having two or three dimensions. We are often *in* areas or *in* interior spaces. Making a very complex perceptual domain a little simpler, we can associate points (*at*) with no dimensions, surfaces (*on*) with one or two dimemsions, and areas or volumes (*in*) with two or three dimensions. Thus, in the examples in [7], one can answer the question, 'Where does Elvis live?' by treating the location as a narrowly specified point in space and using *at* [7a], as some kind of surface or linear concept and using *on* [7b], or as a general area and using *in* [7c].

[7]   a.   *at* 625 Royal Street
       b.   *on* Royal Street
       c.   *in* the old part of town

In providing the answers in [7a, b, c], the speaker has expressed an essentially static relation between the entity 'Elvis' and the locations. The relationship can also be expressed dynamically, focusing on the movement of Elvis (or other entities) in relation to the location(s) as a point [8a], a surface [8b], or an area [8c].

[8] a. Elvis went *to* the lake,
     b. climbed *on(to)* the pier,
     c. and jumped *in(to)* the water.

The location can be the goal of movement, as in [8a, b, c], expressing where the movement is towards. Or it can be the source of movement, as in [9a, b, c], expressing where the movement is from.

[9] a. When Elvis was reaching to get a glass *from* the shelf,
     b. he knocked a bowl *off* the table,
     c. and all the salad spilled *out of* the bowl.

The prepositions used in [9] to indicate movement *(away) from, off,* or *out of* a location are also those used to indicate a position (or state) that would result from such movement, as illustrated in [10].

[10] a. Elvis has been *away from* here for a while.
      b. All his pictures are *off* the walls.
      c. Some people say he's *out of* the country.

Finally, we could also focus on the path of Elvis's movement relative to some space. If that space is treated as a point [11a] or an area [11c], Elvis's path will take him *past* or *through* it. When the space is conceived as a surface [11b], Elvis's path can take him *along* it.

[11] a. Elvis ran *past* the clock tower,
      b. dashed *along* the street,
      c. and made his way *through* the fruit market.

These observed regularities in the use of prepositions for reference to locations in space are summarized in Box 6.3.

Summary Box 6.3 **Prepositions and location**

Position of entity (E)	**Reference location perceived as:**		
	Point	Surface	Area
Connected position	*at* E ●	*on* E	*in* ⌊E⌋
Goal of movement	*to* E →●	*on(to)* E ⌢↘	*in(to)* E⌢↓
Source of movement	*(away) from* ●→E→	*off* ⌐↗E	*out of* ⌊⌡↗E
Path of movement	*past* ●↗E	*along* ⊐E→	*through* ⌐·E⌡→

There are several important aspects of the information summarized in Box 6.3 which should be kept in mind. Some types of spatial references (i.e. locations) may be inherently more 'area-like' (i.e. having volume, or three dimensions) than 'surface-like' or 'point-like' and hence may tend to be used with one set of related prepositions more than another. However, most spatial references can be conceptualized by a speaker differently on different occasions, depending on the nature of the information being conveyed.

For example, a town would seem to represent the kind of location that would most typically be treated as three-dimensional space and lead us to talk of being *in* it, as shown in [12a]. However, from a different perspective, the town may be treated as if it was a kind of surface with sunshine *on* it, as in example [12b], from a morning radio show. And, if that city is treated as one point in a journey, essentially having no relevant dimension, then we can stop *at* it, as in the airline service announcement in [12c].

[12] a. The university is *in* Baton Rouge.
b. The sun is shining *on* Baton Rouge this morning.
c. Flight 410 to Nashville has one stop *at* Baton Rouge.

Although the concept of 'surface' may frequently be taken to mean 'on top of' a horizontal surface, as in [13a], it doesn't mean that the perspective has to be that of the human observer. As shown in [13b], it can be a spider's orientation to the surface that is being described. The relevant space can be also be viewed as the vertical surface on which certain entities are found, as in [13c].

[13] a. The cat was *on* the floor,
b. watching the spider *on* the ceiling
c. which was following the fly *on* the wall.

Spatial locations viewed in terms of a vertical dimension are also the key to the use of *up* and *down* as prepositions indicating a directional path as a surface, illustrated in [14a] and [14b].

[14] a. They climbed *up* the steep side of the hill
b. and walked *down* the other side.

A final point to note is that conceptual distinctions in types of spatial location extend to entities which may not initially seem to be primarily spatial. This is particularly true with regard to the extensions of 'area', or three dimensional concepts. Entities as physically different as *an ocean, a mouth, a box, a drawer, a crowd,* or *a dress,* among many others, can all be treated in English as having the same conceptual status in terms of spatial dimensions. In many respects, such entities are treated as having 'interior' space, or 'container-like' properties, with respect to some other entity that is *in* or *out of* them. It tends to follow that many extensions of these basic relationships between physical or concrete entities and locations will be made into non-physical and abstract relationships. This type of extension can be fairly easily understood by considering some of the ways in which references to location in time in English follow patterns used for location in space, but it goes much further and appears to be at the heart of many metaphorical, or non-literal, references involving simple prepositions in English.

Exercise 6.C

First, circle the prepositions in the following dialogue. (This is from a 'map task' of the type illustrated in Figure 2.3 and described in greater detail in Yule 1997.) Then, using the information in Box 6.3 as a guide, decide whether each reference location after the preposition should be treated as a point, a surface, or an area.

Point/surface/area?

1	**He** Start at the bottom left corner	_____
2	and go to the first intersection.	_____
3	Turn left onto Church Street	_____
4	and go up that street	_____
5	to the bookstore.	_____
6	**She** Do I go into the bookstore?	_____
7	**He** Yeah. Now from the bookstore	_____
8	you turn left and go past the bank	_____
9	and across the next intersection	_____
10	and you'll see a church on the right.	_____
11	**She** Okay, I'm at the church.	_____
12	**He** Good, that's your next stop, in the church.	_____
	She Okay.	
13	**He** Come out of the church,	_____
14	go to the corner and turn right,	_____
15	then go along that street	_____
16	to the school.	_____
17	**She** It's on the left?	_____
	He Yeah.	

Location in time

There are a number of similarities between the way prepositions are used to locate entities in space and the way in which they locate events or activities in time. Many of the conceptual distinctions in spatial reference presented in Box 6.3 are also used in temporal reference. With some concepts, a three-part distinction can be expressed, as in [15] to [17] below, where events can be fixed in terms of very specific 'points' in time, using *at*, through restricted 'units' of time such as dates and days (or their parts), using *on*, to more extended 'periods' such as months, years, and seasons, using *in*.

[15] a. at six o'clock
      b. at noon
      c. at that time

[16] a. on Monday
      b. on March 20th
      c. on Sunday morning

[17] a. in October
      b. in 1947
      c. in summer

It is possible to think of temporal expressions with *at* as answering the question 'What specific point in measured time?'; those with *on* as answering the question 'Which restricted unit of time?', and those with *in* as answering the question 'Which extended period of time?'

As noted already with examples of physical location in [12], the same temporal location can have more than one conceptualization. The same amount of actual time (e.g. between 9 a.m. and noon, next Wednesday) can be treated in two distinct ways when planning a meeting. You may just want to refer to that restricted unit of time (as opposed to another, such as Wednesday afternoon or Thursday morning) and suggest meeting *on* Wednesday morning. Alternatively, you may be thinking that there is an extended period of time (like a container) available and the meeting can take place *in* the morning or even *in* the early part of the morning. The distinction is not between two amounts of time, but between two ways of thinking about location in time.

Some of the other simple prepositions shown in Box 6.3 can occur with temporal reference to events having sources and goals as points in time. In [18a], there are two examples expressing *from* one point *to* another point in time. In [18b], the activity goes *into* a period of time.

[18] a. *From* March to November this office will close *from* 12:30 *to* 1:30 for lunch.
      b. The party started late and lasted *into* Sunday morning.

Simple prepositions can also be used for the 'path' of an activity relative to a specific point, or a more general period of time, as in [19].

[19] a. It was *past* midnight when we got home.
      b. We lived there *through* one very cold winter.

As noted earlier with the conceptualization of spatial reference, speakers can treat a particular temporal reference as having different properties on different occasions. Thus, a temporal expression such as *night* can be conceptualized as a specific point in the day distinct from other times, as in [20a], as a restricted unit of time, as in [20b], or as an extended period of time, as in [20c]. The more extended the period of time being referenced, the more likely that the lexical preposition *during* (lexicalizing the concept of duration) can be used instead of *on* or *in*.

[20] a. *At* night, all your problems can seem much worse.
      b. *On* the night in question, this man was sound asleep.
      c. *In* the night, refugees try to cross the border.

Exercise 6.D

Circle the prepositions in the following dialog. Then try to decide if the time concepts following each preposition should be treated as a specific point (in time), a restricted unit (of time), or an extended period of time.

Point/unit/period?

1	**Ann**	What are you doing on Monday?	_____
2, 3	**Jim**	I'm teaching from 9 to 12.	_____
			_____
4	**Ann**	How about getting together in the afternoon?	_____
5	**Jim**	I'm free at one o'clock.	_____
6, 7	**Ann**	Em, no, I meant later, like from 2 to 4?	_____
			_____
8	**Jim**	No, I have to leave at 2:15.	_____
9	**Ann**	Okay. How about on Tuesday morning?	_____
10	**Jim**	In the early part maybe.	_____
11		I'm always here at 7:30.	_____
12	**Ann**	Oh, no, I'm still asleep at that time!	_____
13	**Jim**	Okay, sometime on Wednesday the 29th?	_____
14	**Ann**	I have a doctor's appointment on the 29th.	_____
15	**Jim**	Okay. What about in early October?	_____
16	**Ann**	This year or the year after next?	_____

17   **Jim**   The year after next? So far I'm free during
           the whole year.   _____

18   **Ann**   Okay. Let's meet at 9 o'clock,   _____

19   in the morning,   _____

20   on October 1st, the year after next!   _____

Location in metaphor

Just as spatial locations can be perceived as containers for entities (*The money is in the bag*) and temporal locations as containers for events (*He shaves in the morning*), so too can other non-physical locations be treated as containers for other referents. For English speakers, linguistic expressions are often treated as being capable of containing thoughts and meanings. As exemplified in [21], words and sentences can be treated as if they were containers.

[21]   a.   His meaning is *in* the words he used.
       b.   Tell us *in* your own words.
       c.   Express yourself *in* complete sentences.
       d.   Try to put your feelings *into* words.
       e.   I can't make any sense *out of* his words.
       f.   He communicated his beliefs *through* words.

The consistency with which the set of prepositions associated with three-dimensional space can be used for linguistic expressions, as in [21], does suggest that this abstract use of prepositions is not simply idiomatic and restricted to isolated cases.

A similar extension of the 'container' concept involves abstract states, particularly states expressing feelings or emotions. As shown in [22], many different states can be treated as having 'interior' space. They are presented as if they are metaphorical containers.

[22]   a.   They're *in* love.
       b.   He's *in* a bad mood.
       c.   Be careful or you'll get *into* trouble.
       d.   At last we were *out of* danger.
       e.   They survived *through* many difficulties.

Thus, one reason we might say that English speakers fall *in love* and not *on love* is because they treat *love* as being more like a container (i.e. having three dimensions) than a surface (i.e. having only one or two dimensions).

Other abstract concepts treated as metaphorical containers in English include the visual field where entities can be *in* or *out of* sight and come *into* or go *out of* view, and discussions where one can get *in* a debate, *into* a controversy, be left *out of* the discussion or convince someone *through* rational argument.

The patterns observed in these examples support the idea that it is the way in which entities, both physical and abstract, are conceptualized that provides a basis for explaining the grammatical uses of prepositions. A similar perspective helps to explain some of the consistent patterns found in the use of particles.

Exercise 6.E

What concepts (e.g. discussion, emotion, vision, words) are being treated as 'container-like', following the prepositions in these sentences?

1   He lay there in despair.
2   I suddenly saw him in a new light.
3   Let's not get into a dispute again.
4   She helped us through the ordeal.
5   Get out of my sight!
6   They reached an agreement through negotiation.
7   He did it out of frustration.
8   I can't express it in just one or two phrases.

Particles

Many of the forms described in the preceding sections as prepositions can also have an adverbial function when they are used as particles in Verb + Particle combinations. These combinations, also known as PHRASAL VERBS, can be used without direct objects, as in [23], with a direct object required *after* the particle, as in [24], with a direct object required *before* the particle, as in [25], and with the option of placing the object before or after the particle, as in [26].

[23]   a.   *Come in!*
       b.   *Get off!*
       c.   *Go away!*

[24]   a.   I *came across* an old photo of you.
       b.   We can *get round* that problem.
       c.   She *ran into* a friend at the store.

[25]   a.   They won't *ask* us *back.*
       b.   This weather *gets* me *down.*
       c.   I wonder if you could *help* me *up.*

[26] a. *Turn off* that radio! *Turn* that radio *off*!
      b. He *chopped down* the tree. He *chopped* the tree *down*.
      c. *Hold up* your hands! *Hold* your hands *up*!

The types of constructions shown in [25] and [26], where the direct object can come between the verb and the particle, are sometimes described as SEPARABLE phrasal verbs. For those in [25], it is obligatory that the verb and particle are separated, whereas for those in [26], it is optional. In some grammar texts, the separation of verb and particle is presented as the defining feature of a phrasal verb, but such a definition would exclude the forms in [23] and [24]. Phrasal verbs of the type shown in [23] and [24] can simply be described as NON-SEPARABLE. The set of structural distinctions among the phrasal verbs in [23] to [26] can be presented as the four basic types which are listed and exemplified in Box 6.4.

Summary Box 6.4 **Types of phrasal verbs**

Type 1: Non-separable: verb + particle (no object)

get up	*pass out* (= faint)	*come to* (= wake)
give in	*sleep in*	*go away*
go on	*carry on*	*break down*

Type 2: Non-separable: verb + particle + object

care for (someone)	*fall for (someone)*	*go against (something)*
hang onto (something)	*look after (someone)*	*stand by (someone)*

Type 3: Separable (obligatory): verb + object + particle

find (someone) out	*shut (someone) up*	*ask (someone) back*
back (someone) up	*ask (someone) out*	*get (someone) down*

Type 4: Separable (optional):

verb + object + particle	verb + particle + object
blow (something) away	*blow away (something)*
block (something) up	*block up (something)*
take (something) down	*take down (something)*
send (something) off	*send off (something)*
turn (something) on	*turn on (something)*
hand (something) out	*hand out (something)*

As pointed out earlier, the structure presented as Type 4 in Box 6.4 can be used with a pronoun in the object position between the verb and the particle (*send it off*), but not after the particle (**send off it*). A possible reason for this is discussed later in terms of information structure.

A list of phrasal verbs, as presented in Box 6.4, does not show the variety of meanings some forms can have with different structures. The phrasal verb *put up*, for example, occurs in a Type 2 structure in an expression like *He put up a good fight*, but has a Type 3 structure in *He put us up for the night*.

Exercise 6.F

Using the structural patterns presented in Box 6.4, identify each of the phrasal verbs in the following sentences as Types 1, 2, 3, or 4.

1   Get off my chair!

2   Cut it out!

3   We'll have to bed down here for the night.

4   The news bowled me over.

5   The changes messed up my schedule.

6   Everyone pitched in to help us.

7   Can you look after the baby today?

8   He chopped the old tree down.

9   Let's invite him over.

10   He always rattles through the exercises.

11   I wish he would slow down.

12   Would you wrap up this present for me?

13   They told him to stay away.

14   You can count me in.

15   I bumped into my old roommate yesterday.

16   Don't throw those books away.

Basic meanings: particles

There is no doubt that many verb + particle combinations have unique (idiomatic) lexical meanings and, like other lexical items in English, should have their separate meanings listed as dictionary entries. If all such phrasal verbs were idiomatic, there would be little point in trying to understand how their whole meanings are related to the meanings of their parts or components.

In many cases, however, it is possible to gain insight into the meaning of some phrasal verbs by examining the consistent meanings associated with some frequently used particles.

Up *and* down

The normal distinction made between *up* and *down* in English is between a physically higher and a physically lower location. This physical distinction is clearly part of the functional difference between asking someone to *jump up* versus *jump down*. Indeed, most verbs denoting physical action can combine with these 'directional movement' particles to produce combinations with fairly clear literal meanings, as illustrated in [27] and [28].

[27]   a.   Can you *lift up* the cover?
        b.   He told them all to *stand up*.
        c.   We'll *come up* when we've finished.

[28]   a.   Can you *climb down*?
        b.   I'll *walk down* the other side.
        c.   We didn't see him *fall down*.

When the concept of 'directional movement' is combined with 'physically higher' and 'physically lower', we can point to a more fundamental conceptual distinction between increase for *up* and decrease for *down*.

In the case of *up*, the sense of 'increase' can extend into a number of different conceptual domains. The examples in [27] convey a sense of 'increase in level' on some kind of vertical scale. By analogy, other scales can be assumed to be the conceptual domain of other expressions associated with an 'increase in level' interpretation (e.g. *The temperature's gone up* and *They've put up the price of bread*). Other conceptual domains can be identified where the use of *up* as a particle conveys a sense of 'increase'. Some examples are 'increase in size' (*Fill it up*), 'increase in activity' (*Business has picked up recently*), 'increase in readiness' (*They're geared up for the game*), 'increase in awareness' (*He woke up*), and 'increase in visibility' (*Your friend showed up this morning*).

In the case of *down* as a particle, the sense of 'decrease' can also be found in terms of 'level' (*His temperature has gone down*), 'size' (*You have really slimmed down*), 'activity' (*They've calmed down at last*), and 'readiness' (*They're trying to wind down the operation*). In some of its uses, *down* can have the implication of 'decrease to the point of ending' which gives a sense of completion to expressions such as *They closed down the factory* and *My car broke down*. The sense of completion associated with *down* is often negative.

With *up* there is a sense of an action being goal-oriented and reaching a state of completion which does not have the possible negative implications of *down*, as in *The wound has healed up* and *We patched up all the holes*. These distinctions in the conceptual domains of *up* and *down* are summarized in Box 6.5.

Summary Box 6.5 **The particles *up* and *down***

***up* = increase in:**	
level	*Things are heating up.*
size	*Fill it up.*
activity	*We will stir things up.*
readiness	*They're all fired up.*
awareness	*He will soon sober up.*
visibility	*I was glad when he turned up.*
***up* = completion:**	*He cleaned up his room.*
***down* = decrease in:**	
level	*Prices have come down.*
size	*The swelling has gone down.*
activity	*We asked them to quiet down.*
readiness	*The troops were told to stand down.*
***down* = completion:**	*All operations have been shut down.*

As illustrated in [29], there are other examples in English of a very clear distinction between the positive and negative implications of *up* and *down*.

[29]   a.   When I'm down, everything seems hopeless.
       b.   But when I'm up, everything seems just fine.

Exercise 6.G

Using the categories listed in Box 6.5, identify the conceptual domains associated with the particles in the following sentences (e.g. increase in level, decrease in activity, completion).

1   A beautiful view opened up before us.
2   All business slows down in a recession.
3   Help me push up this window.
4   I'm going to take down the old signs.
5   I'll try to speed up the deliveries.
6   The engine finally cooled down.
7   He used up all my matches.
8   Keep the noise down!
9   He's made up his mind.
10   Your friend seems to have perked up.

Off, on, out, *and* away

The particle *off* can also be used to signal completion of an action. In its physical sense, *off* conveys a meaning of 'disconnected location' when used with verbs denoting physical action, as exemplified in [30].

[30] a. He *fell off* the horse.
     b. She *jumped off* the wall.
     c. *Get off* that chair!
     d. I *took* my coat *off.*
     e. I *sent off* the parcel yesterday.

The sense of disconnection extends to non-literal uses where the resulting state is to be interpreted as complete or at an end, as in the examples in [31].

[31] a. He *paid off* his debts.
     b. They *broke off* negotiations.
     c. Someone *cut* me *off.*
     d. *Turn off* that light!
     e. The frost *killed off* many plants.

As the opposite of *off,* the particle *on* conveys a sense of physical connection in its most literal uses, as in [32], which extends to a kind of abstract connection exemplified by the verbs in [33].

[32] a. She *put* some clothes *on.*
     b. He *tried* the new jacket *on.*
     c. They've *added on* an extension.

[33] a. I'll *call on* you for some help.
     b. He *caught on* very quickly.
     c. The boys *get on* well together.

The existence of a connection appears to have a further interpretation in terms of something continuing to be the case, and a number of phrasal verbs with *on* convey a sense of actions continuing or, to emphasize the difference with *off,* not being complete, as shown in [34].

[34] a. They *kept on* working.
     b. Could you *hold on* for a minute?
     c. I asked him to stop, but he *drove on.*
     d. Some surrendered, but the others *fought on.*

The particle *out* contributes a basic physical meaning of 'towards an exterior location' when combined with verbs denoting action, as in [35].

[35] a. *Throw* him *out*!
     b. We were lucky to *get out* alive.
     c. Are you *coming out* tonight?

At a more abstract level, *out* appears to have a conceptual meaning involving 'removal'. Thus, the basic meanings in [35] can be interpreted as 'removal from interior space'. This can extend to 'removal from being unknown, or hidden' (*We found out the facts* or *The facts came out*), 'removal from group' (*They picked out the best ones*), 'removal from container' (*He washed the dirt out*), and 'removal from obligation' (*He backed out of the agreement*).

Possibly because of the sense of removal from one situation to another implied in these uses of *out*, there is often a general 'change of state' or 'transition' implication present in many phrasal verbs involving *out*. As a marker of 'change of state', *out* often indicates the beginning of a new state, as in [36], but it is also used in expressions indicating the end of some state, as in [37].

[36] a. We *started out* early in the morning.
b. They *set out* much later.
c. He suddenly *broke out* in a rash.

[37] a. The fire *went out*.
b. One punch *knocked* him *out*.
c. We finally *figured out* the solution.

The last of the common particles under consideration is *away*, which has a basic sense of 'disconnected location', as exemplified in [38].

[38] a. The girl stayed, but the boy *ran away*.
b. Someone *took* the boxes *away*.
c. We chased him, but he *got away*.

When used non-literally, the sense of 'disconnection' involved in phrasal verbs with *away* appears to extend to a meaning like 'unrestrained' or 'without control or direction', as found in the examples in [39].

[39] a. The baby was *babbling away*.
b. He was *carried away* by the music.
c. The soldiers were *firing away* all night.
d. The fool was *throwing away* all his money.

These different functions of the particles are summarized in Box 6.6.

Summary Box 6.6 **The meanings of particles**

Particles	Conceptual meanings
up	increase, completion
down	decrease, completion
off	disconnection, completion
on	connection, continuation
out	removal, change of state
away	disconnection, unrestrained action

In many colloquial phrases, these basic conceptual meanings can receive specific local interpretations. The disconnection in *I'm off* is, in British English, that the speaker is leaving. The disconnection in *He's away* is that someone is not in the present location. The connection in *We're on* is that it is time to join in some performance. And the removal in *You're out!* is that the player is no longer in the game.

Exercise 6.H

Using the categories in Box 6.6, try to identify the conceptual meanings of the particles in the following sentences (e.g. completion, continuation, connection, disconnection, removal, unrestrained action).

   1   He was in the shower, singing away.
   2   We gathered up all the money.
   3   The boss singled me out for criticism.
   4   They moved on to another topic.
   5   It's time to put those toys away.
   6   His parties go on all night.
   7   Will you take out the garbage?
   8   It was hard, but we finally pulled it off.
   9   We finished early, but the others worked on.
  10   One of the cars went off the road.

Meanings in context

When we look at the roles of prepositions and particles in INFORMATION STRUCTURE, there is a noticeable difference. Prepositions and PREPOSITION PHRASES typically represent extra information in an utterance. They don't encode what basically happened, as in [40a], nor who did what, as in [40b]. They generally provide information about where and when something happened. Their normal position is at the edge of the action, in initial [40c] or final [40d] position in the sentence.

> [40] a. The doorbell rang.
> b. Mr Tamashira opened the door.
> c. *In the hallway* he saw a young woman.
> d. She entered his apartment *at exactly twelve thirty*.

In initial position (like this example), preposition phrases create a starting point, a setting, or a framework within which the following information is to be interpreted. In final position, the additional information in the preposition phrase may actually be the focus of interest (i.e. new information) at that point in the discourse, as in the italicized example in [41c].

[41] a. I like music.
      b. I sometimes even like loud music.
      c. But I never like loud music *at seven in the morning*!

The most common function of preposition phrases is to communicate the circumstances or context related to the main event. There is a general pattern in the relationship between what is being talked about in a sentence and contextual information. The context is likely to be in existence prior to the main entity being talked about. The context is typically larger and more complex than the entity. That is, given two concepts such as *car* and *garage*, we tend to treat the larger, more permanent entity (*garage*) as the context, via a preposition phrase. This conceptual pattern is echoed in the information structure preferences of the sentences in [42] and [43]. Even though the basic information content is similar in the a. and b. versions, the preferred organization of information structure predicts that the versions in [42a] and [43a] will always be much more likely than those in [42b] and [43b].

[42] a. There's a car in the garage.
      b. There's a garage round the car.

[43] a. Your cup is on the table.
      b. The table is under your cup.

Whereas prepositions are at the edge of the action in a sentence, particles are often at the center of the action. Particles are part of the verb. They are usually stressed. They often represent new information. If they are part of a separable phrasal verb, the position of the particle depends on the information status of the object. Following the basic pattern of 'given before new', an object that represents given information will occur before the particle. This simple principle helps to explain why it would be very unusual to find object pronouns after particles. As shown in [44a], the given information (*it*) comes before the new information element (*out*). Unless the pronoun (*it* or *him* or *that*) received a lot of stress, the version in [44b] would be very unlikely and, for many people, it would be ungrammatical.

[44] a. We left it out.
      b. *We left out it.

These observations provide an explanation for the most basic patterns found in sentences with separable phrasal verbs. As illustrated in [45a], the particle will appear at the end, after an object that is shorter, unstressed, a pronoun, and represents something already identified (i.e. given information). When the object, as in [45b], is longer, stressed, a full noun phrase, and new information, it is the object that will appear at the end, after the particle.

[45]   a.   He tried *them* on.
       b.   He tried on *some new shoes.*

These points are summarized in Box 6.7.

Summary Box 6.7 **Prepositions, particles, and information structure**

Preposition phrase: information about circumstances of event(s):

(a)   in initial position: starting point, setting, or framework
(b)   in final position: additional (new) circumstantial information

Particle: information that is part of the event(s):

object (before particle)	(particle before) object
shorter	longer
unstressed	stressed
pronoun	full noun phrase
given	new
e.g. *We left* it *out.*	e.g. *We left out* a lot of stuff.

End-weight

It is important to keep in mind that there is a strong tendency in English to put longer chunks of information at the end of sentences. Known as END-WEIGHT, this process will tend to keep particles close to the verb and in front of longer noun phrases. Although it is possible to hear speakers, as they create their utterances, sometimes produce the type of structure shown in [46a], there is a strong preference, based on end-weight, for the version shown in [46b].

[46]   a.   Em, did he leave the part about end-weight in information structure out?
       b.   He was careful not to leave out the part about end-weight in information structure.

It is clear that any discussion of prepositions and particles in English must take both conceptual structure and information structure into account. In Chapter 7, we extend that discussion to look at the use (or non-use) of prepositions in indirect object constructions.

Exercise 6.1

Referring to the discussion of information structure, choose the appropriate version each time there is a choice between a. and b. in the following text. Write a. or b. in the space provided.

Ani	What's the meaning of 'reimburse'?	
Raz	a. I don't know. Let's look up a new word.	I _____
	b. I don't know. Let's look it up.	
Ani	a. Hand over the dictionary and I will.	2 _____
	b. Hand it over and I will.	
Raz	a. I left my dictionary in the computer room.	3 _____
	b. In the computer room I left my dictionary.	
	a. I think I put down the dictionary beside the computer.	4 _____
	b. I think I put it down beside the computer.	
	a. Well. Is the word being used in what kind of context?	5 _____
	b. Well. In what kind of context is the word being used?	
Ani	It says, 'They reimbursed him for his tuition fees.'	
Raz	a. Maybe it means they worked out what his tuition was.	6 _____
	b. Maybe it means they worked what his tuition was out.	
Ani	a. No, it says he enjoyed having more cash in his pocket.	7 _____
	b. No, it says in his pocket he enjoyed having more cash.	
	a. And in the next part he paid off some old debts.	8 _____
	b. And in the next part he paid them off.	
Raz	a. Maybe it means they paid back him some money.	9 _____
	b. Maybe it means they paid him back some money.	
Ani	a. Yeah. How about they gave him back the money for his tuition?	10 _____
	b. Yeah. How about they gave him the money for his tuition back?	
Raz	Sounds good to me!	

Discussion topics and projects

1   Phrasal verbs are common in English and not common at all in most other languages. They are notoriously difficult for learners of English as a second language. Look at the extracts below, from (i) a Hebrew L1 speaker, (ii) a Spanish L1 speaker, (iii) a Korean L1 speaker, and (iv) an American English L1 speaker, all describing the same videotaped event. (For more information on the task involved, see Tarone and Yule 1989.)

(a) List the verbs used by each speaker.

(b) What is the major difference between the English native speaker's verbs and those used by the non-native speakers?

(c) How might you use this type of data with learners to help them become more familiar with the use of phrasal verbs in English?

> (i) a blonde female student entered the class—she put her bag on one of the chairs and she sit—she sat—then she took the magazine from the teacher's table and she started to look at it—it—em—after less than one minute of watching in the magazine she left the class

> (ii) arrived one person and—eh—she sat on a chair—a desk—and she saw the magazine and—took that—and saw the magazine—after that eh—she put the magazine on her purse and went out of the classroom

> (iii) another woman—her hair is blond—come into the classroom—and sit in the front row—at the center and—uh—she stand up—and took the magazine which is—which is on the desk—and she skip the magazine through—and she put the magazine on his—eh—on her bag—and she watch her—she watch—she read her watch—and go out—of the classroom

> (iv) a student walks in and sits down in the front row and sees the magazine and she picks it up and pages through it—and decides she is not too interested—she sets it down and looks at her watch and gets up to leave

2   The conversion of Verb + Particle constructions into nouns is a common process in contemporary English. Below is a partial list of examples collected from newspaper articles and advertisements.

(a) Can you add other examples to this list?

(b) Is there one structural type (from the four presented in Box 6.4) that is preferred as the basis for forming these types of nouns?

> back-up   drop-out   make-up   show-off

breakdown	getaway	mix-up	shutdown
break-in	give-away	pile-up	takeover
cutbacks	kick-off	putdown	touchdown
cookout	knockout	rip-off	walkout
cover-up	lift-off	sellout	warm-up
drive-in	let-down	send-up	write-off

3   It has been claimed (Fraser 1976: 13) that English verbs which can be used in the Verb + Particle construction are single syllable forms or, if more than one syllable, are stressed on the first syllable.

(a) Do all the verbs in the Verb + Particle constructions presented in this chapter fit this pattern?

(b) Can you think of any Verb + Particle combinations which do not fit this pattern?

(c) Can all single syllable verbs in English be used in Verb + Particle constructions?

4   Some phrasal verbs occur with a following preposition, as in these examples:

> They eventually *got down to* work.
> You've been told to *cut down on* cigarettes.
> He likes to *drop in on* his friends.
> She always *comes up with* good ideas.
> It's time for them to *hit back at* their critics.
> He should *do away with* these awful exercises.

(a) Can you add other common combinations of phrasal verb plus preposition to this list?

(b) Looking at your list, plus the examples above, what is the basic structural type of phrasal verb which takes a following preposition? (Check against the four types in Box 6.4.)

(c) One of the most common prepositions used after phrasal verbs is *with*. Conceptually, a construction such as 'X Verb + Particle *with* Y' seems to indicate that X and Y are connected as a result of the event indicated by the Verb + Particle sequence. This analysis seems appropriate for the following sentences:

> I caught up with my friends.
> He gets along with the other students.

You've fallen in with a wild crowd.

To what extent does this analysis apply to the following examples? (Perhaps you can suggest modifications such as 'positive connection' or 'negative connection' or some other conceptual distinctions tied to the meaning of the phrasal verb involved.)

   (i) That kid tries to keep up with the older boys.
  (ii) He always wants to go along with them.
 (iii) Come on, you can join in with us.
 (iv) Well, I hope I'll fit in with your friends.
  (v) Yeah, you'll get on with everyone.
 (vi) Has Freddy made up with his girlfriend?
 (vii) I didn't know he'd broken up with her.
(viii) I heard he's going out with someone else.
 (ix) He thinks he can get away with murder.
  (x) Yeah, he borrowed my pen and just walked off with it.
 (xi) Be careful, he'll make off with whatever he wants.
 (xii) Forget him, will you come out with me?
(xiii) Not tonight, I think I'm coming down with the flu.

Teaching ideas

1 Stand up, sit down

One of the most basic language teaching techniques is very appropriate for introducing prepositions and particles. The technique known as Total Physical Response (Asher 1977) has students following directions from the teacher or other students. In its most elementary form, the teacher can demonstrate the use of a large number of expressions with a few students in front of the whole class. The students and teacher begin by sitting on chairs, facing the rest of the class. The teacher says *Stand up* and does it, then *Sit down* and does it. After a few repetitions, the teacher issues the commands to the students and they perform the actions. Lots of repetition at a fairly slow pace works best in this type of introductory exercise. It doesn't take long, however, for students to understand (and do) all of the following:

> Walk *to* the door.
> Go *to* the window.
>
> Sit *on* the floor.
> Stand *up* again.
>
> Put the book *on* the table.
> Put the pen *in* the box.
>
> Take the pencil *out of* the drawer.
> Give the paper *to* Su-Chen.

Pick *up* the chalk, go *to* the blackboard, and draw a circle *on* it.
Put *down* the chalk, pick *up* the eraser, and rub *out* the circle.

2 Is there a fish on the wall?

This basic-level type of exercise can be done with any picture, photograph, or drawing. It can be a written or spoken exercise. Taking Figures 2.1 and 2.2 as examples (see page 48), a large number of questions, with different prepositions, can be asked. The exercise can be designed to elicit Yes/No (i to iv), True/False (v to vii), or longer phrases (viii to x) as answers. If students are in pairs, each with a different version of the picture, the activity can become a standard 'spot the difference' task.

    (i)   Is there a dog in the picture? Yes/No
   (ii)   Is there a key on the table? Yes/No
  (iii)   Is there a plant beside the table? Yes/No
  (iv)   Is there a fish on the wall? Yes/No
   (v)   There is a woman in the picture. True/False
  (vi)   There is a ball under the table. True/False
 (vii)   There is a clock on the wall. True/False
(viii)   Where's the dog?
  (ix)   How many things are on the table?
   (x)   Where's the telephone?

3 Draw a line under the circle

There are many instructional tasks that require the accurate use of prepositions. Some of those suggested by Brown and Yule (1983b) are presented here.

(a) One student has a diagram with, for example, a line, a circle, a square, a triangle, a number, and a letter in some arrangement. The other students have blank sheets of paper and a pen (or pens, if color is used). The speaker has to describe the diagram so that the others can reproduce it as accurately as possible. (Students may be willing to draw, then describe, their own diagrams.)

(b) One student has a picture of some blocks, wooden or plastic (Lego pieces are excellent for this), and another student has the actual blocks. The speaker has to describe the arrangement so that the listener can assemble the blocks correctly.

(c) One student has a set of pictorial shapes (matchstick figures, geometric shapes, letters, numbers, squiggles, or weird abstract designs). Another student has the same set (or part of the set) in a different arrangement. One speaker has to get the other to identify his or her shapes and their arrangement (*above, below, under, next to, beside*). See Yule (1997) for examples of these types of materials.

(d) The maps presented earlier in Figures 2.3 and 2.4 (see page 50) can also elicit instructions from one student to another. The appropriate use of prepositions of location and direction are needed to accomplish this type of task.

4 At three o'clock on Monday?

Prepositions of time can be introduced, then practiced via a task that involves trying to arrange a meeting among people with different schedules.

(a) The teacher creates three schedules for students, with class times, activity times, other meeting times, and meal times already written in. Every third student in the class gets a copy of the same schedule. The discussion that follows involves groups of three students with different schedules in an attempt to find a slot (lasting an hour, for example) for a meeting of all three of them.

(b) Alternatively, the students can individually create written versions of their own schedules (using a grid design), then get into groups of four or five to discuss when they can arrange a meeting of the group, or a study session.

(c) Another version can be created for pair work as a role play exercise, where members of the pair are attempting to arrange an appointment. Possible roles are hairstylist and customer, medical receptionist and patient, dentist and person with toothache, business secretary and client, or professor and student.

   Note. If the schedules are designed by the teacher in such a way that no clear meeting time is possible, then much more discussion and negotiation are likely to occur.

(d) There are other types of schedules that can be used for practicing appropriate prepositions. Local bus timetables can be used (or modified) for question-and-answer exercises (*from–to* locations, *at* times). If they are available, airline and railway timetables can also be used.

5 Love is a box

The connection between physical location and metaphorical location in English can be explored via an exercise that invites students to create pictures of abstract relations. This can be done by asking students to draw a picture, with labels, to represent *The boy is in the box*. Then, ask them to change the labels to match the sentence *The boy is in love*. If possible, get the students to suggest changes to the box to make it fit the expression better. Then, ask them how they would change the box to fit other expressions, such as *The boy is in trouble* or *The boy is in danger*.

This type of activity can be done in pairs or groups once students understand that creating a physical picture of an abstract concept is the point of the exercise. Before completing class-time, pairs or groups should be encouraged to share their 'images' with the whole class. Here are some other examples of sets that go from the concrete to the abstract. (See Lindstromberg (1996) for others.)

The cat got into the cupboard.
The girl got into an argument.
She got into trouble.

The book is under the box.
The students are under the weather.
They are under stress.

The phone is on top of the TV.
That guy is on top of his job.
He's really on top of the world.

The bird is out of the cage.
You are out of danger.
You're out of your mind!

The tree fell down.
The boy is feeling down.
His plans are going down the drain.

6 Time to get up

Any description (in English) of getting up and getting ready (for school or work) will normally contain phrasal verbs. There are different exercises that can be devised on this theme. It may help students to become familiar with some common verb-particle combinations if the teacher provides an initial description. The following verbs may be included: *wake up, switch off/turn off (alarm/light), get up, get in (shower), turn on/turn off (water), get out, pick out (clothes), try on, take off, put on.*

(a) As an in-class exercise, students in pairs can ask each other (in turn) to describe the beginning of their day. If they can record their descriptions, they can then listen and write down all the verbs used, noting the phrasal verbs. From this material, they have to create, as a pair, a written description of one person's start to the day that contains as many phrasal verbs as possible.

(b) As an out-of-class exercise, students can be given the task of finding proficient speakers of English and asking them to describe how they start their day. If these descriptions are recorded and then played in class, the use of phrasal verbs can be identified. (This exercise usually produces a much wider range of uses of phrasal verbs than the in-class exercise.)

(c) Other themes that can be used for activities in either of the two formats include 'Buying clothes', 'Getting ready to go to a party', or 'Cleaning my room (or apartment)'.

7 Don't (discard that/throw that away)

As illustrated in Discussion topic 1, many language learners use single word verbs (e.g. *enter*) where phrasal verbs (e.g. *come in*) seem more natural in spoken descriptions. It may be a useful exercise to make students aware of this pattern by presenting choices of verbs with roughly similar meaning. This format has been used in second language acquisition research by Hulstijn and Marchena (1989). The primary goal would simply be to make students aware of the available choices, but this type of exercise can lead to a discussion of what is more 'natural' in which type of context (e.g. spoken or written, or careful speech, technical or non-technical texts). Here are some examples:

   (i) It suddenly (appeared/turned up) one morning.
  (ii) They told us to (continue/go on) working.
 (iii) I didn't want to (disappoint them/let them down).
  (iv) Don't (discard that/throw that away).
   (v) I can never (distinguish between them/tell them apart).
  (vi) In London, I (encountered/bumped into) an old friend.
 (vii) You must (extinguish/put out) all smoking materials.
(viii) They were late so they (invented/made up) an excuse.
  (ix) She (refused/turned down) our offer of help.
   (x) We had to (remove/take off) our shoes.
  (xi) I can't wait for them to (return/come back).
 (xii) Didn't you have to (rise/get up) at dawn every morning?

8 I threw it off and got up and put on my clothes

With more proficient students, it may be possible to present longer extracts from texts to illustrate the uses of prepositions and particles. It is worth noting that phrasal verbs are more typically found in the kind of writing that depicts action and speech (e.g. narrative text) than the kind that presents argument or discussion (e.g. expository text). The following example is from a mystery novel (Macdonald 1971: 120).

> It was late at night, almost halfway to morning. I knocked myself out with a heavy slug of whisky and went to bed.
>
> In the dream that took over my sleeping mind I was due to arrive someplace in a very short time. But when I went out to my car it had no wheels, not even a steering wheel. I sat in it like a snail in a shell and watched the night world go by.
>
> The light coming through the bedroom blind changed from gray to off-white and woke me. I lay and listened to the early traffic. A few

birds peeped. At full dawn the jays began to squawk and divebomb my window.

I'd forgotten the jays. Their sudden raucous reminder turned me cold under the sheet. I threw it off and got up and put on my clothes.

Step 1. Students (in small groups) have to read through the extract and identify the prepositions and particles.

Step 2. There should then be a general discussion of any difficult examples, plus a consideration of the 'style' of this kind of writing. (It may help to ask students to try to think of single verb equivalents for each phrasal verb, if they can.)

Step 3. After everyone is familiar with this short text, ask the students (in their groups) to try to create the next paragraph (or two) that would continue in the same style as the extract. Does it include breakfast (what kind?), going to find the car (in what state?), coping with the weather (how is it?)?

Further reading

General reference, with examples

Alexander, L. 1988. *Longman English Grammar*. Appendices 28–37. London: Longman.
Frank, M. 1993. *Modern English*. (2nd edn.) Chapter 9. Englewood Cliffs, NJ: Prentice Hall Regents.
Palmer, F. 1988. *The English Verb*. (2nd edn.) Chapter 10. London: Longman.

More theoretical discussions

Bolinger, D. 1971. *The Phrasal Verb in English*. Cambridge, Mass.: Harvard University Press.
Dixon, R. 1982. 'The grammar of English phrasal verbs.' *Australian Journal of Linguistics* 2: 1–42.
Jolly, J. 1991. *Prepositional Analysis within the Framework of Role and Reference Grammar*. New York: Peter Lang.
Zelinsky-Wibbelt, C. (ed.) 1993. *The Semantics of Prepositions*. Berlin: Mouton de Gruyter.

Preposition diagrams

Quirk, R., S. Greenbaum, G. Leech and J. Svartvik. 1972. *A Grammar of Contemporary English*. Chapter 6. London: Longman.

On spatial and temporal uses

Bennett, D. 1975. *Spatial and Temporal Uses of English Prepositions*. London: Longman.

Herskovitz, A. 1985. 'Semantics and pragmatics of locative expressions.' *Cognitive Science* 9: 341–78.

On metaphor

Lakoff, G. and M. Johnson. 1980. *Metaphors We Live By.* Chicago: Chicago University Press.

Phrasal verbs

Courtney, R. 1983. *Longman Dictionary of Phrasal Verbs.* London: Longman.
Cowie, A. and R. Mackin. 1975. *Oxford Dictionary of Current Idiomatic English. Volume 1: Verbs with Prepositions and Particles.* Oxford: Oxford University Press.

On up *and* out

Lindner, S. 1983. *A Lexico-Semantic Analysis of English Verb Particle Constructions with Out and Up.* Bloomington, Ind.: Indiana University Linguistics Club.

Information structure

Chen, P. 1986. 'Discourse and particle movement in English.' *Studies in Language* 10: 79–95.

On special difficulties for learners

Ijaz, I. 1986. 'Linguistic and cognitive determinants of lexical acquisition in a second language.' *Language Learning* 36: 401–52.
Kaluza, H. 1984. 'English verbs with prepositions and particles.' *International Review of Applied Linguistics* 22: 109–13.
Schumann, J. 1986. 'Locative and directional expressions in basilang speech.' *Language Learning* 36: 277–94.

Language acquisition research

Dagut, M. and B. Laufer. 1985. 'Avoidance of phrasal verbs: A case for contrastive analysis.' *Studies in Second Language Acquisition* 7: 73–9.
Hulstijn, J. and E. Marchena. 1989. 'Avoidance: Grammatical or semantic causes?' *Studies in Second Language Acquisition* 11: 241–55.
Laufer, B. and S. Eliasson. 1993. 'What causes avoidance in L2 learning?' *Studies in Second Language Acquisition* 15: 35–48.

Teaching suggestions

Cornell, A. 1985. 'Realistic goals in teaching and learning phrasal verbs.' *International Review of Applied Linguistics* 23: 269–80.
Lindstromberg, S. 1996. 'Prepositions: meaning and method.' *ELT Journal* 50: 225–36.

7 INDIRECT OBJECTS

1   We can teach learners that *He told us a story* is correct and* *He described us a picture* is not correct. But what do we say if they ask why?

2   Why is * *He said me 'Hello'* ungrammatical?

3   Why do we say *I bet you five dollars* and not * *I bet five dollars to you*?

4   What is the difference between saying *I gave some money to Jack* and *I gave Jack some money*?

5   Given the question, *Where's your bicycle?*, why is *I gave it to a friend* a better answer than * *I gave a friend it*?

Mary: Where did you get those flowers?
George: From your mother's house.
Mary: What! Are you crazy?
George: Why? It was your idea.
Mary: But I asked you to take her flowers.
George: That's what I did!

In this version of an old joke, George acts as if the phrase *take her flowers* means 'take the flowers that belong to her', but Mary obviously means 'take flowers to her'. George doesn't seem to understand the use of *her* as an indirect object in this sentence. Although it may not help characters like George, in this chapter we will try to make sense of how indirect objects work in English.

Overview

After a brief survey of the basic forms, distinguishing between the AFTER-VERB and AFTER-PREPOSITION STRUCTURES, and those with PREPOSITIONS *to* versus *for*, we look at the types of verbs that are found with each of the structures. The historical origins of the structures and pronunciation features of different verbs are reviewed as possible clues to the occurrence of some verbs in only one of the basic structures. Additional clues are then sought in the basic meanings expressed by these structures. The concept of TRANSFER and whether possession is implied as a result of transfer provide one way of distinguishing between the structures. The concepts of creating, getting, and benefiting are used to make sense of those structures where *for* is the preposition used with the INDIRECT OBJECT. The impact of INFORMATION STRUCTURE and the specific effect of END-WEIGHT are then used to explain certain structural choices with verbs that can occur in both. There is a final observation on the connection between LINGUISTIC DISTANCE and conceptual distance as illustrated in structures with indirect objects.

Basic forms

In Chapter 6, we were concerned with the general uses of prepositions. In this chapter, we will focus specifically on a problematic aspect of English grammar where the PREPOSITIONS *to* and *for* are used (some of the time) with INDIRECT OBJECTS. In the following examples, the indirect objects have been italicized.

[1]   I sent some photos to *my friend.*

[2]   I sent *my friend* some photos.

[3]   Give your money to *me*!

[4]   Give *me* your money!

[5]   He told the story to *Sam.*

[6]   He told *Sam* the story.

In each of the examples [1] to [6], there is also a DIRECT OBJECT. In [1] and [2], the direct object is *some photos.* From these examples, it is possible to see two basic structures. In one type (examples [1], [3], and [5]), the indirect object is after a preposition (*to*), that is, in AFTER-PREPOSITION (or 'after prep') position. In the other type (examples [2], [4], and [6]), the indirect object is after the verb, that is, in AFTER-VERB position. These patterns are presented in Box 7.1.

Summary Box 7.1 **Two indirect object constructions**

After-prep:	*I*	*sent*	*some photos*	*to my friend.*
	subject	verb	direct object	indirect object
After-verb:	*I*	*sent*	*my friend*	*some photos.*
	subject	verb	indirect object	direct object

The most common preposition found in the after-prep structure is *to*, but the preposition *for* is also found, as shown in [7].

[7]   Did you get something for me?

[8]   Did you get me something?

Other verbs that are used with *to* and *for* are listed in Box 7.2.

Types of verbs

One of the puzzles of English grammar is that some verbs usually occur in only one of the two basic structures with indirect objects. As shown in Box 7.2, it is possible to create lists of the verbs that occur in both structures (Group 1), of the verbs that typically occur in only the after-prep structure (Group 2), and of those that typically occur in only the after-verb structure (Group 3).

Summary Box 7.2 **Verbs used with indirect objects**

Group 1		Group 2		Group 3
After-verb and after-prep		After-prep only		After-verb only
(+ *to*)	(+ *for*)	(+ *to*)	(+ *for*)	
bring	*build*	*communicate*	*construct*	*bet*
give	*buy*	*describe*	*create*	*cost*
send	*cook*	*donate*	*design*	*fine*
teach	*get*	*explain*	*obtain*	*forgive*
tell	*make*	*report*	*purchase*	*spare*

Verbs from Group 2 have indirect objects in after-prep position, so that [9] is grammatically correct, but [10] is not. Verbs from Group 3 have indirect objects in after-verb position, so that [11] is grammatically correct and [12] is not.

[9]   He described the picture to *us*.

[10]   *He described *us* the picture.

[11]   It cost *me* a lot of money.

[12]   *It cost a lot of money to *me*.

Some explanations for these differences in structure are presented in the following sections.

Exercise 7.A

Using the information in Box 7.1 and Box 7.2, try to decide if the verbs listed below would be grammatical in structures (a), or (b), or both.

(a)   Mary _____ something to/for her friend.

(b)   Mary _____ her friend something.

1   design
2   describe
3   tell
4   bring
5   report
6   buy
7   charge
8   create
9   repeat
10   find

Photocopiable © Oxford University Press

Basic structures: origins and pronunciation

Part of the puzzle with indirect object constructions is that verbs with very similar meanings are not used in the same structures. In Box 7.2, note that *give*, *teach*, and *tell* can be used in both structures with indirect objects (as in [13], [15], and [17]), but *donate*, *explain*, and *communicate* typically occur in only the after-prep structure (as in [14], [16], and [18]).

[13]   a.   They'll give some old books to *the library*.
       b.   They'll give *the library* some old books.

[14]   a.   They'll donate some old books to *the library*.
       b.   *They'll donate *the library* some old books.

[15]   a.   He taught the new rules to *everyone*.
       b.   He taught *everyone* the new rules.

[16]   a.   He explained the new rules to *everyone*.
       b.   *He explained *everyone* the new rules.

[17] a. She told the bad news to *all of us.*
     b. She told *all of us* the bad news.

[18] a. She communicated the bad news to *all of us.*
     b. *She communicated *all of us* the bad news.

One explanation of this puzzle has been presented in terms of the historical origins of both the structures and the verbs involved. In Old English, the after-verb structure was the most common. Those verbs in Modern English which have Old English roots still occur in that original structure. During the late Middle English period, many new verbs (Latin in origin) were borrowed through French, together with a French construction which only used the after-prep form. The new verbs were only used in the new structure. The older verbs were used in both the new (after-prep) structure and the older (after-verb) structure. Thus, in Box 7.2, verbs of Old English origin dominate Group 1 and verbs of Latin origin dominate Group 2 .

Another big difference between verbs in these two groups is their pronunciation. The Old English group are single syllable forms (e.g. *tell*). The Latin forms normally consist of two or more syllables (e.g. *re-PORT, com-MU-ni-cate*), with stress on the second syllable. There are some two syllable forms which have stress on the first syllable (e.g. *OF-fer, PROM-ise*) and have a sound structure closer to the Old English forms. As shown in [19], a verb with first syllable stress is used in both structures, like Group 1 types.

[19] a. Did you offer some coffee to *our guest?*
     b. No, I offered *her* a cold drink.

These differences in pronunciation patterns, summarized in Box 7.3, may provide clues for natural learners as they listen to spoken English structures involving indirect objects.

Summary Box 7.3 **Origins and pronunciations**

Verb origin	Stress	Indirect object position
Old English	First or only syllable stressed	After-verb and after-prep
Latin	Second syllable stressed (two or more syllables)	After-prep only

The general pattern shown in Box 7.3 is a useful guide in deciding which verbs can occur in the after-verb structure. Unfortunately, it is not a completely reliable guide, because a number of verbs do not follow the pattern. For example, the single syllable verb *say* does not occur with indirect objects in after-verb position. The sentence **He said me something* is ungrammatical (while *He said something to me* is okay).

Also, some two-syllable Latin forms, with their first syllables unstressed (e.g. *assign, award,* and *reserve*), do occur in both structures, while others with similar stress patterns (e.g. *announce, admit, repeat*) only occur in the after-prep structure. To distinguish between the types of events described by these verbs requires an analysis, not of pronunciation, but of meaning.

Exercise 7.B

Using the information about number of syllables and stress in Box 7.3, put a circle round the verbs which can be used in the sentence structures provided. Depending on the sentence structure, both verbs, only one of them, or neither of them can be used.

1   Will you _____ us the procedure? *show / display*

2   Please _____ the boxes to me. *return / send*

3   Can you _____ me the magazine? *throw / deliver*

4   Did they _____ you that book? *recommend / offer*

5   Don't _____ this to anyone. *repeat / tell*

6   We'll _____ them some cards. *mail / send*

7   They'll _____ us some new plans. *propose / suggest*

8   Could you _____ me how to do it? *explain / teach*

9   He'll _____ you something to eat. *make / fix*

10   Don't even _____ his name to me! *mention / whisper*

Photocopiable © Oxford University Press

Basic meanings

The previous sections have been mostly concerned with differences in forms and structures with indirect objects. There are also some very clear meaning (or conceptual) distinctions marked in sentences containing indirect objects. Here are three:

Indirect objects will tend to be used to refer to humans.
These humans will generally be in the role of recipients.
The major concept expressed will involve transfer.

In the following sections, we explore how these basic concepts are expressed grammatically and how different results of 'transfer' are to be understood.

Humans, transfer, and having

The concept of TRANSFER, and how its effects are to be interpreted, is crucial to an understanding of indirect object constructions in English. Transfer is movement. Transfer can involve real (concrete) objects, such as *books* in [20a], or mental (abstract) objects, such as *ideas* in [20b].

[20]   a.   She gave the students some new *books.*
        b.   She gave the students some new *ideas.*

In these sentences, the transferred objects (*books, ideas*) are expressed as direct objects. The direct objects are the entities that are affected by the action of the verb. The subject (*she*) expresses where the transfer is from (i.e. the source). The indirect object (*the students*) expresses where the transfer is to (i.e. the goal). The verb of transfer (*gave*) includes the meaning 'cause to go', in the sense that the source causes the transferred object to go to the goal. In the after-verb structure, this transfer implies that a new individual will possess the object being transferred. These basic meanings are presented in Box 7.4.

Summary Box 7.4 **Indirect objects, transfer, and having**

Structure 1: After-prep

Source	Action	Transferred object		Goal/location
A	cause	B	to go to	C
She	*gave*	*some books*	*to*	*the students.*
He	*sent*	*the parcel*	*to*	*a friend.*
I	*taught*	*the new song*	*to*	*the whole group.*

Structure 2: After-verb

Source	Action	Goal/possessor		Transferred object
A	cause	C	to have	B
He	*sent*	*his mother*		*a birthday card.*
I	*sold*	*Ray*		*my old computer.*
You	*told*	*the girls*		*a scary story.*

The after-prep structure is generally used when the indirect object is perceived as a location, and is strongly preferred when a physical location (i.e. a place) is the goal, as in [21].

[21] The Red Cross sent relief supplies to Zaire.

Those verbs which can only be used in the after-prep structure (Group 2, Box 7.2) indicate transfer from the source. Thus, when you *announce, declare, describe, explain,* or *report* something to some person, as in [22], that person is not treated as having come into possession of whatever you said.

[22] a. We reported the results to the crowd.
      b. They explained their plan to the committee.

It is worth noting that many of the verbs that seem only to occur in the after-prep structure have some type of 'communication' meaning in common. This observation may also explain why a large number of verbs expressing 'manner of utterance' have indirect objects only in the after-prep structure. When you *say, shout, scream, murmur,* or *whisper* something to someone, the focus is on the act and manner of utterance. Such actions are not treated, in the grammar of English, as causing any change in the receiver's state. Verbs denoting 'manner of utterance' do not have indirect objects in after-verb position. This would be the simplest explanation for the oddness experienced when a language learner produces utterances like * *He said me 'Hello'.*

Those verbs which do have indirect objects in after-verb position generally convey some (intended) change in the state of the recipient as a result of the action. In the clearest cases, the recipient comes to be in possession, physically or mentally, of whatever is transferred. The recipient is most often human, but the thing that is transferred does not have to be what the human would want, as in experiences like those in [23].

[23] a. The loud music gave me a terrible headache.
      b. These grammar lessons give me a pain in the neck!

Exercise 7.C

(a) In the following sentences, put a circle round the indirect objects that indicate human recipients.

   1   You'll teach one group basic grammar.
   2   She sent her clothes to the laundry.
   3   Don't mention this to anyone!
   4   New paint gives your house a fresh look.
   5   The rain brought us some relief from the heat.
   6   He confessed his guilt to a friend.

7   Pass me the salt, please.

8   She hit the ball to the edge of the grass.

(b) For those sentences where you did not circle the indirect object, what kind of transfer (e.g. physical, mental) is involved?

_____

_____

_____

Transfer and not having

The connection between after-verb position and the idea of possession can also be noted with that small set of English verbs that involve loss of possession. For those verbs in Group 3 (shown earlier in Box 7.2) such as *cost* and *fine*, the indirect object is not a goal or a location. This may explain why these verbs do not occur in after-prep structures. Instead, they are treated in the same way as other 'possession' verbs, with their indirect objects in after-verb position, but indicating a negative effect, as in [24].

[24]   This awful book cost me twenty dollars!

Whereas the verb *buy* has a 'cause-to-have' meaning, a verb like *cost* has a 'cause-not-to-have' meaning. Other examples are shown in Box 7.5.

Summary Box 7.5 **Indirect objects, transfer, and not having**

Structure 3: After-verb only				
Source	Action	Possessor		Entity
A	cause	C	not to have	B
The deal	*cost*	*me*		*a fortune.*
The judge	*fined*	*him*		*fifty dollars.*
I	*bet*	*you*		*five dollars.*

The verb *bet* is included in Box 7.5 in its typical use as a speech act meaning 'offer to bet'. The act of stating *I bet you five dollars* is interpreted here as 'I hereby offer to cause you not to have five dollars'. Notice that you are not the 'goal' of the five dollars, so we don't say **I bet five dollars to you*. In this bet, you are the 'source' of the five dollars (someone hopes).

Exercise 7.D

Put a circle round the verbs in the following set which have conceptual meanings similar to those shown in Box 7.5.

1   We read him his rights.
2   They denied everyone permission to leave.
3   She left him all her money.
4   I offered him a hand.
5   We took them some groceries.
6   The guards refused us entry.
7   You promised me a new computer.
8   He forgave them their sins.

Creating, getting, and benefiting

There is another set of verbs, with meanings of 'creating' and 'getting', that can also be used in both indirect object structures. In these cases, the basic role of the indirect object is that of beneficiary. The receiver benefits from the action, as Keiko does in [25].

[25] I'm getting a present for Keiko.

There are two kinds of benefiting for these indirect objects, but only one of them implies possession. Once again, it is the indirect object in the after-verb position, typically referring to a human, that is treated as both beneficiary and possessor as a result of the event. Several examples are presented in Box 7.6.

Summary Box 7.6 **Indirect objects and benefiting**

Structure 4: After-prep

Source	Action	Created/obtained entity		Goal/
A	cause	B	to be for the benefit of	beneficiary C
I	*cooked*	*dinner*	*for*	*all of them.*
She	*got*	*a present*	*for*	*her friend.*
We	*bought*	*ice cream*	*for*	*everyone.*

Structure 5: After-verb

Source	Action	Beneficiary/possessor		Created/obtained entity B
A	cause	C	to benefit by having	
She	*made*	*her daughter*		*a new dress.*
Hugo	*got*	*them*		*football tickets.*
I	*'ll fix*	*you*		*a nice cold drink.*

Note that verbs such as *create* and *design* would typically be found in structure 4 (Box 7.6), with indirect objects in the after-prep position. Many of these verbs are also of Latin origin (e.g. *compose, devise, establish, organize*) and follow the pattern shown earlier in Box 7.3. One can also see how the actions of these verbs may be for the benefit of some person without resulting in that person actually possessing the created thing. In contrast, the small (one syllable) English verb *do*, has one meaning close to 'benefiting' and can appear in both structures from Box 7.6, as in the common expressions of [26] and [27].

[26] Will you do something for *me*?

[27] Could you please do *me* a favor?

Exercise 7.E

(a) In the following sentences, put a circle round those indirect objects that indicate human recipients.

   I   He designs exhibits for museums.

   2   I'll get my dog a bone.

   3   Don't buy me any more of those.

   4   Let's bake your father a special cake.

   5   Could you heat the water for us?

   6   She organizes supplies for the hospital.

   7   I'll make everyone something to eat.

   8   They got some water for their plants.

(b) In these sentences, what other types of entities can 'benefit' (as indirect objects)?

   _____

   _____

   _____

   _____

Meanings in context

Thus far, we have focused narrowly on basic form and meaning and neglected the ways in which indirect objects occur in discourse. There are certain discourse patterns that result in a strong preference for one structure rather than another. A major source of difference can be described in terms of information structure.

As we have noted already, in English sentences, information that the speaker or writer assumes to be known (or given) to the hearer or reader will generally be placed before information that is unknown (or new) at that point. The simple slogan is 'given before new'. One of the obvious differences between the two versions of the information being presented in [28] and [29] is that the positions of the direct object (*some money*) and the indirect object (*Jack*) are reversed.

[28] I gave some money to *Jack*.

[29] I gave *Jack* some money.

In terms of information structure, [28] is more likely to be said when *Jack* is the new information being presented and [29] will be used when it is *some money* that is new. This pattern is clearer when the given information is presented in a question, as in [30] and [31], and the answer is structured to place the new after the given.

[30] Where's the money? I gave it to *Jack*.

[31] Why is Jack so happy? I gave *him* some money.

Notice that pronouns (*it, him*) are used for given information in the answers in [30] and [31]. The words or phrases used to express given information are generally shorter than those used for new information. Other preferences for expressing given information are definite forms (*the teacher*) rather than indefinite (*a teacher*), as explained in Chapter 2, and specific forms (*that teacher*) rather than non-specific forms (*some teacher or other*).

The indirect object will normally occur in the after-verb position when its grammatical form reflects an information status that is not as 'newsworthy' as the direct object. These typical features are summarized in Box 7.7

Summary Box 7.7 **Indirect objects and information structure**

The indirect object in after-verb position is more likely to be:	The indirect object in after-prep position is more likely to be:
shorter	longer
definite	indefinite
specific	non-specific
a pronoun	a full noun phrase

The differences presented in Box 7.7 are typical patterns which may not always be found because other markers of information structure (e.g. intonation) are in use. However, these patterns do help to explain why it is very unusual in English to find pronouns after full noun phrases in some constructions. For example, in answer to his mother's question, *Where's your bike?*, a boy will probably answer *I lent it to a friend* and will not normally say, *I lent a friend it*. Indeed, the simple distinction between shorter (in after-verb position) versus longer expressions can be easily seen in the typical patterns of some very common English expressions, shown in [32] to [38]. The indirect objects are in italics.

[32] Give *me* a break!

[33] Tell *me* another one!

[34] Read *me* a story.

[35] Buy *me* something nice.

[36] Lend *me* your ears (and I'll sing *you* a song).

[37] Show *them* who's boss!

[38] Send *them* a message they won't forget.

End-weight

Another factor at work in English is the preference for END-WEIGHT in message structure. The length of either the direct or indirect object is sometimes described in terms of its 'weight' within the message being communicated. The more language used to identify a person or thing, the more 'weight' it will tend to have in the message. The strong tendency towards end-weight in English sentences clearly influences the positions of the direct and indirect objects. The longer expression tends to be placed at the end. This can be seen in typical spoken expressions such as [32] to [38] and also in written language examples such as [39] and [40].

[39] He handed *her* a large brown manilla envelope stuffed with hundred dollar bills.

[40] Later, she gave that envelope to *a short bedraggled man sitting by the side of the road holding a sign that read 'Will Work for Food'*.

Notice that the longer expression of new information placed at the end of the sentence is the direct object in [39] and the indirect object in [40].

Exercise 7.F

(a) Put brackets round the direct objects in the following sentences. Then draw a line under the indirect objects.

e.g.   If you are not completely satisfied with this product, return (it) to <u>our Customer Services Department</u> immediately.

1   Could you pass me some mustard, please?

2   We wrote letters to everyone in the government.

3   The man showed Mrs Weir an old faded photograph of his son.

4   He handed a note to one of the guards.

5   Sorry, you're too late. I can't rent you a car today.

(b) As a simple measure of length, count the number of syllables in the direct and indirect objects in the spoken versions of sentences 1–5 in (a). For each sentence, fill in the space below that matches the position of the indirect object (before or after the direct object). What do you notice about the number of syllables in the indirect objects in relation to their position?

	indirect	direct	indirect
e.g.	-	_1_	_10_
1	____	____	-
2	-	____	____
3	____	____	-
4	-	____	____
5	____	____	-

Linguistic distance

The appropriate use of indirect objects in English seems to require an explanation that involves both conceptual meaning and information structure. When the referent of an indirect object is treated as given information, denotes a human, and comes into possession of some entity, there is a powerful tendency to place that indirect object in after-verb position. When the referent is new information and represents the goal of an act of transfer, the indirect object will typically occur in after-prep position.

By placing the indirect object in after-prep position, the speaker or writer also creates greater LINGUISTIC DISTANCE, and hence a much looser connection, between the action of the verb and the recipient or beneficiary of that action. When the indirect object is in after-verb position, there is much less linguistic distance, and hence a much closer connection, between the action of the verb and the recipient or beneficiary of that action. As is often the case in English, linguistic distance signals a type of conceptual distance. The result of an extremely close connection between one verb (*give*) and its most common indirect object (*me*) is that they have combined into a single spoken form (*gimme*), one of the earliest indirect object constructions acquired by English speaking children.

Discussion topics and projects

1   A number of new expressions are being used in contemporary English to talk about 'transfer' by means of new technology. Words like *fax* and *e-mail* are regularly used as verbs with indirect objects. In your experience, do these verbs occur with their indirect objects in after-prep or after-verb position, or both? What about indirect objects used with forms like *express-mail, fed-ex, memo, photocopy, radio, telegraph, telephone, telex, wire,* and *xerox* when they are used as verbs? Have you noted any others that could be added to this list?

2   There are two related topics that derive from common mistakes produced by English language learners.

(a)   Many learners of English as a second or foreign language say and write ungrammatical sentences like the following:

   *I explained him the problem yesterday.
   *He recommended me this new book.
   *Our teacher suggested us some good topics.
   *I would like to introduce you my cousin.

   How would you explain to one of those learners why these are considered ungrammatical, particularly in written work? What basic rule or rules might be most useful for such learners to know? Perhaps you would devise different types of explanations for higher proficiency and lower proficiency learners: what would they be?

(b)   There seems to be a limitation on which 'recipients' or 'beneficiaries' can become the subjects of English sentences. In some cases, there is no problem, as in (ii), but (iv) is one type of ungrammatical sentence produced by language learners.

   (i)   Dr Overstreet taught us some German expressions.

   (ii)   We were taught some German expressions by Dr Overstreet.

   (iii)   Dr Overstreet explained some German expressions to us.

(iv) *We were explained some German expressions by Dr Overstreet.

Is this pattern just found with these verbs (*teach, explain*) or also with other verbs considered in this chapter? Can you think of an explanation for this phenomenon?

3   Most of the examples presented in this chapter have been simple sentences where the direct and indirect objects are easy to identify. In discourse, these patterns may not always be so clear. Read through the following extracts from texts and try to identify the direct and indirect objects in each case. Can you find any points where a 'recipient' is understood, but no indirect object is actually stated?

   (i) The twins say, 'Give us a date—any time in the last or next forty thousand years.' You give them a date, and, almost instantly, they tell you what day of the week it would be.

   (ii) Only five years earlier, Ochoa had been awarded the title of Hero of the Revolution—the highest honor conferred to a military man in Castro's Cuba.

   (iii) For a small sum, Madame Thibaut loaned Felicia high heels and a silver sequined gown sleek as a fish.

   (iv) Abuela gives me a box of letters she wrote to her onetime lover in Spain, but never sent. She shows me his photograph too.

   (v) I gave him the highlights of what we found. He asked what I thought of Yeltsin and he said he admired his guts for seeing him when Clinton was a candidate.

   (vi) I told him that with Yeltsin what you see is what you get. He said that he has spoken to Yeltsin twice and Yeltsin sounded worried. Clinton suggested that they meet earlier than the April 4th date, but Yeltsin wanted to wait until after his struggle with the Parliament had been resolved. He said that Yeltsin told him to see me.

   (vii) The same learners transferred negative interrogatives, a common syntactic mitigator in Danish, to their German requests, but not to English.

   (viii) Brooke's father, Frank Shields, a former cosmetics industry executive, gave Agassi a medal that Brooke's grandfather Francis Xavier had been awarded as a member of a US Davis Cup team.

Example (i) is from Sacks (1986: 186), (ii) from Oppenheimer (1992: 18), (iii) and (iv) from Garcia (1992: 79, 235), (v) and (vi) from Crowley

(1996: 47), (vii) from Kasper (1992: 216) and (viii) from *People Magazine* (5th May, 1997, page 51).

4   How many indirect objects, in which positions, can you identify in the following text?

> I can't remember who told me this awful joke, but you asked for one. Okay, one day this guy goes into a bar with a dog and says to the bartender, 'Hey, give me a whiskey, and my dog a beer.'
> 'Sorry,' says the bartender, 'but we don't serve dogs alcohol'.
> The guy says, 'But this is a special dog. He not only drinks, he talks. Tell him what you want, Rover.'
> 'Beer,' growls the dog.
> The bartender is amazed, but he's still not sure. 'How old is that dog?'
> 'Just turned four.'
> 'Ah,' says the bartender and gets the dog a bottle of Pepsi.
> The dog drinks it down, then stands and stares at the bottle.
> 'Want to buy him another?' asks the bartender.
> 'Sure, give us a couple more,' says the guy, 'but this time don't show him the bottle.'
> 'Why not?'
> 'Well, he's just starting to read and he already wants to bet me that beer doesn't start with a P.'

Teaching ideas

1 Rearrange these sentences

The basic forms of sentences containing indirect objects are typically presented in exercises where one version (e.g. the after-verb form) has to be rewritten as another (the after-prep form), as shown in (i) and (ii).

> (i)   Mark sold Sally his old car. → *Mark sold his old car to Sally.*
> (ii) I made you a snack. → *I made a snack for you.*

Most textbooks provide written exercises of this type. It is important to remember that such exercises will only be possible with those verbs that can be used in both structures (Group 1, Box 7.2).

It may be possible to practice both structures more interactively via the following activity, based on an idea from Marianne Celce-Murcia and Sharon Hilles (1988: 93).

Collect one object from each of six students (by asking, for example, *Could you lend me a pen?* or *Would you give me one of your books?*). You are then going to return the objects to their owners. Hold up each object and use one of the following patterns (the pen actually belongs to Mehta):

Teacher   Should I give this pen back to Sun Lee?
Student(s) No, give it to Mehta.

Teacher   Should I give Mehta the book?
Student(s) No, give her the pen.

It should be possible to get students to follow the pattern of this exercise in small groups, each student taking a turn as the one asking questions.

Note. In essence, this exercise is practicing not only the two basic structures, but presenting them in a way that also shows the information structure differences of each basic form. It may be possible to discuss this pattern (with some written examples) after the oral activity.

2 Com-MU-ni-cate

It is possible to help students notice the pronunciation clue for remembering many verbs that only appear in the after-prep construction. Indeed, helping students develop a feel for the rhythm and stress of English words may have wide-ranging benefits beyond indirect object structures.

Explicitly draw students' attention to the syllable structure of a set of longer verbs (e.g. *communicate, contribute, introduce, recommend*) in contrast to some single syllable verbs (e.g. *give, hand, send, teach*). If necessary, exaggerate the structure by saying the syllables separately (com-MU-ni-cate). Then, explicitly show them how the longer verbs can only be used in the first of the following structural frames.

(a) She already _____ that stuff to us.

(b) She already _____ us that stuff.

Once they recognize the contrast, provide them with the following set of verbs and ask them to decide, via pronunciation, which structures the verbs will fit. (Point out that the same pattern works if the preposition *for* is used in (a).)

(verbs with *to*) *bring, deliver, donate, explain, tell, write*
(verbs with *for*) *assemble, cook, get, manufacture, organize, purchase*

Note. Some researchers have used nonsense words to investigate these pronunciation clues. If you think your students will benefit from this kind of exercise, ask them to decide whether crazy forms like *bambalize, ket, magwanate, zirk* (and others) would fit into (a) or (b) above.

3 Hand the book to Kazuko

The 'transfer' meaning of indirect object structures can be practiced in a type of activity associated with the method called Total Physical Response. In its simplest form, this is a speaking and listening exercise, with a number of objects on a table and students sitting in a circle/semi-circle. The goal is to have each student give an instruction to another, such as: *Hand the book to Kazuko* or *Throw the ball to Kim.*

With lower proficiency students, it may be necessary for the teacher to say the instructions initially, or to provide a list of verbs (e.g. *give, hand, pass, take, throw*) and some warm-up examples. As the students become comfortable with the exercise, the recipients can be asked each time to express what just happened, using the alternative structure (e.g. *Maria just handed me the book*).

4 Tell us a story

A writing/reading version of the type of activity just described can be designed with students writing instructions on small pieces of paper that are then placed on the table. The teacher may have to write some of the first notes or give some guidance on instructions through examples such as:

> Write your name on this paper and pass it to the person on your left.
> Stand up and introduce yourself to the class.
> Explain the meaning of your name to everyone.
> Whisper your address to another student.
> Describe your home to the student across from you.
> Tell us a story or a joke.

Students can usually create entertaining instructions (but may need some guidance in verb choice in order to focus on indirect object constructions).

5 Cathy, John, surprise, give

The following two exercise types were used by Kate Wolfe-Quintero (1998) in one of her research projects on indirect objects. The first is a sentence construction task and the second is described as a free production task.

(a) Students are given four words and asked to write a sentence that includes all those words (following an example or two like: *Cathy gave John a surprise*). The set of words contains two human names, an object name, and a verb that is naturally used with indirect objects. The following examples represent a very small sample of the wide range of possibilities.

  (i)   Cathy, John, surprise, give
  (ii) Mary, Kula, ball, throw
  (iii) Lee, Dave, salt, pass
  (iv) Jim, Pam, screwdriver, buy
  (v)   Fred, Jean, poem, write

One big advantage of this type of exercise is that a large number of different verbs (e.g. *describe, explain, mention, recommend*) can be included and practiced. It is often difficult to create tasks that elicit such a wide range of verbs naturally.

(b) Students are given a paper with pictures of a family, showing Tom and Sue, who are married, their daughter Ann, and their dog Spot. Students are asked to write sentences about this family, using the verb given each time.

    (i)   take _____

    (ii) construct _____

    (iii) hand _____

    (iv) tell _____

    (v) whisper _____

This task is reported to be successful in eliciting sentences with indirect objects and can be used to check if (and how often) students are using both the after-verb and the after-prep structures.

6 Special occasions

This exercise is based on an idea from Victoria Badalamenti and Carolyn Henner-Stanchina (1993: 241). Get the class to list some major life events (e.g. birth, death, engagement, marriage) and other special occasions (e.g. birthday, Christmas, anniversary, St Valentine's Day).

The task then is to describe what people *do for* or *give to* each other on these occasions. This can be a speaking or writing activity.

For lower proficiency students, it may be helpful first to list a number of items that will be expressed as direct objects (e.g. *cards, presents, money, flowers*). Illustrative examples might be:

> At Christmas, we buy presents for our friends and family.
> We send cards to people on their birthday.

One version of this exercise can be based on common American or British customs. Another can be based on customs from other countries, including those personally familiar to some students.

7 Could you get me a Coke?

This activity may work best with students in small groups. The 'benefiting' meaning of indirect objects with *for* can be practiced through an exercise in which each group is planning to send one person to *get* lunch or snack items *for* them.

List (preferably by eliciting from students) a number of food items that can be *picked up* (e.g. *hamburger, sandwich, candy, chips, French fries, Coke, Pepsi, coffee, juice*). Also list a number of useful verbs that take indirect objects with *for* (e.g. *bring, buy, get, order*). It may be useful to provide structural frames such as:

> Would you _____ a _____ for me?

Could you _____ me a _____?

The students in each group give their orders to one member of the group who writes them down. When the orders are complete, the student reads out the list to make sure it is correct. If there is time and interest, all the lists from the groups can be combined at the front of the class into one large order, with comments perhaps (*Hungry today, huh?*) by the teacher.

8   Extracts from texts

For higher proficiency students, it may be helpful to present extracts from texts and invite them to identify both direct and indirect objects. The text presented in Discussion topic 4 earlier is particularly rich in examples and could be used. More complex examples can be found in newspaper and magazine articles. The following types of examples, from a magazine article about a businessman called Donald Trump (Klein 1994), can be used to help students recognize more complex forms of indirect object constructions, as they appear in texts.

(i) 'Ivana still loves you,' Donald Trump's mother was telling him. 'I know,' said Trump. 'I talk to her all the time.'

(ii) I remember hearing a champ after a fight say to the cameras, 'I want to thank the Lord, my savior, who gave me the ability to beat the shit out of my opponent.'

(iii) My father would tell people, 'Do yourself a favor.'

(iv) He told me how, more than 20 years earlier, Lewis Rudin had given him the idea of leaving the small-time world of Brooklyn.

(v) He had to hand over the Shuttle to Citicorp. He had to turn back his 282-foot yacht, the *Trump Princess*, to the Boston Company. He had to give up the Trump Palm Beaches condo to Marine Midland. 'I had to put my ego aside for a while,' he told me.

Further reading

A note on terminology

Several different terms have been used in the study of indirect objects. The forms are often called 'datives' and the different structures are sometimes discussed in terms of 'dative alternation', 'dative movement', 'dative shift', 'the ditransitive construction', and 'the double object dative.'

General reference, with examples

Celce-Murcia, M. and D. Larsen-Freeman. 1983. *The Grammar Book*. Chapter 18. Rowley, Mass.: Newbury House.
Willis, D. 1991. *Collins COBUILD Student's Grammar*. Unit 73. London: HarperCollins.

Wolfe-Quintero, K. 1993. 'The dative alternation in English.' *University of Hawaii Working Papers in ESL* 11: 91–120.

More theoretical discussions

Goldberg, A. 1992. 'The inherent semantics of argument structure: The case of the English ditranstive construction.' *Cognitive Linguistics* 3: 37–74.
Herriman, J. and A. Seppänen. 1996. 'What is an indirect object?' *English Studies* 77: 484–99.
Hudson, R. 1992. 'So-called "double objects" and grammatical relations.' *Language* 68: 251–76.

Types of verbs

Wierzbicka, A. 1988. *The Semantics of Grammar*. Chapter 6. Amsterdam: John Benjamins.

Origins and pronunciation

Green, G. 1974. *Semantics and Syntactic Regularity*. Bloomington, Ind.: Indiana University Press.
Visser, F. 1963. *An Historical Syntax of the English Language. Part One: Syntactical Units with One Verb*. Leiden: Brill.

Basic meanings

Gropen, J., S. Pinker, M. Hollander, R. Goldberg, and R. Wilson. 1989. 'The learnability and acquisition of the dative alternation in English.' *Language* 65: 203–57.
Pinker, S. 1989. *Learnability and Cognition*. Cambridge, Mass.: MIT Press.

Information structure

Collins, P. 1995. 'The indirect object construction in English: An informational approach.' *Linguistics* 33: 35–49.
Givon, T. 1984. 'Direct object and dative shifting: Semantic and pragmatic case.' In F. Plank (ed.): *Objects*. (pp. 151–82). New York: Academic Press.
Smyth, R., G. Prideaux, and J. Hogan. 1979. 'The effect of context on dative position.' *Lingua* 47: 27–42.

End-weight

Erteschik-Shir, N. 1979. 'Discourse constraints on dative movement.' In T. Givon (ed.): *Syntax and Semantics, Vol. 12: Discourse and Syntax*. (pp. 441–67). New York: Academic Press.

Linguistic distance

Thompson, S. and Y. Koide. 1987. 'Iconicity and indirect objects in English.' *Journal of Pragmatics* 11: 399–406.

Acquisition research

Bley-Vroman, R. and N. Yoshinaga. 1992. 'Broad and narrow constraints on the English dative alternation.' *University of Hawaii Working Papers in ESL* 11: 157–99.

Le Compagnon, B. 1984. 'Interference and overgeneralization in second language learning: The acquisition of English dative verbs by native speakers of French.' *Language Learning* 34: 39–67.

Mazurkewich, I. 1984. 'The acquisition of the dative alternation by second language learners and linguistic theory.' *Language Learning* 34: 91–109.

Tanaka, S. 1987. 'The selective use of specific exemplars in second language performance: The case of the dative alternation.' *Language Learning* 37: 63–88.

Teaching suggestions

Carroll, S. and M. Swain. 1993. 'Explicit and implicit negative feedback: An empirical study of the learning of linguistic generalizations.' *Studies in Second Language Acquisition* 15: 357–86.

Fotos, S. and R. Ellis. 1991. 'Communicating about grammar: A task-based approach.' *TESOL Quarterly* 25: 605–28.

8 INFINITIVES AND GERUNDS

1 Every language teacher knows there's a difference in meaning between *He forgot to shave* and *He forgot shaving*. Is there a simple way to explain the difference?

2 Language learners always want to say *She enjoys to go*. Why do we have to say *She enjoys going*, but we can't say *She wants going*?

3 English can seem crazy sometimes. The sentence *He denied to take it* is wrong and *He denied taking it* is correct. However, *He refused to take it* is good and *He refused taking it* is wrong. Can anyone explain this?

4 If *They chose to stay* is correct, why can't we say *They considered to stay*?

5 The sentences *She loves to dance* and *She loves dancing* seem to communicate the same thing. Is there ever a difference in their uses ?

'*The infinitive seems more appropriate than the gerund to denote the imaginative (unreal).*'

This quotation from Otto Jespersen (1940: 166) would seem to suggest that any explanation of these English structures will lead us into the realms of the imaginative and the unreal. That certainly sounds more interesting than most grammar topics!

Overview

After a brief survey of basic structures involving NON-FINITE verb complements, illustrated by the *to*-INFINITIVE, the BARE INFINITIVE, and the GERUND, we consider some of the basic meaning differences as exemplified by the use of different complement types after a number of common MAIN VERBS. A possible 'verb before *to* verb' (V before *to*- V) versus 'verb after verb *-ing*' (V after V -ING) contrast in interpretation is explored. A distinction is noted between the more noun-like properties of gerunds and the more verb-like properties of infinitives as a way of interpreting the type of information typically presented in each form. A large number of main verbs identified as COMMITMENT VERBS (*plan, persuade*) are shown to prefer infinitive complements in either a SELF-DIRECTED or OTHER-DIRECTED commitment. There is also a consideration of the different interpretations of complements after ASPECTUAL VERBS (*start, quit*) and SENSORY-PERCEPTION VERBS (*hear, see*). There is a final note on the connection between LINGUISTIC DISTANCE and CONCEPTUAL DISTANCE with regard to the complements of sensory perception verbs.

Basic forms

In Chapter 7, we looked at how nouns are used as objects, following a verb, to refer to people and things. In this chapter, we will look at how verbs are used in the same position, as COMPLEMENTS, to refer to actions and events. We will focus on two kinds of complements, infinitives and gerunds. As illustration, the complements (*to see, to get, walk*) in the examples in [1] have the base form of the verb and are described as INFINITIVES. The complements (*walking, leaving, being*) in the examples in [2] have the participle form of the verb and are described as GERUNDS.

[1]   a. He wanted to see her again.
      b. She told him to get lost.
      c. He watched her walk away.

[2]   a. She continued walking.
      b. He couldn't bear her leaving him.
      c. She resented his being such a wimp.

The infinitives and gerunds in [1] and [2] are described as NON-FINITE forms because they carry no grammatical information such as tense. That is, the non-finite form *to go* does not have a finite version, with tense, such as **to goes* or **to went*. There are other types of complements with finite forms of the verb marked for tense (i.e. *goes, went*). These are called FINITE clause complements and often begin with *that*, as shown in [3].

[3]   a. He hopes that she goes insane without him.
      b. She regrets that she ever went out with him.

Whereas the finite complements in [3], with or without *that*, can take a wide range of different verb forms, there is a very limited set of verb forms in non-finite complements, as shown in [1] and [2]. The basic structural pattern involves a MAIN VERB occurring first, followed by the complement verb. The complement, or second verb in the sequence, can take the form of a *to*-infinitive (*to-* V), as in examples [1a, b], a bare infinitive (V), in example [1c], or a gerund (V *-ing)*, in examples [2a, b, c]. The complement verb can come immediately after the main verb, as in [1a] and [2a], or there can be a noun or an OBJECT PRONOUN between them, as in [1b, c] and [2b]. With the gerund, that noun or pronoun can also occur in the possessive form, as in [2c]. These basic structural distinctions are presented in Box 8.1.

Summary Box 8.1 **Structures with infinitive and gerund complements**

Main verb			Complement verb	Examples
NP	V		*to*-V	*I want to sing.*
NP	V	NP-object	*to*-V	*I want Joe/him to sing.*
NP	V	NP-objcct	V	*I heard Joe/him sing.*
NP	V		V *-ing*	*I hate singing.*
NP	V	NP-object	V *-ing*	*I hate Joe/him singing.*
NP	V	NP-possessive	V *-ing*	*I hate Joe's/his singing.*

For some people, the NP-possessive form in the last line of Box 8.1 is 'better' or more correct than the NP-object version in the second last line. That is, *I remember his saying that* may be valued higher (by some) than *I remember him saying that*. However, in contemporary English usage, the second version is certainly much more frequent than the first.

Exercise 8.A

The following sentences are based on a description of a doctor who was rather unusual. Underline each of the main verb + complement verb sequences and, for each one, identify the structural pattern, using the categories from Box 8.1.

> Doctor Wong was strange, but everyone liked him.
> He really didn't care very much about money.
>
> e.g. Those people who couldn't <u>afford to pay</u> him didn't have to.
> Unlike most other doctors, he wasn't very serious.

1 He loved to make jokes, even when he prepared his will.
2 He persuaded his lawyer to include the sentence:
3 'Try real hard to revive me if I only look dead.'
4 In his office, he liked to take his shoes off and wander round
5 in his socks. People often heard him talking to himself.
6 His wife said she didn't like his singing the same song over
7 and over. She didn't want to go anywhere with him.
8 He had mentioned retiring

9   and she had encouraged him to do it.

10   He didn't stop working until his eightieth birthday last week

11   when he decided to hang up his stethoscope for good.

e.g. afford to pay (*V to- V*)

1 _____	7 _____
2 _____	8 _____
3 _____	9 _____
4 _____	10 _____
5 _____	11 _____
6 _____	

Basic meanings

The structural patterns illustrated in Box 8.1 are not found with every verb. Some main verbs take only an infinitive or only a gerund as complements, some can take both, and some verbs occur with neither. It is possible to treat these differences as a basic structural feature of each verb individually (as a main verb) and simply create lists of which verbs have each of the complement types, as shown in Box 8.2.

Summary Box 8.2 **Verbs and their complements**

	Non-finite complements		
1 Only finite complements	2 Only	3 Only	4 Both
that ...	*to-*V	*V -ing*	*to-*V/*V -ing*
argue	agree	avoid	begin
assume	allow	consider	cease
believe	arrange	detest	continue
contend	beg	enjoy	dread
guess	choose	fancy	forget
know	decide	finish	hate
realize	decline	keep	like
say	hope	postpone	love
state	offer	practice	prefer
suppose	promise	resent	regret
think	tell	resist	remember
wonder	want	suggest	stop

In many language teaching texts, lists of the type presented in Box 8.2 may be the only information supplied to students. We can provide more support than this. It may actually help students if they can focus on one or two key verbs that are clear examples of each of the four sets, as numbered in Box 8.2. Good clear examples are offered in [4], [5], [6], and [7]. Let us begin with the type of complement that follows verbs in the first column of Box 8.2.

Group 1: Verbs with only finite (that ...) *complements*

As listed in column 1 of Box 8.2, verbs such as *know* and *realize* indicate mental states and have finite complements that represent thoughts or propositions. That is, in a sentence of the type *He knows that X*, the information in the complement *X* is presented as an idea, a fact, or a proposition. Main verbs of this type are normally found with finite clause complements, as in [4].

[4] a. He knew that she was seeing someone else.
     b. She realized that he had been spying on her.

The meaning represented in [4a] is not expressed by the other non-finite complement types. Sentences like *He knew her to see someone else* and *He knew her seeing someone else* are ungrammatical.

Group 2: Verbs with only to- V *non-finite complements*

There are some main verbs, such as *hope* or *want*, which indicate that the action of the complement verb will be in the future (expressing future possibilities) and hence refers to something that has not yet taken place. Main verbs of this type, listed in the second column of Box 8.2, tend to be followed by the infinitive, as in [5].

[5] a. He hoped to change her mind.
     b. She wanted him to forget her.

The meaning of [5a] is never expressed via a gerund complement. That is, *He hoped changing her mind* is ungrammatical. When a meaning similar to [5a] is expressed in a finite clause, the complement verb is usually marked by a MODAL VERB, indicating some kind of non-factual status (e.g. *He hoped that he could change her mind*).

Group 3: Verbs with only V *-ing non-finite complements*

Looking at the third column of Box 8.2, we can find a further contrast in meaning associated with the gerund complements that appear after verbs such as *detest* and *enjoy*, as in [6]. The meaning of these gerund complements is that the situations described are to be treated as already established. Hence they are the opposite of those future possibilities associated with the infinitive.

[6]   a.   She detested him spying on her.
       b.   He enjoyed watching her all the time.

The main verbs used in [6] are not found with infinitive complements. The sentence *She detested him to spy* is ungrammatical. When these verbs are used with finite complements, they often occur with nouns (e.g. *the fact*) that indicate the established state of the action (e.g. *She detested the fact that he spied on her*).

Group 4: Verbs with both to- V *and* V -ing *non-finite complements*

In the fourth column of Box 8.2, there are some verbs, such as *forget* and *remember*, which illustrate rather clearly the different meaning relationships with infinitive and gerund complements, as illustrated in [7].

[7]   a.   He forgot to take his medicine.
       b.   He forgot taking his medicine.

In [7a], the infinitive complement means that he didn't take his medicine, indicating its non-factual status (i.e. *He forgot that he should take it*). In contrast, in [7b], the gerund complement means that he did take his medicine, indicating its past, 'actually happened' status (i.e. *He forgot that he had taken it*). Thus, in *He forgot to shave*, we know he didn't shave, and in *He forgot shaving*, we know he did shave.

In the clearest cases of such differences, it is possible to treat the different complements as indicators of different sequences of actions. In many cases, a V *to-* V sequence can be interpreted with a V before *to-* V meaning, as illustrated in [8].

[8]   a.   You must remember to pay the bills. (remember *before* pay)
       b.   He stopped to buy magazines. (stop *before* buy)
       c.   We regret to say this. (regret *before* say)

In other clear cases, a V V *-ing* sequence can be interpreted with a V after V *-ing* meaning, as illustrated in [9].

[9]   a.   You must remember paying the bills. (remember *after* pay)
       b.   He stopped buying magazines. (stop *after* buy)
       c.   We regret saying that. (regret *after* say)

These marked distinctions in the meaning of different complements following verbs like *forget* and *remember* do not extend to all the verbs in column 4 of Box 8.2. We clearly need to look for other meaning distinctions. There are also some other puzzles in the relationship between structure and meaning for other verbs in Box 8.2. For example, if you suggest going to the park, the *suggest* time must be before the *go* time. With the V before V interpretation, we would expect to find the infinitive. Yet, it is common to use *suggest* with a gerund complement. The same problem exists with verbs like *consider* and *fancy*.

In addition, the difference in meaning between *I love to dance* and *I love dancing* doesn't really seem to be a matter of future action versus past action, nor is the difference between *I'll begin to cook dinner* and *I'll begin cooking dinner*. These puzzles will be explored in the following sections.

Exercise 8.B

Underline the main verbs in these sentences and, using the category headings in Box 8.2, identify the types of complement structures that follow them.

e.g. The Post Office was <u>reminding</u> everyone to post early for Christmas.
  (*to-* V)

  1   Don't delay sending those Christmas parcels! (_____)

  2   Don't be tempted to wait until the last minute! (_____)

  3   Their advertisements implored us to think ahead. (_____)

  4   They challenged us to get busy. (_____)

  5   Don't put off buying that special gift! (_____)

  6   Avoid waiting in long lines later! (_____)

  7   They encouraged us to think of our friends. (_____)

  8   They inspired us to spend and send. (_____)

  9   And, of course, we proceeded to ignore them. (_____)

  10   Well, people abhor getting Christmas cards in November. (_____)

  11   And we dislike thinking about Christmas in September. (_____)

Meanings in context

One way to approach the distinction between infinitives and gerunds is in terms of the type of information generally presented in each form in their normal contexts of use. It is helpful to remember that infinitives and gerunds are both derived from verbs, but have a syntactic function normally associated with nouns. It is to be expected that they will have both verb-like and noun-like properties. By looking at how they are used, we can work out the extent to which each of them has more verb-like or more noun-like aspects, in terms of the type of information conveyed. Properties that are more verb-like involve actions and the performance of those actions. There is an assumption of an agent, or performer of the action. Somebody does something. In contrast, the more noun-like properties involve events, and the treatment of those events as separate from their actual performance, almost as propositions. There may be no assumption of an agent, or performer. The event tends to be treated as a specific thing that can be referred to. Something happened.

Given these differences, it is possible to see that infinitives have retained more verb-like properties and gerunds have developed more noun-like properties.

Noun-like events

In the case of the gerund, the possibility of using a possessive form (*Joe's* or *his*), as illustrated in [10a], is one strong piece of evidence for its noun-like status. The 'go' element in both sentences of [10] is presented as a specific kind of event rather than as the performance of an act.

> [10] a. She resented his going there without her.
>   b. He enjoyed going there alone.

It is the definite sense of 'the going there' in [10] that conveys the implicated meanings of 'actually happened' or 'established activity' as the kind of information often associated with gerund complements. In many cases, a simple noun phrase (e.g. *the walk*) can be used instead of a gerund in reporting an event (e.g. *We enjoyed the walk to town* or *We enjoyed walking to town*).

With this perspective, it is possible to make better sense of constructions of the type shown in [11].

> [11] a. He considered going to the beach.
>   b. She suggested going to the museum.

In terms of simple verb sequence, the *consider* or *suggest* action would come before the *go* action and hence one might expect an infinitive complement for *go*. Yet, these main verbs never take infinitive complements. Their occurrence with a gerund complement may be explained by thinking of the object of *consider* and *suggest* as an event (something more noun-like) than as the performance of an act. Also, if we think in terms of the performer of the *go* action, notice that in [11b], the *she* is not necessarily the only one *going*. Indeed, it is possible for *she* to *suggest going* without ever *going* herself. It may be useful to think of the complements in [11] as having definite event status ('the going') by analogy with the definiteness found in 'his going' or 'their going'. This definite quality is sometimes overt in expressions containing gerunds with definite articles like *It's there for the taking* and *The hardest part is the waiting*.

Verb-like actions

With infinitive complements, it is the association with performing an action that creates implied meanings. In the examples in [12], the focus is on the *go* act, and not on the event. The agency or performer of the act, is also mentioned in each case. There is no sense of a definite action or any markers of definiteness possible in these structures.

[12]   a.   She told him to go without her.
       b.   He wanted her to go too.

These properties of indefinite potential performance of an act are at the source of the meanings 'non-factual' and 'possible' often associated with infinitive complements. In terms of information structure, infinitive complements are indefinite and gerund complements are definite.

Deny *and* refuse

Some aspects of this distinction between the types of information presented by the two complements may be illustrated with the verbs *deny* and *refuse*. These verbs both have negative meanings (i.e. they add a 'not' to the interpretation of their complements). We would expect verbs with such similar meanings to take the same type of complement. However, as shown in [13], they don't.

[13]   a.   Peter denied going to the party.
       b.   Peter refused to go to the party.

The difference between [13a] and [13b] provides a useful clue to the different kinds of information expressed by the infinitive versus the gerund. To explain the use of these different forms, we have to think about what kinds of things are denied and refused.

In the case of *deny*, the information in the complement is presented as not true. In order for a complement to be treated as true or not true, it must have the status of a proposition (i.e. a statement of fact). The use of the gerund after *deny* suggests that the gerund is used to express propositions. Of course, a proposition can also be expressed in a finite *that*-clause (e.g. *He denied that he went to the party*).

In contrast, the information in the complement following *refuse* is typically presented as an action, often a physical act. Performing an action is not a proposition and cannot be true or not true. It can be done or not done. The appearance of the infinitive after *refuse* suggests that the infinitive is used to express actions. It is worth noting that there is no possibility of using a finite *that*-clause as the complement of *refuse*. That is, any version of *He refused that he went/goes/will go to the party* is ungrammatical.

The different types of information generally conveyed by the two complements are summarized in Box 8.3.

Summary Box 8.3 **Information in infinitives versus gerunds**

	to- V	V *-ing*
Features:	more verb-like	more noun-like
	no possessive modifier	possessive modifier possible
	specified agent likely	specified agent less likely
Meanings:	acts	events
	more performance-like	more proposition-like
	performer assumed	performer not assumed
	less definite	more definite
	possibly happens	actually happens

The different meanings associated with the two types of complement, as listed in Box 8.3, may help to explain the typical interpretation of sentences like [14a] in contrast to those in [14b].

> [14]   a.   I like to box / to dance / to swim / to ski.
>   b.   I like boxing / dancing / swimming / skiing.

In [14a], the speaker has to be talking about herself as agent performing the acts indicated in the complement. In [14b], it is the event, not the act, that is the focus of attention, with the possibility existing that the speaker herself is not a performer in the events mentioned. That is, if you just watch the event on TV and enjoy it, you have to use [14b]. And, even if you are a non-smoker, you can say *I don't like smoking* because, with the gerund, you don't have to be the one doing it.

Exercise 8.C

Underline the infinitive and gerund complements in the following sentences. Then, using the information in Box 8.3, decide whether their implicated status is more like the performance of an action (write 'act') or more like an event or proposition (write 'event').

> e.g.   The man proposed <u>spending</u> their vacation in London. (event)
>
> 1   The woman said she'd prefer to see the Eiffel Tower. (_____)
>
> 2   He said that they couldn't afford to fly to Paris. (_____)

3 'Don't you fancy visiting Buckingham Palace?' (_____)

4 'I really dislike going on conducted tours of things.' (_____)

5 'Don't you remember taking that tour around Scotland?' (_____)

6 'Yes, and I hated spending two weeks in a raincoat.' (_____)

7 'Let's arrange to rent a car!' (_____)

8 'I dread being stuck in a car for hours.' (_____)

9 'Hmm. Okay. We'll postpone deciding until next week.' (_____)

Types of verbs

Having explored a basic distinction in the type of information represented by the different complements, we can now turn to a consideration of the range of verbs that take such complements. They can be described as COMMITMENT VERBS, ASPECTUAL VERBS, and SENSORY-PERCEPTION VERBS.

Commitment verbs

The largest group of verbs occurring in main verb position and followed by infinitive complements may be best described as involving some kind of commitment to future action. In many cases, the commitment comes through someone else *persuading* a person *to do* something and some of these verbs have been called 'suasive' verbs. Conceptually, the act of commitment comes before the act to be performed (or not performed). It may be this common conceptual organization of two actions in sequence that leads to the V before *to-* V interpretation often associated with sentences containing infinitive complements. Because a commitment can be verbal, as well as non-verbal, many verbs denoting linguistic action (e.g. *demand, tell*) are found in this construction. A commitment can also be strongly positive (*consent*) or strongly negative (*decline*) or somewhere in between (*offer*).

More significant from a structural perspective, a commitment can be either SELF-DIRECTED (*decide*) or OTHER-DIRECTED (*allow*). That is, you yourself (self-directed) can *decide to go* or someone else (other-directed) can *allow you to go*. When the commitment is self-directed, there is usually no need for a direct object. That is, we say *I decided to go*, and not **I decided me to go*. When the commitment is other-directed, the structure will include a direct object, italicized in [15].

> [15] a. He ordered *us* to get out.
>   b. He convinced *us* to leave immediately.

As in all constructions involving commitment verbs, there is variation in the strength of the other-directed commitment. This is expressed via different linguistic action verbs, from the very forceful type (*command*), through the less forceful (*persuade*), to the non-forceful (*permit*).

Other-directed action is also characteristic of the *for* NP *to-* V structure. Main verbs such as *arrange, long, pray* and *yearn* that occur with the *for* NP *to-* V complement pattern can also be used with simply *for* NP (e.g. *We prayed for rain*). These verbs typically express a desire of the main verb subject that the action in the infinitive will take place, as illustrated in [16].

> [16] a. We arranged for him to leave at once.
>   b. She longed for him to return.

When the commitment is self-directed, the NP V *to-* V pattern is used with both verbal and non-verbal commitments, as in [17].

> [17] a. They threatened to shoot us.
>   b. We decided to surrender.

Variation in the strength of the self-directed commitment can result in a range of likelihood of the second action being performed. There is a range from strong likelihood (*decide, determine*), through the less likely (*aim, expect*) and the purposeful (*plan, prepare*), to the simply desirable (*hope, seek*). It may be the implied meanings of commitment verbs of this type, to do with the likelihood and desirability of future action, that has created the 'unrealized possibilities' interpretation often associated with infinitives.

Some of these commitment verbs were presented earlier in column 2 of Box 8.2. More of the different types of commitment verbs are presented in Box 8.4. Each group is arranged in columns from strongly to weakly implied likelihood of future action in the infinitive (*to-* V) being performed.

Summary Box 8.4 **Commitment verbs**

Self-directed action				Other-directed action	
NP V *to-* V				NP V NP *to-* V	
demand	*agree*	*decide*	*apply*	*order*	*command*
ask	*consent*	*aim*	*attempt*	*tell*	*convince*
beg	*offer*	*hope*	*prepare*	*persuade*	*urge*
plead	*decline*	*want*	*plan*	*advise*	*ask*
pray	*refuse*	*wish*	*struggle*	*permit*	*beg*

There is a use of verbs such as *come* and *go* that appears to follow the pattern proposed here for self-directed action, as illustrated in [18].

> [18]   a.   The little boy *went to open* the door, but decided not to.
>   b.   He had *come to realize* that the monster wanted to get him.

In these uses, the verbs of motion actually convey some aspectual properties (i.e. beginning and concluding) of the action expressed by the infinitive. There really aren't two separate actions being performed. We will explore this pattern in the following section.

Exercise 8.D

In the examples below, there is a main verb followed by the description of an action in brackets. Combine the two verbs to create a verb plus infinitive complement sequence (with pronouns as required).

    e.g.   You promised (you go) *You promised to go.*

    1   They expect (we come early)

    2   I intend (I leave tomorrow)

    3   She claims (she is innocent)

    4   He convinced us (we stay at home)

    5   We chose (he will represent us)

    6   He longs (she will visit him)

    7   They aspire (they win)

    8   Can you allow (we come in)?

    9   She's threatening (she will leave)

   10   We swore (we get revenge)

   11   He taught us (we write better)

Aspectual verbs

As already noted in Chapter 3, on TENSE and ASPECT, situations can be described from perspectives that focus on their beginning, their continuing, or their ending. Verbs used to indicate such perspectives are treated as aspectual verbs (or aspectualizers). Because these verbs do not denote separate actions, their occurrence with complement verbs cannot be interpreted as two actions in sequence. Instead, as shown in [19], there is one 'working' event which is described from three different perspectives.

> [19]   a.   We started working just after dawn.

      b. We stopped working around noon.
      c. Then we continued working after lunch.

There is a strong preference for gerund complements following aspectual verbs, with many of those verbs only taking gerunds. This is particularly noticeable with phrasal verbs (e.g. *start out, give up, carry on*), but is also the case with some simple verbs (e.g. *finish, keep, remain*), as shown in [20].

[20] a. She finished singing, but the band carried on playing.
       b. He had to give up smoking, but the others kept doing it.
       c. Many started out dancing, but by the end only a few remained standing.

In the examples in [20], it is not possible to replace any of the gerunds with an infinitive. It seems that activities and processes have their starts, ends, and continuings within an overall perspective that is ongoing. Activities and processes are events that have duration, and we could simply say that the gerund is strongly preferred when we refer to duration in time.

Infinitives can be used with some aspectual verbs (e.g. *begin, cease, continue, start*). The infinitive seems to be preferred when a point in time (i.e. not duration) is being referred to as a beginning or an end, as exemplified in [21].

[21] a. I turned the key and the engine suddenly started to splutter into life.
       b. Just as suddenly it died and ceased to make a sound.

When that point in time is the start of a possible series (i.e. indicating possible repeated action), the infinitive will also be used, as in [22a]. However, if the repeated action is treated as an ongoing event, then the gerund is preferred. Indeed, the implication with the gerund is that there are more instances of the repeated action over a period in time, as in [22b]. Repeated action over time can be perceived as an activity with duration.

[22] a. He begins to sneeze if a cat comes near him.
       b. He begins sneezing if a cat even comes into the same room.

There is also a preference for the infinitive when the complement verb indicates a state, that is, with non-dynamic verbs such as those italicized in [23].

[23] a. The old leader continued *to be* in charge.
       b. We began *to understand* his political power.
       c. And the people ceased *to believe* that things would change.

These observations are summarized in Box 8.5.

Summary Box 8.5 **Aspectual verbs and complements**

Aspectual verbs

begin	*commence*	*finish*	*remain*
burst out	*complete*	*give up*	*resume*
carry on	*continue*	*go on*	*start*
cease	*discontinue*	*keep (on)*	*stay*
come out	*end up*	*quit*	*stop*

With complements

to-V	V *-ing*
point in time	period of time
single act	ongoing event(s)
state	activity, process

On a separate note, there is one preference that seems to be motivated by aesthetics (i.e. it just sounds better) rather than grammar. The gerund is often avoided when the aspectual verb is in the progressive. For some speakers, having a gerund (*-ing*) form after a progressive (*-ing*) may also seem redundant. That is, a V-*ing* V-*ing* sequence tends to be avoided. Rather than write *are beginning wanting* or *are continuing insisting,* English speakers seem to prefer the sound of the structures shown in [24].

[24]   a.   The students are beginning to want change.
         b.   The teachers are continuing to insist on the old ways.

Exercise 8.E

Underline the complement verb in the main verb + complement verb sequences in the following text. Then, decide whether the meaning of the complement is best analyzed as 'point' (in time) or 'duration' (in time).

Some old men were playing golf. I sat and watched them <u>wandering</u> past a small clump of bushes. They moved like wooden puppets that had ceased being supported by their strings. I noticed one of them turn round suddenly as a rabbit started to run towards the bushes. I heard the man shout something to his friends and they all burst out laughing. They kept on laughing and talking as they continued stumbling in the direction of a flat green area. They all stopped to look towards a distant flag. Then they began pulling their golf clubs out. One of them sat down, but the others remained standing. I could see the sitter wearily taking off one shoe and then the other. It was the kind of day when your feet feel like hot wood.

e.g. wandering (duration)   6 _____

1 _____   7 _____

2 _____   8 _____

3 _____   9 _____

4 _____   10 _____

5 _____   11 _____

Sensory perception verbs

There is a small set of verbs in English that can take either bare infinitive or gerund complements. These verbs generally convey the sensory experience (e.g. *see, hear, feel*) of actions or events, as illustrated in [25]. In [25a], there is a bare infinitive (*trip*), and in [25b], there is a gerund (*cursing*).

[25] a. She saw him trip over the cat.
      b. Seconds later she heard him cursing.

Generally, the pattern involves one person perceiving another, but in some situations, that one person can be described as having two different experiences, with the second marked by a reflexive form, such as *herself* in [26]. In these examples, the same person perceives and experiences the action.

[26] a. In the dream she saw herself falling.
      b. Suddenly she felt herself jerk awake.

The difference in meaning of the two complement types seems to be based on an implication that the perceived event is ongoing (at the time of perception) in gerund complements [26a] and not so in the bare infinitives [26b].

More specifically, we might say that there is no time limitation placed on the perceived event expressed via the gerund and so it tends to favor an interpretation of non-completion. Notice that, in [27], the events being experienced are presented as ongoing and incomplete.

[27] Sunday morning in England. We could smell breakfast cooking as we lay in bed and listened to the church bells ringing.

In contrast, the bare infinitive does seem to have an implication that the action of the complement is being presented as limited in time and hence complete. This is most obvious when the perceived action happens once and is over, as in [28a]. If the gerund is used in the same situation, the typical interpretation is that the action was ongoing or happened several times, as in [28b].

[28] a. I saw you blink.
      b. I saw you blinking.

These basic distinctions are summarized in Box 8.6.

Summary Box 8.6 **Sensory perception verbs and complements**

Sensory perception verbs

feel	*look at*	*overhear*	*smell*
hear	*notice*	*see*	*spot*
listen to	*observe*	*sense*	*watch*

With complements

Bare infinitive (V)	Gerund (V *-ing*)
limited in time	unlimited in time
completed	incomplete
single act	series of acts

Linguistic distance

One final puzzle exists with regard to why we use the bare infinitive, and not the *to-* infinitive, with sensory perception verbs. This puzzle may be explained by referring to a phenomenon already noted with other features of English. There seems to be a recurring pattern in English whereby LINGUISTIC DISTANCE reflects CONCEPTUAL DISTANCE. The more linguistic material between two forms, the less connected are the actions or events designated by those forms. When two actions are perceptually separate, the *to* element comes between the main verb and the infinitive form (e.g. *I told her to leave*). When the perception is at exactly the same time as the action, there is no separation of the two actions, and so the *to* element does not come between the verbs (e.g. *I saw her leave*). The same observation applies to perception verbs with the gerund, where there is no marked separation of perception and action (e.g. *I saw her leaving*). Less conceptual distance is reflected in less linguistic distance.

In the extended (non-literal) uses of perception verbs, when the meaning is not about immediate sensory perception of an action, quite a lot of linguistic distance can be placed between the main verb and the second verb. In such cases, finite *that-* clauses of the type shown in [29] are common.

[29] a. I see that we've reached the end of the chapter.
      b. Yes, but I hear that he's included projects and other topics.

Discussion topics and projects

1   The following extract is from a magazine article (Isaacson 1992: 227–28) describing some historical events involving one ex-president (Ford) and one president-to-be (Reagan) of the United States.

(a) Identify and list all the verb + complement verb sequences, including both finite and non-finite examples.

(b) Did you find any structures that were not discussed in the chapter? Can you find a way to analyze them, given the basic information in the chapter?

> Later that year, at the Republican convention in Detroit, Kissinger was involved in an audacious set of political negotiations—never before fully revealed—that almost resulted in a restructuring of the American presidency and, though this was one of the touchiest points of contention, his own return to power. Nominee Ronald Reagan was casting around for a running mate and began toying with the notion of a dream ticket: former president Ford might be persuaded to accept the vice-presidential slot. Ford had previously rejected the idea, but on the second day of the convention he met with Reagan and agreed to reconsider.
>
> Kissinger got a call from William Casey, who was Reagan's campaign director, inviting him up to the Reagan staff suite. When Kissinger arrived, he found Casey and Reagan's other top aides, Edwin Meese and Michael Deaver. They wanted Kissinger to persuade Ford to join the ticket. Kissinger, who had a genuine affection for Ford, was excited to be asked for help by his old conservative tormentors and enticed by the prospect of an arrangement that could call him back into power.
>
> From the outset, the role that Kissinger would get to play in the new administration was a sticking point. Reagan did not trust him. Aware of the animosity he engendered, Kissinger told Ford that no 'personalities or names' should keep the deal from being done. But Ford made it clear that he wanted Kissinger to become secretary of state again. 'I decided,' Ford recalls, 'that if I was going to be on the ticket, I was going to insist pretty strongly that Henry be secretary of state. I told Henry that was one of the things we were going to negotiate.'

On Wednesday, as rumors of the possible dream ticket began rippling across the convention floor, Ford authorized Kissinger and three other advisers to meet with Reagan's top aides and see if a deal could be struck.

Late that afternoon, Ford called and asked if he could come see Reagan. He had decided it was time to press the Kissinger issue. 'Ron, I'm making a sacrifice here,' he said when he arrived. 'And now I'm asking you to make a sacrifice. I want you to appoint Henry Kissinger as secretary of state.'

'I was pretty insistent,' Ford recalls. 'But Reagan wouldn't commit to it.' After less than fifteen minutes of conversation with Reagan, Ford left to go back to his room and mull the matter over.

But the magic had gone from what was, as most participants admitted in retrospect, a somewhat wild notion. The Kissinger issue had pricked the balloon and spared the nation a rather unpromising effort to restructure the executive branch. That evening, Ford went on television to ruminate publicly about what Walter Cronkite called 'a co-presidency.' Impatiently, Reagan called Ford and said he needed a decision that night. An hour or so later, Ford came by to say he had decided against joining the ticket.

2   Many adjectives in English can also be followed by complement forms. The infinitive seems to be much more frequent, but the gerund is also possible in some constructions. Here are some examples:

> It's hard to find/finding a parking place here.
> I was sorry to miss you.
> It's awful working there.
> He was wrong to criticize you.
> We're ready to help.
> She's nice to talk to.
> It was good seeing you again.

Now consider the following list of adjectives:

afraid	curious	first	kind	slow
annoying	delighted	free	quick	stupid
careful	difficult	glad	reluctant	unkind
certain	eager	impossible	ridiculous	unlikely
crazy	easy	keen	rude	willing

(a) What kind of complements do these adjectives take?

(b) Can you add other adjectives (plus their complements)?

(c) What is the meaning difference (in terms of who helps whom) between *He is hard to help* and *He is quick to help*?

(d) Given the meaning difference in (c), which adjectives in the list above must be interpreted in the pattern of the 'hard' sentence and which in the pattern of the 'quick' sentence?

3   For many learners of English as a second or foreign language, there is a definite puzzle presented by sentences such as the following:

> I'm looking forward to seeing you soon.
> We object to doing all the work.

At first glance, it looks as if the *to* particle associated with the infinitive can also appear with the gerund form. It is rather confusing. However, the *to* in these cases is a preposition. And after prepositions, we usually have nouns. Main verb + preposition sequences strongly favor the gerund (confirming its noun-like status). Some common verbs of this type are presented below.

(a) Try to complete these sentences with complements.

   (i)   He left without _____.
   (ii)   I thought about _____.
   (iii) He asked about _____.
   (iv)   He stopped me from _____.
   (v)   I dream of _____.
   (vi)   We decided against _____.
   (vii) They resorted to _____.
   (viii) She insisted on _____.
   (ix)   I'm used to _____.
   (x)   They won by _____.
   (xi)   They play at _____.
   (xii) We succeeded in _____.

(b) How many other (different) verb + preposition + complement examples can you think of?

(c) Which prepositions do not take complements?

(d) How many adjective + preposition + complement sequences can you think of? Some examples are *He's fond of talking about himself* and *We're close to winning the prize*.

4   Some nouns in English can also be followed by infinitive and gerund complements. Here are some examples:

   (i)   It's a nice change to go somewhere different.

   (ii)   He regrets his decision to sell the land.
   (iii) Her determination to succeed was amazing.
   (iv)   Do you have enough money to pay for all this?
   (v)   She never has a kind word to say about him.
   (vi)   He's too much of a gentleman to criticize them.
   (vii) There's little hope of finding any survivors.
   (viii) We appreciated their kindness in helping us.
   (ix)   There's no likelihood of him coming early.
   (x)   Our plans for taking an early vacation have been shelved.

(a) Can any of these examples be expressed, with similar meaning, by a main
    verb + complement sequence?

(b) What types of nouns seem to occur most readily in these constructions?
    Can you think of other examples to support your analysis?

(c) What types of nouns never occur in such constructions?

Teaching ideas

1 Invite/visit

A common type of exercise used to practice the basic forms of infinitive and
gerund complements simply presents two verbs in sequence. The basic
structural frame (NP V NP *to-* V) can be illustrated with *invite/visit* and the
sentence *I invited my friend to visit me.*

(a) Some care should be taken initially that verbs with only *to-*V complements
    are listed as the first of the two verbs. Here are some examples:

   (i)   encourage / stay
   (ii)   warn / be careful
   (iii) tell / keep quiet
   (iv)   convince / stay
   (v)   teach / play poker
   (vi)   remind / work hard
   (vii) ask / hurry up
   (viii) advise / wait

(b) Once the basic structure seems to be familiar, students can be encouraged
    to use the first verbs from (a) to create sentences of their own. Other verbs
    (e.g. *love, hate, like, prefer, dread*) can be included.

2 We tell (they come early)

A more complex exercise for practicing basic forms with infinitive complements
provides two simple clause elements and asks students to combine them into a
sentence (see Exercise 8.D earlier). Two structural frames (NP V NP *to-* V and
NP V *to-* V) are illustrated in the first two examples below.

We tell (they come early)   We told them to come early.
We ask (we leave)   We asked to leave.

   (i)   You promise (you help)
  (ii)   He order (we stand up)
 (iii)   She pretend (she is ill)
 (iv)   They permit (we enter)
  (v)   I offer (I make lunch)
 (vi)   He allow (they go early)
 (vii)   We agree (we work harder)
(viii)   I expect (you come sooner)

3 I want to be a dentist

The large number of commitment verbs with infinitive complements can be practiced in an activity that focuses on personal plans and goals. As a first step, the students can read over a short text such as the following:

> Rosa Lopez isn't happy. She wants to get out of school. She has decided to be a dentist and she hopes to start work as soon as possible. She has asked her parents to help her, but they always tell her to finish school first. She has begged them to let her quit, but they have persuaded her to stay. She has agreed to study one more year and then, when she is nine, she plans to start her career as a dentist.

(a) Attention can first be focused on the V *to-* V structures in this text, either in a general discussion or by getting students to underline them, count them, or write them down.

(b) Additional verbs that are used to talk about plans and goals can be elicited or introduced (see Box 8.4).

(c) Some students can be asked to talk about their personal plans as a way of activating the vocabulary needed to refer to kinds of careers or educational goals.

(d) Students, in pairs, can then interview each other, making notes on their answers to questions such as:

> What do you plan to do after studying?
> What kind of career do you want to have?
> Who advised you to study here?
> Why did you decide to study this subject?

(e) Later, given time, some individuals can be asked to report to the whole group on what they learned during their interviews. Alternatively, a short written report can be assigned on the same topic.

4 Turning over a new leaf

Introduce the idea of 'Turning over a new leaf' or 'Changing for the better' as a topic for student consideration. Elicit what they think are bad habits (e.g. being lazy, eating junk food, smoking, watching too much TV, etc.) and good habits (e.g. eating well, exercising, getting up early, studying, etc.). Beside these two lists (perhaps on the blackboard), provide another list with some aspectual verbs (i.e. *begin, start, stop, quit, give up*).

(a) As a first structure, start with the frame *I should* _____ , and use or elicit expressions such as *I should stop watching so much TV* or *I should start exercising more.*

(b) As a second structure, elicit or provide some examples that begin with the following structural frames:

> I'd like to …
> I want to …

This can lead to examples such as *I'd like to quit smoking* or *I want to start eating better food.*

(c) Then, in pairs or groups, students are given the task of creating sets of things they would like to do, or they think others (such as their teacher, their roommate, their brother or sister) should do to 'turn over a new leaf'. The final product can be a spoken or written report.

Note. For those students who might benefit from reflecting on the language being produced during this task, it can be pointed out that some complements take other complements, as in *I'd like to quit smoking* where an infinitive complement is followed by a gerund.

5 The following are prohibited

The noun-like qualities of gerunds can be seen in many public signs. Some examples are presented in the accompanying photograph.

Looking at this sign, students could be asked to identify the words for things (or objects) and those for activities. It can be noted that the 'doing' words are gerunds. They may also be able to provide other examples of gerunds they've seen in public notices. Follow-up activities can be in-class and out-of-class.

(a) In class, with students in small groups, give them the task of creating a set of rules for the classroom that can be displayed on a sign. Some of the groups have to create signs that begin with *The following are encouraged.* The other groups have to create signs that begin with *The following are prohibited.* Later, the different types of signs can be compared (and perhaps displayed).

(b) Out of class, students have to write down examples of gerunds from signs and notices. Good locations are parks, public facilities, buses, subways, police stations, and, of course, schools. (It's even better if students can take photographs of examples and bring them to class.) As a spoken exercise in class, they have to present their discoveries and try to explain why people aren't allowed to do those things in those places. As a written exercise, they can use their examples in a composition on 'The following are prohibited'.

(c) Another natural context for gerunds (and other nouns) is in questionnaires used for surveys. You can create a scale of never–sometimes–often–always beside a series of descriptions. Some examples are listed below from a health questionnaire that had the general heading: How frequently do you experience the following?

> headaches, tingling in fingers and hands,
> feeling exhausted, feeling short of breath,
> heaviness in arms or legs, reacting with annoyance to others,
> having bad dreams, crying easily,
> trembling or shaking, having your mind go blank

In this list, the examples are all negative. Students may be able to think of positive examples. In class, some groups could create questionnaires with positive, and some with negative symptoms, then use those questionnaires as a basis for a survey (i.e. members of each group interview members from the other).

6 Blond, enjoys running

This exercise is based on an idea from Heidi Riggenbach and Virginia Samuda (1993: 106). It focuses attention on gerunds as they appear in personal ads. Current examples from a local newspaper can be used, if possible, or you could create examples such as the following. These examples are based on typical ads in newspapers in the USA. There may be variations, of course, in other regions. For each person, students have to identify the kinds of activities preferred.

    (i) DWF, 40s, loves walking on the beach, listening to the waves and feeling the earth move.

   (ii) Blond, enjoys running, swimming, biking, and playing lots of games. SF, 27, seeking SM with similar interests. Let's go!

  (iii) SM, 34, likes hanging out, eating, drinking beer, smoking, and having a good time. Are you looking for me?

  (iv) Do you enjoy dancing and dining out? Do you think about loving and caring for just one special person? I'm the one, DM, 58, very fit.

After discussing the examples, noting the main verbs and gerunds used, students can be asked to write their own or, in pairs, to create one for some fictional character.

7 Try to use a good learning strategy

This is an exercise that can be used to practice expressions with complements and also may foster awareness of how to be a more effective learner. It is based on learning strategies. With higher proficiency students it should be possible to elicit (or the teacher can offer) some of the following types of strategies:

Guess the meanings of words in context.
Ask for repetition of new words.
Repeat new words silently many times.
Listen for the general meaning of what's said.
Say only what is exactly correct.
Look up every new word in the dictionary.
Think in your first language then translate.
Use gestures when you're stuck.
Read a magazine article in English every night.
Create flashcards to remember new words.

Using these examples, and others they can think of, students have to create (perhaps in groups) two lists, one of learning strategies they think are effective and the other of strategies they don't recommend. Provide them with the following structural frames. (Notice that the first two in each group use infinitives and the last requires a gerund.)

Try to …
It's a good idea to …
Think about …

Don't try to …
It's a waste of time to …
There's no point in …

In a spoken exercise, after creating their lists, each group can report their ideas to create a comprehensive list. In a written exercise, students can be asked to write a short report on 'How to be a better learner'.

8   What a wannabe!

With higher proficiency students who may be trying to develop their listening/speaking fluency, there may be some interest in the typical spoken version of the verb *want* + infinitive. As found in everyday talk and in many songs (*I wanna hold your hand, Do you wanna dance? I wanna be loved by you*), the combination *want* + *to* is often pronounced as *wanna*. It may be useful practice for the students to hear, in perhaps a small dictation exercise, a number of common expressions, including: *D'ya wanna?, Wanna bet?, What a wannabe!* Their subsequent task is to listen for forms of this type and report any examples in class.

Note. In the expression *a wannabe*, it is worth pointing out to students that the V *to-* V (*want to be*) verb structure has been converted to a noun for the type of person who is always trying to be cool, fashionable, important, or sexy (but not succeeding).

Further reading

General reference, with examples

Azar, B. 1993. *Chartbook. A Reference Grammar.* Chapter 4. Englewood Cliffs, NJ: Prentice Hall Regents.
Palmer, F. 1988. *The English Verb.* (2nd edn.) Chapter 9. London: Longman.

More theoretical discussions

Duffley, P. 1992. *The English Infinitive.* London: Longman.
Mair, C. 1990. *Infinitival Complements in English.* Cambridge: Cambridge University Press.
Ransom, E. 1986. *Complementation: Its Meanings and Forms.* Amsterdam: John Benjamins.
Rudanko, J. 1989. *Complementation and Case Grammar.* Albany, NY: SUNY Press.

The possessive (or not) with gerunds

Nunnally, T. 1991. 'The possessive with gerunds: What the handbooks say, and what they should say.' *American Speech* 66: 359–70.

Bare infinitives

Mittwoch, A. 1990. 'On the distribution of bare infinitive complements in English.' *Journal of Linguistics* 26: 103–31.

Meaning differences

Bolinger, D. 1968. 'Entailment and the meaning of structures.' *Glossa* 2: 119–27.
Wierzbicka, A. 1988. *The Semantics of Grammar*. Chapter 1. Amsterdam: John Benjamins.

Verb-like and noun-like properties

Hopper, P. and S. Thompson. 1985. 'The iconicity of the universal categories "noun" and "verb".' In J. Haiman (ed.): *Iconicity in Syntax*. (pp. 151–83) Amsterdam: John Benjamins.

Aspectual verbs

Brinton, L. 1988. *The Development of English Aspectual Systems*. Cambridge: Cambridge University Press.
Freed, A. 1979. *The Semantics of English Aspectual Complementation*. Dordrecht: Reidel.

On V -ing V -ing sequences

Bolinger, D. 1979. 'The jingle theory of double *-ing*.' In D. Allerton, E. Carney, and D. Holdcroft (eds.): *Function and Context in Linguistic Analysis*. (pp. 41–56) Cambridge: Cambridge University Press.

Sensory perception verbs

Kirsner, R. and S. Thompson. 1976. 'The role of pragmatic inference in semantics: A study of sensory verb complements in English.' *Glossa* 10: 200–40.

Language acquisition research

Mazurkewich, I. 1988. 'The acquisition of infinitive and gerund complements by second language learners.' In S. Flynn and W. O'Neil (eds.): *Linguistic Theory in Second Language Acquisition*. (pp. 127–43). Dordrecht: Kluwer.
Roeper, T. 1982. 'The role of universals in the acquisition of gerunds.' In E. Wanner and L. Gleitman (eds.): *Language Acquisition: The State of the Art*. (pp. 267–87). Cambridge: Cambridge University Press.

Shirahata, T. 1991. 'The acquisition of English infinitive and gerund complements by Japanese EFL learners.' *Annual Review of English Language Education in Japan* 2: 41–50.

Teaching suggestions

Mills, D. 1987. 'Infinitival verb complementation: Theory and usage as a basis for pedagogy.' *World Englishes* 6: 227–39.
Ur, P. 1988. *Grammar Practice Activities*. Chapters 14 and 33. Cambridge: Cambridge University Press.

9 RELATIVE CLAUSES

1 Some learners produce sentences like *Did you enjoy the film which you saw it?* Is there any explanation for this type of mistake?

2 What is the difference between (a) and (b)? Is (a) better than (b)?
(a) *That's the person to whom I talked.*
(b) *That's the person I talked to.*

3 How can we decide if the structure in (a) does or doesn't need commas, as shown in (b)?
(a) *My friend who's Japanese is coming.*
(b) *My friend, who's Japanese, is coming.*

4 Aren't *who* and *whose* just for people? Isn't it a mistake to talk about *a house whose roof is leaking* and *a dog who makes us laugh?*

5 Given the two sentences in (a) and (b), how do we decide which one is easier to learn?
(a) *I met a man who had a cat.*
(b) *The man I met had a cat.*

'I am not against reforming the Corruptions of Speech You mentioned, and own there are proper Seasons for the Introduction of other Words besides That; but I scorn as much to supply the Place of a Who or a Which at every turn.'

Given this extract from *The Spectator*, published in 1711 (quoted in Bond 1965), it seems that the appropriate choice of *who, which*, or *that* has been a matter of some concern for almost three hundred years. We no longer write these pronouns, or nouns, with initial capital letters, but we are still sometimes puzzled by questions concerning the appropriate use of these forms in relative clauses. In the course of this chapter, we shall try to answer some of those questions.

Overview

After an introductory survey of the basic forms of English RELATIVE CLAUSES, distinguishing between the ANTECEDENT, typically in a MAIN CLAUSE, and the RELATIVE PRONOUN in the relative clause, we look at the different grammatical roles of SUBJECT, OBJECT, AFTER-PREPOSITION, and POSSESSIVE RELATIVES. We also consider phenomena such as RESUMPTIVE PRONOUNS, ZERO RELATIVES, and structures with FRONTED or STRANDED prepositions. The basic structural relationships between main clauses and relative clauses are explained in terms of medial and final position, noting the frequent connection between main clause objects and subject relatives. Differences between RESTRICTIVE and NON-RESTRICTIVE RELATIVE clauses, with their SEPARATION MARKERS, are listed. Basic meaning distinctions are noted in the use of different relative pronouns and also RELATIVE ADVERBS. Finally, there is an explanation of the roles of relative clauses in introducing NEW INFORMATION, connecting with GIVEN INFORMATION, including the process of GROUNDING, and the effect of END-WEIGHT in sentence structures.

Basic forms

RELATIVE CLAUSES are typically found after a NOUN PHRASE and provide some information about the person or thing indicated by that noun phrase. They are sometimes called 'adjective clauses' because, like many adjectives, they often describe and help to identify the person or thing being talked about. In the following examples, the adjective *new* in [1a] and the relative clause *that doesn't make me fall asleep* in [1b] both provide information about the *book*.

[1]   a. For the grammar class, we need a *new* book.
       b. I'm talking about a book *that doesn't make me fall asleep*.

In English, adjectives typically come before the noun, but relative clauses come after the noun. Also, the information in [1a] is in a single clause, whereas the information in [1b] is presented in two clauses. There is a MAIN CLAUSE (*I'm talking about a book ...*) and a relative clause (*... that doesn't make me fall asleep*). There is always a close connection between the noun phrase (e.g. *a book*) in the main clause, known as the ANTECEDENT, and the RELATIVE PRONOUN (e.g. *that*) in the relative clause. When a relative pronoun is used in English, there is a strong tendency to place it immediately after the antecedent noun. There are, as shown in [2], several different relative pronouns.

[2]   a. I'm the kind of person *who* is always losing things.
       b. Right now, I can't find a book *that* I need for school.
       c. It's a brand new book *which* I just bought last week.

    d. It's for a class with a teacher *whom* I really like.

    e. She's the first teacher *whose* classes I actually look forward to.

These five relative pronouns (*who, that, which, whom, whose*) are used in different grammatical roles within the relative clause. We will consider the roles of subject, object after-preposition and possessive relatives.

Subject relatives

It is common in grammar texts to treat the relative pronoun as a form that substitutes for a noun and to present sentences like [3b] and [4b] as derived from [3a] and [4a]. It is worth noting that the whole noun phrase (*the man*) and not just the noun (*man*) is replaced by the relative pronoun (*who*) in [3b].

[3]   a. Did you see the man? *The man* was here.

      b. Did you see the man *who* was here?

[4]   a. Did you take the book? *The book* was on the desk.

      b. Did you take the book *which* was on the desk?

In these examples, the relative pronouns *who* and *which* are the subjects of their clauses. In addition to these forms, we often find *that* being used as a SUBJECT RELATIVE, as shown in [5].

[5]   a. I didn't see the man *that* was here.

      b. And I didn't take the book *that* was on the desk.

In contemporary spoken English, *that* is found much more often than *which* in these constructions.

Object relatives

In examples [6b] and [7b], the relative pronouns *whom* and *which* are the objects of their two clauses.

[6]   a. Did you like the woman? You met *the woman*.

      b. Did you like the woman *whom* you met?

[7]   a. Did you enjoy the film? You saw *the film*.

      b. Did you enjoy the film *which* you saw?

It is worth noting that the noun phrases *the woman* and *the film* are after the verbs, as objects, but the relative pronouns *whom* and *which* are placed at the beginning of their relative clauses.

In a number of other languages, there would typically be a pronoun after the verb in these relative clauses. Using such a construction in English results in an ungrammatical sentence.

[8] *Did you enjoy the film which you saw *it*?

The extra pronoun, italicized in [8], is called a RESUMPTIVE PRONOUN and may be used by some language learners in the early stages of learning English. In many ways, it is a 'good' kind of mistake because it reveals a basic knowledge of how English actually works. As the learner's experience and knowledge develop, this type of mistake normally disappears.

In addition to *whom* and *which*, the relative pronoun *that* is frequently used as an OBJECT RELATIVE, as shown in [9].

> [9]   a.   I didn't like the woman *that* I met.
>   b.   I didn't like the film *that* I saw.

In casual conversational speech, there is often no relative pronoun, or a ZERO RELATIVE, in the object relative position, as illustrated in [10].

> [10]   a.   I don't want to talk about the woman *ø* I met.
>   b.   And I'm tired of talking about the film *ø* I saw.

In object relative position, the forms *whom* and *which* are associated with more formal language than the *that* and *ø* forms. The zero relative occurs most often in short object relatives with pronoun subjects, of the type shown at the end of both [10a] and [10b].

After-preposition relatives

As shown in [11] and [12], the forms *whom* and *which* are also used when relative pronouns come directly after prepositions.

> [11]   a.   Where is the person? You talked to *the person.*
>   b.   Where is the person to *whom* you talked?

> [12]   a.   Where is the hotel? You stayed in *the hotel.*
>   b.   Where is the hotel in *which* you stayed?

Note that, in [11a] and [12a], the prepositions and noun phrases are at the end. In [11b] and [12b], the prepositions and the relative pronouns are at the beginning, or the front, of their relative clauses. In these structures, the prepositions *to* and *in* have been FRONTED along with the relative pronouns. This is one position where the form *that* cannot be used instead of *whom* or *which*. A sentence such as **I can't remember the hotel in that I stayed* is ungrammatical.

However, if the preposition is placed at the end of the sentence, then the form *that* can be used at the beginning of the relative clause. As illustrated in [13], the relative pronoun *that* is next to the antecedent, but the prepositions *to* and *in* have been left, or stranded, at the end of the clause. This is generally called a STRANDED preposition.

[13] a. Can I meet the person *that* you talked to?
      b. Can we find the hotel *that* you stayed in?

When a preposition is stranded, it is even more common to find clauses with zero relative, as in [14].

[14] a. Mary knows the person *ø* I talked to.
      b. And she'll remember the hotel *ø* we stayed in.

It is still possible to find grammar handbooks that warn students not to end a sentence with a preposition, as happens in [13] and [14]. However, these structures with stranded prepositions are much more frequent in contemporary English usage than the AFTER-PREPOSITION RELATIVE in [11b] and [12b] with fronted prepositions. Neither is 'better', but those with fronted prepositions (*to whom*, *in which*) can sound very formal and stuffy.

Possessive relatives

The possessive form *whose* is used to introduce POSSESSIVE RELATIVES, as illustrated in [15] and [16].

[15] a. Did you talk to the girl? *Her* bag was stolen.
      b. Did you talk to the girl *whose* bag was stolen?

[16] a. Have you ever lived in a house? Its *roof* was leaking.
      b. Have you ever lived in a house *whose* roof was leaking?

There is an alternative form possible for [16b], using *of which* after the noun (*the roof of which*) rather than *whose* before it (*whose roof*). We might think of the basis of this construction as shown in [17a]. Another example with a similar structure is offered in [18].

[17] a. Have you ever lived in a house? The roof *of the house* was leaking.
      b. Have you ever lived in a house the roof *of which* was leaking?

[18] He had stomach pains the cause *of which* was unknown.

In possessive relatives, the *whose* form is more frequent (occurring three times more often) than the *of which* form. Both of these possessive relatives are typically found in written English and are not common in everyday spoken English.

These different forms of relative pronouns are summarized in Box 9.1. They are listed in columns, from the most frequent at the top to least frequent at the bottom. Grammar texts tend to focus on *who*, *which*, and *that*, but it is worth noting that the zero relative is the most frequent choice in two very common structures.

Summary Box 9.1 **Uses of relative pronouns**

Subject relatives	Object relatives	After-preposition relatives		Possessive relatives
		Fronted	Stranded	
who	*ø*	*(to) which*	*ø ... (to)*	*whose*
that	*that*	*(to) whom*	*that ... (to)*	*of which*
which	*which*		*who ... (to)*	
	whom		*which ... (to)*	

The list of basic forms in Box 9.1 provides a general view of relative pronouns in English. It should be noted, however, that the form *whom* may actually be disappearing from contemporary spoken English. In some cases, as illustrated in [19], it is being replaced by *who*.

[19] That isn't the woman *who* I talked to.

In many more situations, however, the sentence in [19] would be spoken, not with *whom* or *who*, but with zero relative.

Exercise 9.A

Read over the following text and bracket each of the relative pronouns, including places where you think there is zero relative (mark with ø). Then, in the spaces provided, write whether the relative pronoun is subject, object, after-prep (indicate whether fronted or stranded), or possessive.

A woman (whose) bank card was stolen didn't know   e.g. <u>possessive</u>

there was a problem until she received a call from

the bank that handles her account. The checking   1 _____

account that Dorothy Hall had with the Central Bank   2 _____

was overdrawn by about $10,000. Someone she didn't suspect   3 _____

had been withdrawing money with a bank card

that had her name on it. Last week, the Central Bank   4 _____

sent her a new card which she should have received on   5 _____

Friday morning. Unfortunately, the card fell into

the hands of another person who suddenly did a lot of   6 _____

shopping. Police suspect one of Mrs. Hall's

neighbors with whom she shares a mailbox and   7 _____

who has been missing since Friday. The elderly neighbor   8 _____

police are now looking for is not considered dangerous.   9 _____

___

Photocopiable © Oxford University Press

Basic structures

In the preceding section, we focused mainly on relative pronouns and their grammatical roles inside relative clauses. In this section, we consider some of the structural relationships between relative clauses and main clauses.

Medial and final position

When a relative clause is connected to a main clause, it can be placed in medial position (i.e. in the middle) or in final position (i.e. at the end) of the main clause. If we have two separate items of information, such as [20a] and [20b], we can combine them, as in [20c], with one clause in the middle of the other.

[20] a. The man has a cat.
      b. The man lives next door.
      c. The man *who lives next door* has a cat.

The italicized relative clause in [20c] is in medial position. Notice that the relative clause in [20c] is modifying the subject (*The man*) of the main clause.

Given the two pieces of information in [21a] and [21b], we can combine them, as in [21c], to create another relative clause (in italics) in medial position.

[21] a. The woman has a large dog.
      b. The man wants to marry the woman.
      c. The woman *that the man wants to marry* has a large dog.

Notice once again that the relative clause in [21c] is modifying the subject (*The woman*) of the main clause. Relative clauses typically occur in medial position when they are modifying the subject of the main clause.

If we look more carefully at these examples, we can see that the relative pronoun in [20c] is a subject relative and, in [21c], it is an object relative. Relative clauses tend to occur in medial position when there is a subject–subject (S–S) and a subject–object (S–O) relationship between the antecedent noun and the relative noun.

When relative clauses occur in final position, the relationship tends to be object–subject (O–S) or object–object (O–O) between the antecedent noun and the relative noun. For example, taking the two pieces of information in [22a] and [22b], we can combine them, as in [22c], with the (italicized) relative clause at the end.

[22] a. The man has a cat.
      b. The cat likes the large dog.
      c. The man has a cat *that likes the large dog.*

In [22c], the structural connection is between the object of the main clause and the subject of the relative clause (O–S). In the following example [23c], notice how the connection is between the object of the main clause and the object of the relative clause (O–O).

[23] a. The woman has a large dog.
      b. The cat likes the large dog.
      c. The woman has a large dog *that the cat likes.*

Relative clauses are found in final position after direct objects of the main clause, as in [23c], and also after antecedents that are objects of prepositions in the main clause, as is the case with both relative clauses in [24].

[24] The cat has started to sleep with the dog *that belongs to the woman that the man wants to marry.*

As illustrated in [24], one relative clause can be connected to an antecedent in another relative clause.

These observations on the structural connections between main clauses and relative clauses are summarized in Box 9.2. The O–S combination at the top is certainly the most frequent, and the S–O combination at the bottom is the least common.

Summary Box 9.2 **Positions of relative clauses**

Relative clause in final position

O–S *I met **a man** **who** has a small cat.*
        object subject

O–O *I also met **the woman** **that** he wants to marry.*
        object   object

Relative clause in medial position

S–S ***The man***   **who** has the small cat likes the woman.*
        subject subject

S–O ***The woman*** **that** the man likes has a large dog.*
        subject object

These different structures in medial and final position may help explain why some relative clauses are harder to learn to use than others. Second language learners are generally much more successful at learning to use those in final position than those in medial position. They are most successful with relative clauses in structures of the O–S type, where the connection is made between the last element (object) of the main clause and the first element (subject) of the relative clause. They also have some success with O–O structures, connecting the objects of both clauses. They have most difficulty producing the S–S and the S–O connections, that is, the two medial position structures. This type of basic structural information may help teachers recognize what kind of relative clause (and the level of difficulty) they are asking their students to cope with.

Exercise 9.B

Read over the following text and draw a line under each relative clause. Then try to identify the connection between each antecedent noun and the relative pronoun as O–S, O–O, S–S, or S–O. (In this exercise, treat the after-preposition relatives as objects.)

e.g.	Place your computer on a surface that is clean and flat.	(O–S)
1	The power cord that grounds the computer has two ends.	(___)
2	The end that has a socket is plugged into the computer.	(___)
3	The other end has a three pin plug which connects to the power supply.	(___)
4	Find the cable with which the monitor is connected to the computer.	(___)
5	The monitor cable is connected to the monitor port which is at the back of the computer.	(___)
6	Some monitors have a port to which you can connect the keyboard.	(___)
7	The keyboard also has a port that is used for the mouse.	(___)
8	The port that the mouse connects to is on the side of the keyboard.	(___)
9	The plug that connects the mouse to the keyboard should be inserted with the arrow pointing down.	(___)

Restrictive and non-restrictive

In all the examples discussed so far, we have been looking at RESTRICTIVE RELATIVE clauses. These are also called 'defining' relative clauses because they define or restrict the reference of the antecedent noun. They help to identify or classify the person or thing being talked about. There is another, less common, structure known as a NON-RESTRICTIVE RELATIVE or 'non-defining' relative clause. A non-restrictive relative clause gives extra information about an antecedent. It provides additional information, not identifying information. In writing, a non-restrictive relative clause is usually marked by commas, dashes, or parentheses, as shown in [25]. In speaking, these non-restrictive clauses would be marked by pauses and a change in intonation. These commas, dashes, brackets, and pauses are generally known as SEPARATION MARKERS.

[25] a. My neighbor, who is an English teacher, plays very loud music.
     b. The man—whose name is Johnny Jensen—also likes to have weekend parties.
     c. These parties (which are very rowdy) seem to go on all night.

These distinct separation markers around non-restrictive relative clauses make them easy to recognize. In writing, they also help to make a distinction between some extra information about an antecedent, as with *my friend* in [26a], and some necessary information, as in [26b], that identifies a particular *friend who's Japanese*.

[26] a. My friend, who's Japanese, is coming.
     b. My friend who's Japanese is coming.

We can paraphrase [26a] as 'My friend is coming and, by the way, she is Japanese', whereas [26b] will communicate that 'My friend who is Japanese, not my friend who is Chinese, is coming'. The commas in the non-restrictive clause in [26a] actually signal that this clause could easily be omitted.

Separation markers are found more often with names and other proper nouns, as in [27a], with additional comments on previous statements, as in [27b], and with clauses that begin with quantity expressions (e.g. *many of whom, none of which*), as in [27c].

[27] a. Mrs Britos, who is the librarian, reported that some books were missing.
     b. Someone said that I took the books, which was not true.
     c. I had never touched the books, most of which were in German.

As we noted back in Chapter 2, however, there are some uses of proper nouns with articles (e.g. *I'm talking about the John Park who was here before*) that are, as in this example, followed by a restrictive relative clause. Most of the time, however, we find non-restrictive relative clauses after names of people, as in [27a].

There are some aspects of restrictive relative clauses that are not normally found with non-restrictive types. The relative pronoun *that* and the zero relative are typical features of restrictive relative clauses. Also, with antecedents such as *anyone, any person, everyone*, and *everything*, a restrictive relative clause is typically used to identify more specifically who or what is being talked about. It would be unusual to find a non-restrictive relative clause after any of those general antecedents. Thus, the italicized examples in [28] are all restrictive relatives.

[28] a. Is there anything *you can't do*?
      b. Well, I can't help every person *who needs help*.
      c. But those *that you help* are usually satisfied.
      d. I'm sure there are some people *who are never happy*.

Generally speaking, restrictive relative clauses are also shorter than non-restrictive relative clauses.

These differences between the two types are summarized in Box 9.3.

Summary Box 9.3 **Restrictive and non-restrictive relative clauses**

Restrictive	Non-restrictive
defining	non-defining
necessary information	extra information
no separation markers	separation markers (e.g. commas)
not usually after proper nouns	after proper nouns
not as additional comments	provide additional comments
not with quantity expressions	with quantity expressions
initial *that* and zero relative	not with *that* or zero relative
with general antecedents	not with general antecedents
shorter and more common	longer and less common

As may have become clear, restrictive relatives are closely tied to their antecedents and non-restrictives are quite separate. The commas or pauses before non-restrictives create more LINGUISTIC DISTANCE between the antecedent and the relative clause. As we have noted elsewhere, more linguistic distance conveys a much looser connection. This distance is also noticeable when both a restrictive and a non-restrictive relative are used with the same antecedent. The restrictive comes first, closest to the antecedent noun, as shown in [29].

[29] The person who left this bag, who must be very careless, will
      probably come back for it.

Generally, in most discussions of English grammar, the basic term 'relative
clause' is normally understood to mean restrictive relative clause.

Exercise 9.C

Read through the following text, finding and underlining each relative clause. Then,
in the space provided, write 'R' beside those that are restrictive and 'NR' for the
non-restrictive types.

e.g. I have a friend <u>who was born in China</u>,	R
which always surprises people, because he doesn't	1 _____
look Chinese at all. His mother, who was English,	2 _____
and his father, whom he never met, were both working in China	3 _____
just before the war.	
There were many foreigners who couldn't leave the country,	4 _____
most of which was suddenly in chaos when war	5 _____
broke out. There was nothing his mother could do. She	6 _____
eventually had a healthy baby, which was a miracle in the circumstances,	
	7 _____
but the father, who had gone on a field trip,	8 _____
was never seen again.	
Mother and baby managed to survive with the help of some people	
who risked their lives in those terrible times.	9 _____

Basic meanings

The most obvious meaning distinction in English relative clauses is between
human and non-human referents. The forms *who*, *whom*, and *whose* are
strongly associated with human or humanlike entities, whereas *which* tends to
be reserved for non-human entities. Some examples are presented in [30].

[30]   a.   Mary is a woman *who* loves her life.
     b.   She has a boyfriend *whom* she adores.
     c.   She has a group of friends *whose* company she enjoys.
     d.   She has a crazy dog *who* makes her laugh.
     e.   And she has a new job *which* she finds exciting.
     f.   But she also has an old car *that* can cause small problems, and a new boss *that* may be the source of some big problems.

As illustrated in [30], the human (*who*) versus non-human (*which*) distinction is mostly straightforward. There are occasional non-humans such as family pets, as in [30d], *who* can be treated as human-like. As shown in [30f], *that* is used with both human and non-human antecedents.

Who, which, that

This basic meaning distinction between relatives can be supplemented by a number of observations. As we have already noted, *whom* is becoming rare in contemporary English and *whose* can actually be found with a range of non-human antecedents, as shown earlier in example [16]. The only relative marker with frequent and consistent human reference is *who*. Yet, *who* is not the only relative pronoun used when an antecedent is human. There are a number of identifiable situations where *who* is clearly preferred with human antecedents and others where it is not.

As noted in Box 9.1, *who* is the most common subject relative. This suggests that it must be used in the typical subject function, as the human individual(s) performing the action of the verb in the relative clause. We might say that *who* is preferred for reference to human agents in relative clauses, as shown in [31].

[31]   a.   The man *who* knocked me down just ran away.
     b.   The people *who* helped me were very kind.

It isn't necessary that the agents should be specifically identified. Indeed, a very common use of *who* is for general reference, or to classify people *who* do certain things, as in [32].

[32]   a.   I get tired of people *who* are always complaining.
     b.   People *who* live in glass houses shouldn't throw stones.

It is important to distinguish between this type of general reference of *who* and the more specific reference that may be associated with groups. One very noticeable type of human reference that often does not use *who* involves collective nouns as antecedents. As illustrated in [33], there are some groups of humans that can be referred to by the relative pronoun *which*.

[33]   a.   I was part of the crowd *which* was waiting for the bus.
     b.   There was a small group *which* kept pushing to the front.

      c. I think they were part of a teenage gang *which* just wanted to
         cause trouble.

Similar examples to those in [33] can be found with other collective noun antecedents (e.g. *audience, class, club, committee, government*) and can have *that* instead of *which*, but tend not to occur with *who*. There seems to be a requirement, in the use of *who*, that the entity should be classified as identifiably human or human-like. An entity such as *a government* may consist of humans, but *the government which passed the new law* can be treated, in terms of its relative pronoun, as if it had non-human status.

It may be useful to think of *who* as being preferred when we want to emphasize the human or human-like aspect of a referent. When there is no need for that emphasis, there may be a tendency in contemporary English to use *that* as the relative pronoun, as in [34].

    [34] a. My sister has a baby *that* cries all night.
        b. Is she the one with the husband *that* never helps her at all?

These examples provide a clue to the very general function of the relative pronoun *that*. Speakers use *that* in relative clauses when there is no need to mark the referent as having special properties. The relative pronoun *that* neutralizes the normal distinction between *who* and *which* (i.e. human versus non-human) and the distinction between *who* and *whom* (i.e. between subject and object). In essence, the relative pronoun *that* signals that all relevant properties of the referent are already known from the antecedent, or are otherwise irrelevant at that point.

Going one step further and signaling that the relative marker itself is irrelevant results in a zero relative. The forms *that* and zero relative are used when no crucial meaning content has to be indicated by the relative pronoun. The opposite situation, *where* a very distinct type of meaning is carried by the relative marker, is illustrated in the following section.

Where, when, why

There are some occasions *on which* (or *when*) the non-human reference of *which* is marked more explicitly for place, time, and reason. If the antecedent is treated as a location, the relative clause can begin with *where*. Reference can be to a physical location, as in [35a], or to an abstract location, as in [35b]. If the antecedent is a time expression, the relative clause can begin with *when*, as in [35c]. And if the antecedent is the reason for something, then the relative clause can begin with *why*, as in [35d].

    [35] a. That's near the town *where* I was born.
        b. I grew up in an atmosphere *where* everything was easy.
        c. The problems started during the period *when* I was a teenager.
        d. That's probably the major reason *why* I left that place.

These forms (*where, when, why*) are sometimes described as RELATIVE ADVERBS because they appear to take the place of adverbial expressions (e.g. *at that time* or *then*). Perhaps because they convey their meaning content so explicitly, they can in fact be used without antecedents. If speakers can assume that a place, in [36a], and a time, in [36b], are already the topics, then the antecedents can be omitted.

[36]   a.   That's near *where* I grew up.
       b.   I can remember *when* I was a small child.

These general observations are summarized in Box 9.4.

Summary Box 9.4 **Meanings of relative pronouns**

Form	Meaning
who	identifiably human
	human-like (e.g. pets)
	often agent of action
	often general reference, classifying
which	identifiably non-human
	non-human-like (e.g. with collectives)
that / ø	neutral (no differentiation required)
where	reference to place
when	reference to time
why	reference to reason

There is an interesting preference in English for *who* and *which*, rather than *that* (and zero), when other linguistic material comes between the antecedent and the start of the relative clause. Some examples, with antecedent and relative clause italicized, are shown in [37].

[37]   a.   I met a *student* yesterday over in the cafeteria *who said he knew you.*
       b.   I wanted to talk about *problems* in my class and in the office generally *which really bother me.*

The distance created by the other linguistic material seems to require clearer marking of the relative pronoun in order to maintain the connection with the antecedent. We shall consider other related aspects of relative clause formation in the following section.

Exercise 9.D

Which relative forms would you put in the spaces provided in the following text? More than one form may be possible in some places.

Jean Barnett had grown up in a place (1) _____ everyone

knew everything (2) _____ everyone else was doing. Anyone

(3) _____ wanted to keep a secret, (4) _____

was not easy, had to create a story (5) _____ would distract

everyone's attention. On that special day (6) _____ she

discovered she was pregnant, Jean decided to tell the women

(7) _____ worked in the local grocery store that she was

trying to put on some weight. She bought lots of butter and cakes. There was

a special reason (8) _____ she had made this decision, she

told them. She came from a family (9) _____ had always been

famous for being too thin. She wanted to change that. She was going to be

the first Barnett (10) _____ size would equal the importance

and wealth of that prosperous family. That reminded her. She should tell her

parents too.

Meanings in context

As we noted already, there are two primary antecedents for relative clauses. Either the relative clause connects to an object in the main clause (final position) or it connects to the subject of the main clause (medial position). These differences in structure are tied to differences in how information in the speaker's (writer's) message is being presented. The basic organization of English sentences containing relative clauses can best be explained in terms of INFORMATION STRUCTURE. In final position, the relative clause is typically used to introduce NEW INFORMATION. In medial position, the relative clause is used to make a connection with already established, or GIVEN INFORMATION.

Introducing new information

Relative clauses in final position are by far the most common and it is possible to explain their typical structure as an outcome of how some messages are organized in English. We can start with the basic information status of each referent in two separate clauses, shown in [38].

[38] a. I have   a friend.
          (given)   (new)
      b. That friend   works in a bookstore.
          (given)   (new)

In any situation, the speaker (writer) is normally assumed to be known and hence *I*, in [38a], can be treated as given. The noun phrase *a friend* is, at this point, being presented as new. As noted in Chapter 2, indefinite noun phrases usually indicate new information. In [38b], *that friend* is no longer new, having been introduced already in [38a], but a *bookstore* is new information at this point. If we combine these clauses, using a relative pronoun, we can have [38a] as the main clause and [38b] as the relative clause, shown in [39].

[39] I have a friend *who works in a bookstore.*

Notice that the relative clause, in italics in [39], is being used here to introduce new information about the antecedent (*a friend*).

The antecedent may be an indefinite noun phrase, as in [39], or indefinite pronouns like *anyone* or *someone* in [40]. Once again, in the examples in [40], the relative clause is being used to introduce new information.

[40] a. Do you know anyone *who has a truck?*
      b. I'm looking for someone *who can fix computers.*

This type of structure is designed to characterize, describe, or create a relevant identity for the person or thing presented as the antecedent. It is very common in sentences beginning with *There is/are* ... , as in [41].

[41] a. There's a man here *who's acting very strange.*
      b. There's also something outside *that looks like a spaceship.*

This 'presentation' type of structure, introducing new information via relative clauses, can be found in texts as varied as children's stories [42a], business reports [42b], and advertisements [42c].

[42] a. Once upon a time there was a king *who had three sons.*
      b. There will be a downturn *that may extend into next year.*
      c. Here's good news about a product *that will change your life.*

All these examples announce or assert something new. As we will see in the next section, relative clauses can also be used to remind us of something already known.

Connecting with given information

Relative clauses in medial position typically modify the subject. In terms of information structure, they are used to identify what is already assumed to be known or given. That given information, expressed in a relative clause, is generally placed inside the main clause, as illustrated in [43].

[43] a. The computer   is a Macintosh.
          (given)   (new)
      b. I have   that computer
          (given)   (given)
      c. The computer *which I have* is a Macintosh.
      d. The computer *I have* is a Macintosh.

The main clause in [43a] treats the subject referent (*The computer*) as given information. As noted in Chapter 2, definite noun phrases usually indicate given information. The clause in [43b] contains reference to the speaker *I* (already given) and the same *computer* (already given). Once the relative clause is embedded in the main clause, as in [43c], it simply identifies which computer the speaker is referring to. The fact that a zero relative can be used, in [43d] (*ø I have*), is further evidence that this object does not have to be mentioned explicitly because it is given information. The structure in [43d], with given information in a medial relative clause (italicized), is often found with zero relative, as in [44].

[44] a. That report *you read* was done on my new computer.
      b. The old computer *I was using* always took such a long time.

The examples in [44] are direct object relatives, but after-preposition relatives, as in [45a, b], and subject relatives, as in [45c, d], are also used to include given information.

[45] a. That book *you were looking for* is in the library.
      b. The new teacher *I told you about* is originally from India.
      c. The person *who did this* will be punished.
      d. The part *that broke* has to be replaced.

The process illustrated by the relative clauses in examples [43] to [45] is sometimes called GROUNDING. This means that the relative clause provides a way of connecting the referent to information already established. It is treated as part of the 'common ground' shared by speaker (writer) and listener (reader).

These observations on the basic information structure of sentences with relative clauses are summarized in Box 9.5.

Summary Box 9.5 **Information structure and relative clauses**

Final position: introducing new information

Main clause		Relative clause	
I have	*a friend*	*who*	*works in a bookstore.*
given	new	given	new
	(antecedent)	(relative)	

Medial position: connecting with given information

Main ...	relative	clause ...	clause
This friend	*ø*	*I have*	*works in a bookstore.*
given	given	given	new
(antecedent)	(relative)		

End-weight

It is noticeable that relative clauses in final position are generally much longer than those in medial position. Relative clauses in medial position, particularly those with zero relatives, as italicized in [46], are often very brief.

> [46] a. The movie *we saw* was really boring.
> b. The book *I read* had a much better story.

As noted before (in Chapters 5, 6, and 7), there is a strong tendency in English to put longer chunks of information at the end of the sentence. Thinking of these longer chunks of information as representing more 'weight', we say that English has a strong preference for END-WEIGHT in message organization.

If there is a lot of information being used to create the identity of an antecedent, then the resulting long relative clause will typically be in final position, as illustrated in [47].

> [47] a. Did you see *a movie that* was set in France with Harrison Ford as an American cop or something?
> b. They always make *a huge breakfast which* nobody ever wants to eat first thing on Christmas morning with a hangover.

It is often noticeable, as in [47b], that longer relative clauses in final position are more often introduced by *which* or *who* than by *that* or zero relative. That is, end-weight clauses are more clearly marked as relative clauses than those brief medial clauses, with zero relatives, shown in [46].

These factors, explicit relative pronoun and longer clause, are also commonly found in non-restrictive relative clauses, *which may account for the placement (like this example) of non-restrictive relatives much more often at the end than in the middle of English sentences.*

Exercise 9.E

Read over the following text, underlining the relative clauses, and decide whether they represent 'given' or 'new' information.

e.g. The first time <u>I met her</u>, Mariki Pusa was carrying a huge	_given_
painting that she'd just finished. The paint was still wet.	1 _____
It was for a class she was taking at the university. The	2 _____
painting showed a large face that had apples instead of eyes.	3 _____
It was odd. There was a nose that looked like a banana	4 _____
and a smiling mouth which was made of white sticks.	5 _____
The sticks she had painted looked like the short kind	6 _____
you get in lollipops. She said she was looking for someone	7 _____
who had a car or a truck because they wouldn't let her on the	8 _____
bus. The truck I had seemed big enough so I offered	
to drive her and her face to the university.	9 _____

Discussion topics and projects

1   It is quite common in texts to encounter what are called 'reduced relatives'. These can occur in both restrictive and non-restrictive forms and seem to be very common in newspaper reporting.

(a) If the examples in (ii), (iv), and (vi) are taken as reduced versions of the relatives in (i), (iii), and (v), can you propose a basic description of what parts are 'removed', and under what conditions, to create reduced relatives?

   (i)   The person who is sitting over there is next.
  (ii)   The person sitting over there is next.
 (iii)   He showed me a letter which was written in Chinese.
 (iv)   He showed me a letter written in Chinese.

(v) Don't sit on the small chair that is next to the window.

(vi) Don't sit on the small chair next to the window.

(b) Read through the following text and identify (by underlining) all examples of reduced relatives.

> We ate in a nice little restaurant near the zoo. We started with shrimp arranged in a small salad and covered with a light sauce. The main course was chicken sizzling in a shallow pan, still too hot to touch. There were also vegetables cooked lightly and portions of brown rice mixed with wild rice. Nobody sitting there could deny that the food being served was quite wonderful. We finished with hot apple pie, baked to perfection, and vanilla ice cream, slowly melting beside it.

(c) Having identified the reduced relatives, can you recall what clues you used to recognize them? What do you think would be the best way to help learners become familiar with these kinds of structures?

(d) There is a rather special problem for English language learners with some reduced relatives. For example, in the following sentences, notice how *do* and *does* are followed by the *-ing* form of the verb.

> How do people driving expensive cars manage to afford them?
> Where does someone looking for fresh fruit find it round here?

First, identify the problem in this type of 'input' that might confuse English language learners. Then, try to think of ways to organize an explanation, or a set of teaching steps, that might help learners make sense of these structures.

2 There is one use of the infinitive in English that is treated as a 'relative infinitive'. Instead of the relative clause italicized in (i), a speaker may say or write the relative infinitive italicized in (ii).

(i) I need someone *who can help me.*

(ii) I need someone *to help me.*

(a) One obvious question is whether the two sentences in (i) and (ii) actually mean the same thing. Do you think there is a difference? Another related question is whether all relative infinitives can be translated into relative clauses. What do you think? (Some examples are provided below.)

(b) Is it possible to use relative infinitives with all grammatical roles listed in the chapter (e.g. subject relative, object relative)? For example (ii) above, we can look at (i) and see that it must be a subject relative. Which grammatical roles would you say are relativized in the following examples?

(i) There's someone here to see you.

(ii)   A good place to study is the Reading Room.
(iii)   We want something to drink.
(iv)   The best person to ask is Liz.
(v)   I can never find time to relax.
(vi)   There's nowhere to sit.
(vii)   We'll find a way to solve these problems.
(viii)   You have ten questions to answer.
(ix)   I'll give you twenty minutes to finish them.
(x)   She has nothing to worry about.
(xi)   Please send me an angel to love.
(xii)   We have a range of colors to choose from.

An extended discussion of relative infinitives can be found in Geisler (1995).

3   In everyday spoken English, there are many points where speakers create forms that would be treated as ungrammatical if written down. It is quite useful to recognize some of the different relative clause constructions that will occasionally be heard in speech, especially if we are encouraging learners to listen to spoken English outside the classroom. The following examples are all from recordings (some from radio and TV programs) of educated native speakers of American English. Try to identify which aspects of these relative clauses make them different from those already described in the chapter. Why do you think the constructions were formed this way?

(i)   we now have governors who when they run for office one of the first things they mention is how they are going to fix the schools
(ii)   now there's Craig Livingstone whom we still don't know who hired him
(iii)   there are still some people that if they are so immune-depressed nothing can help them
(iv)   they weren't unwashed—they smelled rather good—they had patchouli oil all over them actually which after a while it did become almost nauseating
(v)   'We have one left leg which we don't know where it belongs', said Oklahoma State Medical Examiner Fred Jordan.
(vi)   well I did have a friend that her sister was in the parade so we went with her
(vii)   the older workers had put up with such bad conditions which it was amazing when I think of what they survived
(viii)   if I don't find a place that I can afford or a place that I can abide whoever else is going to be living there I'll go stay in the YMCA
(ix)   I have one brother lives up in Minnesota but we never talk at all

(x) there was somebody here wanted to meet you yesterday—where were you all day?

4 There is a concept called 'the noun phrase accessibility hierarchy' which, many have argued, provides an explanation of how relative clauses are learned. Basically, the idea is that, because a subject noun phrase can become a relative form more easily than an object noun phrase, it is more 'accessible to relativization'. In addition, a direct object is more accessible than an indirect object, which is more accessible than an object of a preposition, and so on. This creates a hierarchy, illustrated from top to bottom, in the following examples.

> Subject: The ring *that* is missing was my mother's.
> Direct object: The ring *that* I'm describing is a small gold one.
> Indirect object: The person *that* I loaned the ring to may have lost it.
> After-preposition object: The small case in *which* she kept the ring was black.
> Possessive: Another case *whose* contents are unknown is also missing.
> Object of comparison: There is nothing *that* this ring is less important than right now.

It has been claimed that, beginning with subject relatives, relative clauses at each point in this hierarchy are more common (than those below them) in the languages of the world, are more frequent within languages, and are easier to learn.

(a) Do you believe that the claims concerning frequency and 'easier to learn' apply to English (spoken and written)? How would you go about testing the frequency claim?

(b) It has also been claimed that we should be able to teach a structure that is lower in the hierarchy and, if we are successful, the structures above it will be learned automatically, without being taught. What is your opinion on this?

For background reading, look at Keenan and Comrie (1977) for the basic hierarchy, and Fox (1987) for some disagreement. Second language acquisition studies on this issue are presented in Doughty (1991), Eckman, Bell, and Nelson (1988), and Gass (1980).

Teaching ideas

1 Fill in the blank

A very common exercise for developing familiarity with the basic forms presents sentences with blank spaces for relative pronouns. A traditional format is exemplified in (a) and another version is suggested in (b).

(a) Traditional exercise format. Fill in the blanks with *who, which,* or *whose.*

  (i) There was someone here _____ was looking for you.

  (ii) The woman, _____ was very angry, kept saying your name.

  (iii) She was holding a book _____ had your name on the cover.

  (iv) She kept waving the book, _____ didn't seem heavy, like a flag.

  (v) The woman, _____ accent sounded Spanish, eventually left.

  (vi) But she seemed to be the kind of woman _____ anger wouldn't go away easily.

(b) Another version. This type of exercise can be made more puzzling (and perhaps more involving) by using some fairly well-known expressions that contain relative clauses. In this exercise, each sentence has two blank spaces, as shown below. The students' task, either in groups or as an assignment out of class, is to think of the missing words. Some examples to get started might be:

  (i) There was an old woman _____ lived in a _____.

  (ii) There's a book called 'The Man _____ Mistook his Wife for a _____'.

  (iii) People _____ live in glass houses shouldn't throw _____.

  (iv) There was an old lady _____ swallowed a _____.

  (v) The one _____ laughs last, laughs _____ .

  (vi) We were like ships _____ pass in the _____.

  (vii) It was the straw _____ broke the camel's _____.

  (viii) We were talking about things _____ go bump in the _____.

2 Combine these sentences

A common exercise format for practicing basic structures provides students with two sentences and invites them to combine those sentences into a single sentence containing a relative clause. One noun phrase has to be identical in each of the sentence pairs. A few examples should be provided to help students understand their task.

(a) Traditional version:

  e.g. I want to catch the plane. The plane leaves at noon.
      I want to catch the plane that leaves at noon.

  e.g. I enjoyed the story. I read the story last night.
      I enjoyed the story that I read last night.

  (i) The money has been stolen. I left the money in a box.

  (ii) The song is my favorite. The song is playing on the radio.

  (iii) Do you know the people? They live next door to me.

  (iv) Where's the old man? I was talking to him yesterday.

Note. After completing a number of examples of this type, it may help to discuss with students the fact that there are several choices in some examples and those choices fit different contexts. For example, in (iv), the formal *to whom* and the informal zero relative are both possible.

(b) Another version. This exercise begins with a set of statements of the following type. (Notice that each person or thing appears in both a subject and an object position.)

The girl was sitting beside the boy.
The boy was carrying a box.
The old woman had a dog.
The box belonged to the old woman.
The dog was looking at the girl.

Students are then provided with a set of questions which have to be combined with identifying information in the sentences above to create two different questions each time.

e.g. Have you seen the boy	*who was carrying the box?*
	who / whom / that the girl was sitting beside?
(i) Where is the box	… ?
	… ?
(ii) Does anyone know the girl	… ?
	… ?
(iii) What happened to the dog	… ?
	… ?
(iv) What's the name of the old woman	… ?
	… ?

(c) Another version. The basic format can be designed to elicit uses of *whose* and *where*, as in the example.

  e.g. Do you remember the couple. Their son got sick?
        Do you remember the couple whose son got sick?

  (i) What's the name of that woman. Her car was stolen?

  (ii) Where did you meet the people. We visited their house?

    (iii) Do you know the store. We bought our TV in that store?

    (iv) Is there any place near here. We can get some coffee in that place?

    (v) Who knows the building. Our class was scheduled to meet in the building?

3 A mechanic is someone who …

This traditional type of exercise is based on common structures used for definitions. There are many possible variations, three of which are illustrated here.

(a) In one column there is a list of examples of the first half of some definitions. In another column, there is a list of the second half of each of those definitions. The order of entries in each list does not match the other. The students' task is to connect the two parts, either by drawing lines or by saying or writing the complete definition.

      (i) A mechanic is a person …   who works in a hospital.

     (ii) A nurse is a person …   who steals things.

   (iii) A janitor is someone …   who doesn't eat meat.

   (iv) A vegetarian is a person …   who repairs cars.

    (v) A thief is someone …   who cleans offices.

(b) Students are given only the first half of each definition and must complete the sentences after discussions in groups or looking in a dictionary.

      (i) An astronomer is a person …

     (ii) A corkscrew is a thing …

   (iii) A dentist is someone …

   (iv) A garage is a place …

Once the structural frame is established, the terms to be defined can simply be offered in a list (e.g. *architect, cemetery, fan, microphone, plumber, rebel, refrigerator, tomboy, zoo*). This may be one way to combine an exercise on relative clauses with the introduction of some new vocabulary that is needed.

(c) The same material can be used in other formats. For example, the structural relationship can be changed to practice subject–subject connections, as illustrated in the first set (i) to (iii), or the second set (iv) to (vi), of sentences below.

      (i) Someone (*who*) … is called a mechanic.

     (ii) A person (*who*) … is a baker.

   (iii) A thing (*that*) … is called an answering machine.

   (iv) A machine … is used to cut grass is called … .

    (v) A person … flies airplanes is called … .

   (vi) Something … brings you good luck is known as … .

4 'Mary's father, who is in his seventies, plays golf'

The 'extra information' status of non-restrictive relative clauses can be demonstrated or practiced via a simple sentence-combining type of exercise, such as (a), or by a more interesting text-elaborating type of exercise, as in (b).

(a) In this exercise, some extra information is provided in brackets after each sentence. This extra information has to be made into a relative clause and added to the main sentence, with punctuation.

> e.g.   Mary's father plays golf every day. (He is in his seventies)
> *Mary's father, who is in his seventies, plays golf every day.*

- (i)   Mr Bones is your new teacher. (He used to work in Brazil)
- (ii)   She told me her name. (I wrote it in my address book)
- (iii)   My friend buys a lot of books. (He doesn't read most of them)
- (iv)   He says he can speak Arabic. (That is hard to believe)
- (v)   There's a man looking for you. (I can't remember his name)
- (vi)   I bought ten lottery tickets. (None of them won)
- (vii)   Her parents arrived here in 1950. (Both of them were refugees)

(b) In this exercise, the text has to be rewritten to include all the extra information (in non-restrictive relative clauses).

> Mr Larry Hayden has an unusual hobby. He collects caps. His house (It is in Pensacola, Florida) is full of caps. Mr Hayden (He has just retired) started his collection after the war. He now has over two thousand caps (Most of them advertise products) and he is still collecting. His wife (Her bedroom walls even have rows of caps) keeps telling him he should grow some more heads, but Larry (He always giggles at this idea) has other plans. He wants to build a special room (The room will have hooks in the ceiling) for his collection. It will be built next to the garage (There are already boxes of new caps waiting in the garage). Despite retirement (Most people are thinking about slowing down during this time), Mad Cap Hayden (His wife calls him this) shows no signs of going any slower.

5 Twenty questions

The twenty questions format can be used for a number of teaching points. In the following speaking task, it can be used to elicit restrictive relative clauses. This can be used as a warm-up activity at the start of any class.

One student (at a time) has to think of a well-known person, place, or thing and the other students, in some organized way (perhaps in teams of three or four), can ask up to a total of twenty questions in order to discover the identity. It is helpful to establish some structural frames (on the blackboard) to encourage the use of relative clauses.

Are you thinking of someone who ... ?
Is this something that ... ?
Is it a place where ... ?
Is this a person who/whose ... ?

6 The luckiest person is someone who ...

In the chapter we noted that *that* and zero relative seem to be chosen when relevant properties are already sufficiently signaled by the antecedent. We can focus on that aspect of relative pronoun use in the following exercises.

One preferred environment for *that* and zero relative (rather than *who* or *which*) is after expressions that identify entities with a special or unique property. Those expressions often contain words like *best, biggest* (and other superlatives), *most, first,* or *only.* Exercises based on this observation can be more closed, as in (a), or more open, as in (b).

(a) Provide students with three words that they have to use to start a description. It will help to start with some examples.

e.g.   best, meal, had
The best meal I ever had was at home.

e.g.   worst, movie, saw
The worst movie I ever saw was called 'Werewolf'.

   (i)   first, time, flew
  (ii)   funniest, person, know
 (iii)   biggest, mistake, made
  (iv)   longest, trip, took
   (v)   most, money, saw
  (vi)   most, interesting, met
 (vii)   lowest, grade, got
(viii)   last, time, cried

Note. If students enjoy this exercise and seem eager to continue, they can be encouraged to create more examples by writing them down (three words only). These are all put together to create another set for the whole class to work with (as either a spoken or a written exercise).

(b) Another version. Students in groups have to create short descriptions from the following beginning phrases (given out on cards to each group). It may be helpful to work through some examples with the whole class to show how relative clauses are useful structures for this task.

e.g.   The best teacher
The best teacher is someone who ...

e.g.   The most important ideas
The most important ideas are those which ...

(i)   The most useful objects (are things which …)
(ii) The worst people (are those who …)
(iii) The least interesting places (are those which/where …)
(iv) The luckiest person (is someone who …)

7 OK, or not OK?

This exercise is designed to focus attention on specific problems with relative clauses discovered by writing teachers. (See Tarone and Yule 1989, pages 74–6, for more details.) The goal of the exercise is to discover, and then focus attention on, those aspects of English relative clauses that learners are consistently getting wrong. A set of sentences with relative clauses is first created (using vocabulary that the students know well). Then, in some of the sentences, the relative pronoun is removed (see ii, v, ix below), in others, part of the verb phrase is removed (see iv, x), and in others, both relative pronoun and part of the verb are removed (see vi, xi). In all these examples, the focus is on the subject–subject connection, but other relationships (particularly object–subject) can be given attention in a similar way.

Step 1. Students are given copies of the sentences and asked to decide if they are correct (circle OK) or incorrect (circle not OK).

Step 2. For each sentence that is not OK, students have to add or remove words to make it correct.

(i)   The people who were coming by bus arrived late. OK / not OK
(ii)   The boy was waiting here has left. OK / not OK
(iii) The book that was lying on the table isn't there now. OK / not OK
(iv)   The woman who frightened ran away. OK / not OK
(v)   The program was on TV seemed really boring. OK / not OK
(vi)   The person making that noise should stop! OK / not OK
(vii) Anyone who is late will just have to wait. OK / not OK
(viii) The one who isn't here yet will talk about that later. OK / not OK
(ix)   Everyone is working hard will do well. OK / not OK
(x)   The dog that barking lives next door. OK / not OK
(xi)   All passengers leaving today must pack up now. OK / not OK
(xii) Anybody who is feeling tired can stop for a rest. OK / not OK

Step 3. The teacher reviews the answers, drawing attention to those points where students seem to think incorrect forms are correct and, even more interesting, where they seem to think correct forms (often examples like vi and xi) are incorrect.

8 Recognizing your relatives

With more proficient students, it should be possible to set a task that requires them to identify a range of relative forms in different types of texts. This exercise may help them identify different styles of writing. In one study, for example, it was noted that different preferences for relative pronouns can be found in different sections (e.g. World News versus Sports) of the same newspaper (cf. Biesenbach-Lucas 1986). A replication of that exercise with any English language newspaper may develop students' awareness of some aspects of the composition of extended discourse in English.

As an in-class exercise, invite students to identify and compare the relative clauses in the following two texts, the first from a news magazine (*Newsweek*, February 3, 1997, page 53), and the second from an academic text (Larsen-Freeman and Long, 1991, page 221).

> (i) Poet James Dickey, 73, who died of lung disease last week in Columbia, S.C., was one of that breed of grandiloquent Southerners who could make good on every boast. A football and track star who graduated magna cum laude from Vanderbilt, he flew 100 missions in World War II. He was a successful advertising writer (Coca-Cola, Lays potato chips), an expert archer, a white-water rafter and a guitar player. He also published more than 20 volumes of poetry, for which he won a National Book Award and a seat in the American Academy of Arts and Letters. The irony is that outside of the small audience for American poetry, Dickey was famous not as a poet but as the author of the gripping novel 'Deliverance' (1970) and the script for the movie based on it.

> (ii) There are various ways in which data-based work is less productive for being theoretically unmotivated. Thus, some studies are still only descriptive, with the 'issue' addressed appearing to have occurred to the investigator after the data were collected. This seems to be the explanation for research reports which end by saying that, 'of course', no conclusions can be drawn about X (the issue which supposedly motivated the study) because of the unfortunate lack of certain crucial data or some missing element in the design (such as a control group), and which then go on to suggest how future research on the issue should be conducted, presumably by someone else.

Further reading

General reference, with examples

Azar, B. 1993. *Chartbook*. Chapter 6. Englewood Cliffs, NJ: Prentice-Hall Regents.
Celce-Murcia, M. and **D. Larsen-Freeman.** 1983. *The Grammar Book.* Chapters 26–27. Rowley, Mass.: Newbury House.

More theoretical discussions

de Haan, P. 1989. *Postmodifying Clauses in the English Noun Phrase.* Amsterdam: Rodopi.

Givon, T. 1993. *English Grammar.* Volume 2. Chapter 9. Amsterdam: John Benjamins.

Guy, G. and R. Bayley. 1995. 'On the choice of relative pronouns in English.' *American Speech* 70: 148–62.

Distribution and frequency

Ball, C. 1996. 'A diachronic study of relative markers in spoken and written English.' *Language Variation and Change* 8: 227–58.

Kikai, A., M. Schleppegrell and S. Tagliamonte. 1986. 'The influence of syntactic position on relativization strategies.' In K. Denning, S. Inkelas, F. McNair-Knox and J. Rickford (eds.): *Variation in Language. NWAV-XV at Stanford.* (pp. 267–77) Stanford, Calif.: Stanford University Press.

Quirk, R. 1957. 'Relative clauses in educated spoken English.' *English Studies* 38: 97–109.

On who *versus* whom

Aarts, F. 1994. 'Relative *who* and *whom:* Prescriptive rules and linguistic reality.' *American Speech* 69: 71–9.

On whose *versus* of which

Johansson, C. 1995. *The Relativizers* whose *and* of which *in Present-day English.* Stockholm: Almqvist & Wiksell.

On information structure

Fox, B. and S. Thompson. 1990. 'A discourse explanation of the grammar of relative clauses in English conversation.' *Language* 66: 297–316.

On end-weight

Yamashita, J. 1994. 'An analysis of relative clauses in the Lancaster/IBM spoken English corpus.' *English Studies* 75: 73–84.

On second language acquisition

Doughty, C. 1991. 'Second language instruction does make a difference.' *Studies in Second Language Acquisition* 13: 431–69.

Pavesi, M. 1986. 'Markedness, discoursal modes, and relative clause formation in a formal and an informal context.' *Studies in Second Language Acquisition* 8: 38–55.

Schumann, J. 1980. 'The acquisition of English relative clauses by second language learners.' In R. Scarcella and S. Krashen (eds.): *Research in Second Language Acquisition.* (pp. 118–31) Rowley, Mass.: Newbury House.

Teaching suggestions

Fotos, S. 1994. 'Integrating grammar instruction and communicative language use through grammar consciousness-raising tasks.' *TESOL Quarterly* 28: 323–51.

Ur, P. 1988. *Grammar Practice Activities.* Cambridge: Cambridge University Press.

10 DIRECT AND INDIRECT SPEECH

1 In most ESL texts, indirect speech seems to be just another version of a direct speech sentence with the same meaning. Is there any difference in meaning associated with these forms?

2 Isn't there a rule for indirect speech that the verbs should both be in the past tense, as in *He said that she* was *ill*? Why, then, isn't this sentence ungrammatical: *He said that she* is *ill*?

3 ESL learners sometimes produce utterances of the type shown as (b). If (a) is okay, why is (b) ungrammatical?
   (a) He said, 'Hello.'
   (b) *He talked, 'Hi, nice to meet you.'

4 In short stories and novels, there are sometimes dialogs reported in some mixture of speech forms. What are the grammatical features of this style?

5 English speakers seem to use direct speech forms at times when they're not actually reporting someone's speech. What are the other uses of direct speech?

'… *students often find indirect speech to be a problematic area of English grammar. What also complicates the area is that native speakers do not consistently abide by the grammar-book rules for producing indirect speech.*'

As this quotation from Celce-Murcia and Larsen-Freeman (1983: 459) suggests, the different ways of reporting what was said in English can present problems for language learners. Just what those native speakers are doing, as they fail to abide by the grammar-book rules, will be explored in the following discussion.

Overview

After a brief review of the basic forms of DIRECT and INDIRECT SPEECH, including BACKSHIFT in tense, we consider the conceptual difference between the *narrative* function of indirect speech and *dramatic* function of direct speech, noting the preferred uses of different REPORTING VERBS. Those verbs used in summarizing previous talk are also noted. The mixed structures found in news reporting are then described, along with the use of direct speech to represent thoughts and reactions. Features of FREE INDIRECT DISCOURSE in written English and CONSTRUCTED DIALOGUE in spoken English are explored. Finally, the grammatical structures of some new QUOTATIVES in contemporary spoken English are described and illustrated.

Basic forms

There are some clear differences in English between the basic forms of DIRECT (or quoted) SPEECH and INDIRECT (or reported) SPEECH. The major differences are usually presented in grammar texts through sentence pairs such as those shown in [1] to [3], where the direct speech forms within quotation marks in (a) are converted to the indirect speech forms in (b).

[1]   a. 'I am waiting here for you.'
       b. He said that he was waiting there for her.

[2]   a. 'Have you seen this report?'
       b. The boss asked if they had seen that report.

[3]   a. 'Can we leave these exercises until tomorrow?'
       b. She asked if they could leave those exercises until the following day.

The indirect forms have no quotation marks and are introduced by a QUOTATIVE FRAME which consists of an attributed speaker (*he, she, the boss*) and a verb of saying (*said, asked*), followed by a conjunction (*that, if*). The intonation of the indirect form will be noticeably different from the direct speech form, particularly in the case of reported questions. Within the reported clause, a number of distinct shifts can be found. The change from present tense in [1a] to past tense in [1b] is described as a BACKSHIFT. There are similar backshifts with *have* (-> *had*) in [2] and *can* (-> *could*) in [3]. Other shifts are illustrated by changes in the forms *I* (-> *he*), *this* (-> *that*) and *here* (-> *there*), plus a reversal in word order from the direct question (*Can we ...*) to the indirect (*they could ...*). These typical features of indirect speech reports are summarized in Box 10.1.

From the kinds of changes listed in Box 10.1, it might seem that the relationship between any direct speech event and its reported version is a straightforward conversion of certain forms. It isn't always so simple. The forms used in a reported version of previous talk can vary a great deal and typically depend on the perspective of the reporter. If the speaker thinks that the situation being reported is still true at the time of the report, then there may be no backshifting (e.g. *He said that Jean is ill*). Also, in situations of immediate reporting, as shown in Mary's report in [4], there may be no changes at all in the indirect speech version.

[4]   **Steve**   The new director is coming here tomorrow.
       Liz   Em, I missed that, what did he say?
       Mary   He said that the new director is coming here tomorrow.

Summary Box 10.1 **Features of indirect speech**

Quotative frames:	*He said ... ; She asked ...*
Conjunctions:	*that; if*
Shifts:	
Tense:	*am -> was; can -> could; have -> had*
Personal pronouns:	*I -> he; you -> her; we -> they; you -> they*
Demonstratives:	*this -> that; these -> those*
Place adverbials:	*here -> there*
Time adverbials:	*tomorrow -> the following day*
Word order:	*Can we ... -> they could*
	Have you ... -> they had

Generally, the form of the indirect speech version will reflect the reporter's sense of closeness or distance between the situation being reported and the current reporting situation. The greater the distance between them, the more likely it is that the types of shifts listed in Box 10.1 will be found.

Exercise 10.A

Following the patterns shown in Box 10.1, write out an indirect speech report of this recorded conversation between a security guard and a young man called Jimmy. Begin *The guard asked Jimmy what he ...*

Guard   What are you doing here?
Jimmy   I work in this building.
Guard   Do you have any identification?
Jimmy   I left it in my office.
Guard   Where is your office?
Jimmy   It's on the fourth floor. I can show you.
Guard   I'll go with you.

Basic meanings

The emphasis in most descriptions of direct and indirect speech is on the differences in forms associated with each, as represented in Box 10.1. There is, however, a subtle distinction in meaning signaled by these differences in form. Notice that the indirect forms are those typically used to mark something as 'distant from speaker'. Notice also that the effect of backshift in tense creates a sense of 'more remote', as described in Chapter 3. Thus, the general meaning signaled by a choice of shifted forms (i.e. *that was there and then*) marks an indirect speech report as more distant from the speaking event being reported. The direct speech forms are those associated with 'near to speaker'. These forms (i.e. *this is here and now*) are clearly connected more closely to the moment of utterance, typically with reference to the speakers (*I* and *you*) as participants in the actual interaction.

The indirect speech forms move the reported speaking event to another time and clearly mark that there is some distance between the time of the report and the time of the speech being reported. This effect makes the indirect speech forms more like a narrative account of an event ('telling') and distinct from the dramatic presentation of the event marked by the direct speech forms ('showing'). Indirect speech functions like narrative and direct speech functions like drama.

Direct speech as drama

When a speaking event is reported via DIRECT SPEECH forms, it is possible to include many features that dramatize the way in which an utterance was produced. The quotative frame can also include verbs which indicate the speaker's manner of expression (e.g. *cry, exclaim, gasp*), voice quality (e.g. *mutter, scream, whisper*), and type of emotion (e.g. *giggle, laugh, sob*). It can also include adverbs (e.g. *angrily, brightly, cautiously, hoarsely, quickly,, slowly*) and descriptions of the reported speaker's style and tone of voice, as illustrated in [5].

[5]   a. 'I have some good news,' she whispered in a mischievious way.
      b. 'What is it?' he snapped impatiently.
      c. 'Can't you guess?' she giggled.
      d. 'Oh, no! Don't tell me you're pregnant!' he wailed, with a whining nasal sound in his voice.

The literary style of the examples in [5] is associated with an older tradition. In contemporary novels, there is often no indication, other than separate lines, of which character is speaking, as the direct speech forms are presented like a dramatic script, one after the other. Extract [6], from a novel by Cormac McCarthy (1993: 9), illustrates this pattern, with the written version of the speech attempting to show how these characters express themselves.

[6] You know it aint what I wanted dont you?
Yeah. I know that.
You lookin after Rosco good?
He aint been rode.
Why dont we go Saturday.
All right.
You dont have to if you got somethin else to do.
I aint got nothin else to do.

In [6], the reader hears only the direct speech of the dialog, with no quotative frames determining what kind of voice or emotion was involved.

Indirect speech as narrative

In contrast, when a speaking event is reported via INDIRECT SPEECH, there is less drama. There is also a tendency to include, in the quotative frame, verbs which indicate the purpose of the utterance (e.g. *admit, agree, deny, explain, promise, respond, suggest*). Such verbs present an interpretation by the reporter of the speech act being performed. As illustrated in [7], the reporter not only tells us what was said, but what kind of action (e.g. *protest*) was performed by the utterance.

[7] a. The teacher announced that there would be extra homework.
b. Many students protested that they already had too much.
c. One student declared that she couldn't do any more.

Indirect speech forms tend to be found when the reporter is more concerned with conveying an interpretation of the content of what was said. Direct speech forms can be used to show the spontaneous nature of how something was said.

Summarized reports

The functional distinction between the dramatic nature of direct speech and the narrative effect of indirect speech is made more extreme when the structure associated with indirect speech is used to summarize a speaking event as a way of reporting it. The difference between what was actually said, as in [8a], and how it was reported, as in [8b], can be quite large.

[8] a. 'I am waiting here for you. Where are you? You're never on time!'
b. He complained about her being late.

The summarized report in [8b] creates an even greater distance between the speaking event and the reporting event. It also results in much greater control being taken by the reporter for the interpretation of the speaking event. There is, then, a conceptual distinction between three types of reporting formats in English, as shown in Box 10.2.

Reporting verbs

Also listed in Box 10.2 are examples of the types of verbs generally associated with the three different formats. Whereas a verb like *say* can be used for summarizing (*He said too much*), reporting (*He said that he was sick*) and quoting (*He said, 'I'm feeling awful'*), many other verbs are associated with only one of these functions. It is worth noting that two of the most widely used verbs associated with speech (i.e. *speak, talk*) have a summarizing function and are not used to introduce direct or indirect speech. This information is rarely presented to second language learners. The learner of English who produces utterances like ** He talked to me, 'How are you? Nice to see you'* is trying to report a specific instance of speaking with a verb that is only used to describe or summarize a speaking event.

Summary Box 10.2 **Reporting formats and verbs**

<------ more distance, greater reporter control ------		
Summarized report	**Indirect speech**	**Direct speech**
Erin called us about the project.	*She asked if they could postpone her part until Monday.*	*'Oh, Mary, can we please postpone my part of the project until next Monday?'*
Summarizing verbs	**Reporting verbs**	**Quoting verbs**
chat, describe, discuss, gossip, speak, talk	*claim, deny, imply, maintain, pretend, propose*	*beg, exclaim, remark, reply, shout, whisper*

The structural sequence from left to right in Box 10.2 can actually be found, in that order, in spoken reports of previous conversations. Example [9] is from a tape-recorded conversation and begins with a summary, continues in the second line with an indirect speech report, and finally presents direct speech.

[9]   He told her about what happened—
        he said he'd been tired—
        he was, 'I'm sorry—I didn't mean to forget the meeting—
        I was so tired I just didn't keep track of everything.'

'The teachers were saying ...'

There is also one type of structure that seems to combine an indirect speech report with a summarizing function in order to mention a previous discussion.

As illustrated in [10], the verbs *say* and *tell* can be used in the progressive to both report and summarize. The plural subject in [10a] is worth noting because it seems unlikely that there was a single direct speech utterance as the source in this case. That is, we are not expected to believe that the exact words (of all those teachers, perhaps in chorus) are being reported.

[10] a. The pre-school teachers were saying that they had trouble with him before.
       b. Cathy was telling me about a new restaurant in town.

We shall return to the issue of the accuracy of what is being reported in both direct and indirect speech.

Exercise 10.B

Underline the ten reporting verbs in the following text and then identify the reporting formats in each case as 'summary', 'indirect', or 'direct'.

> Yesterday I went with Zee to a lecture on the English language. The professor was talking about negation in different languages. He was describing one language that had a double negative. For a while he was really going on about how the double negative in that language was still a negative. Then he proposed that English was very different. 'For example,' he said, 'if you say, "It isn't not important," you are actually communicating that it is important.' He claimed that the English double negative could convey a positive meaning. I was puzzling over that, but he didn't stop there. 'However,' he exclaimed in his high squeaky voice, 'there is no language in which a double positive can be used to express a negative!' Everybody was busily writing this down. Zee turned to me with a smile and whispered, 'Yeah, right.'

Meanings in context

Those clear distinctions in form and meaning that we have noted between direct and indirect speech in English are not always present in written reports. It is important to recognize a range of mixed structures and variations of the basic forms and functions described already.

News reports

One of the most common sources of reported talk is the daily newspaper, which can present that talk in different ways. In the newspaper report (about a protest against a university's investments) in extract [11], there is a strong preference for placing the quotative frames (italicized) after the quoted material.

> [11]   The vote will 'add to a growing mandate from all members of the University community for total divestment,' *said Clare Woodward*, a biochemistry professor and one of the protestors who occupied University President Ken Keller's outer office last week. The regents cannot ignore the overwhelming opinion of students and faculty on this issue, *she said* after the meeting.
>
> 'The vote was impressive,' *said Ron Edwards*, president of the Minneapolis Urban League, who sat in on the Senate meeting. 'It will give an upbeat message to students, faculty and their supporters.' The vote was significant, but only advisory, *Edwards said*. The regents will take final action in June, *he said*.

A number of observations can be made about this type of reporting. The speech directly reported within quotation marks may only be part of the sentence in which it occurs. Notice also how difficult it is on some occasions to decide whether the speech reported without quotation marks is in fact direct or indirect speech. When no quotation marks are used, one assumes initially that an indirect speech format is being used. However, at the end of the first paragraph, the reported speech occurs without quotes, yet shows no shift of the verb form (*cannot*) or of the demonstrative (*this*). This is, in fact, direct speech being reported without quotation marks.

The main pattern in [11] seems to be one in which a speaker's words are reported as direct speech in quotation marks, followed by a quotative frame identifying the speaker by name and status, then continuing with further remarks from that speaker without quotation marks. When there is descriptive material identifying the speaker, the typical sequence of constituents in the quotative frame is reversed (e.g. *said Clare Woodward*).

The mixture of direct and indirect forms within single sentences is not uncommon in newspaper reporting. Extracts [12], [13], and [14] are brief examples of the style and show how the topic character, called *MacLaine* in [12], *Kennedy* in [13], and *Louie* in [14], can be the referent of both third person (*she/he*) and first person pronouns (*I/my*) within the same sentence.

> [12]   MacLaine concedes that one of the reasons she has had no major romantic involvement 'for a while' is that she 'would have to find a man who shared my spiritual beliefs'.
>
> [13]   Kennedy has toned down the punk look and vows 'not to blurt out exactly what I think'.

[14] When he was in the fourth grade at St. Joseph of the Palisades Elementary School, his teacher warned Louie's father, William, a real-estate broker, 'that I might be hanging round with the wrong types of boys'.

The quotation marks in examples [12], [13], and [14] represent major shifts of perspective for the reader. The reader is expected to recognize that the non-quoted parts represent the reporter's perspective whereas the parts in quotation marks are a direct presentation of the speaker's perspective.

Thoughts and reactions

In other written genres, quotation marks can be used, not for speech, but for thoughts or reactions. In some cases, this function is clearly indicated by the type of verb (e.g. *think*) in the quotative frame, as illustrated in [15].

[15] a. He thought for a moment, 'There's something wrong here.'
      b. 'Why me?' she wondered.
      c. He was puzzled, 'Where can she be?'

However, in other texts, writers can include thoughts in quotation marks without an explanatory quotative frame, as in [16], from Seinfeld (1995: 47).

[16] Why is it difficult and uncomfortable to be naked? It's because when you have clothes on, you can always make those little adjustments that people love to do. Hitching, straightening, adjusting. You know, you feel like you're getting it together. 'Yeah, pretty good. Feeling good, feeling pretty good.' But when you're naked, it's so final. You're just, 'Well, this it. There's nothing else I can do.'

Quotation marks as an indication of speech and thought are not always present, however, as we shall see in the next section.

Exercise 10.C

(a) Direct speech forms can occur in written text with no punctuation and no quotative frame. Can you find and underline an example of this phenomenon in the following extract from a magazine article (Caputo 1991: 163)?

The predictable configurations of the rooms and corridors, the presence of modern conveniences bearing well-known brand names created the cozy impression that one was in a place where the people and events were also familiar and predictable, as easily understood as a room-service menu. Why, this country isn't so different from home, Ethel, and these folks are just like us. That fallacy was safe enough in Brussels.

(b) Identify three or more aspects of your underlined example that are clear
indicators of direct speech.

_____

_____

_____

Free indirect discourse

Another mixture of features from direct and indirect speech can occur in texts,
particularly in narrative, and is described as FREE INDIRECT DISCOURSE. This
style of reporting combines the shifted tenses and third person pronouns of
indirect speech with the direct speech versions of non-shifted expressions of
time and place, inverted questions, and interjections. These features are listed
in Box 10.3, with examples from a version of the Little Red Riding Hood story
(from Yule, Mathis, and Hopkins 1992) which is presented as extract [17].
Although this extract reports a conversation between two speakers, there are
no quotative frames to introduce and attribute the utterances as indirect
speech, nor any quotation marks to indicate if some parts are direct speech.

> [17] Little Red Riding Hood objected to her mother's advice. Why
> should she always take the same path from here to Granma's? She
> might see something different if she could cut through the woods.
> Her mother was unmoved. She might get lost too. She might
> meet someone who would hurt her, or heaven forbid, even kidnap
> her.
> But goodness how could she learn about the world if she never did
> anything new or different?
> She would learn in plenty of time. She was too young now.

The characteristic features of free indirect discourse, as illustrated in this story,
are summarized in Box 10.3.

Summary Box 10.3 **Features of free indirect discourse**

No quotative frames
Backshifted tenses: *should, might, could, did, was*
Shifted (third person) pronouns: *she, her*
non-shifted time/place adverbials: *here, now*
non-shifted order in questions: *why should she, how could she*
Interjections included: *heaven forbid, goodness*

For readers who aren't used to this style of reporting, there is the possibility of some misunderstanding. The reference of *she* throughout example [17] is Little Red Riding Hood. However, the reader has to realize that, in the second paragraph, it is the mother's speech to her daughter that is being reported. If the reader does not notice this change of speaker, then the *she* (who might get lost) could easily be misinterpreted as the mother.

Complete stories can be written in this style, with characters' speech being represented with neither the quotative frames of indirect speech nor the punctuation marks of direct speech. In extract [18], from a short story called *Rope*, by Katherine Anne Porter (1958), a young married couple are having a disagreement.

[18]   She looked so forlorn, so lost and despairing he couldn't believe it was only a piece of rope that was causing all the racket. What *was* the matter, for God's sake?

Oh, would he please hush and go away and *stay* away, if he could, for five minutes? By all means, yes, he would. He'd stay away indefinitely if she wished. Lord, yes, there was nothing he'd like better than to clear out and never come back. She couldn't for the life of her see what was holding him, then.

The first sentence in [18] appears to be a reported thought of the man, followed by a representation, in the second sentence, of what he said to the woman. The first sentence of the second paragraph is the woman's response, followed by three sentences attributable to the man. The final sentence is the woman's response. Although the referential devices (pronouns and tenses) are consistently in the form associated with indirect speech, the idiomatic expressions (*for God's sake*), the interjections (*Oh*; *yes*; *Lord, yes*), the inverted word order of the questions and the total absence of quotative frames give a direct speech flavor to the reported interaction. Yet there are no quotation marks or separate lines used to guide the reader in interpreting where one speaker ends and another begins.

The mixture of direct and indirect speech forms can appear in less literary contexts. Extract [19] is from the published minutes of a university faculty meeting and extract [20] from the official record of a town council meeting.

[19]   Professor G asked further about the mechanics; specifically, how many nominations the committee typically received and were they automatically carried over.

[20]   Mr H asked didn't the town get 2% of sales from the company and wasn't it a 15 year contract with a 10 year option.

In [19], the report puts the first question into the word order of indirect speech, but presents the second question in the order associated with direct speech. In

[20], both questions are in the direct speech form, but not marked as such by punctuation.

Exercise 10.D

The following extract is from the published record of a town council meeting (from data described in more detail in Yule 1993). Read through the text and identify the different parts as 'direct speech' or 'not direct speech' by writing 'D' or 'ND' in the spaces provided.

Mr L moved to grant a beer and liquor license to Club Atlantis   e.g. ND

located at 215 Oak Street, providing everything is in order.

Mr B wants as part of records I am going to vote for the license,   1 ___

but I told him and I said it at the last meeting that if he wavers   2 ___

just a wee little bit and not keep up with what he has promised the Council,

keep it clean, keep people off the streets   3 ___

and have no problems, or the license will be pulled.

Mr H stated that he is not in favor of things continuing as is.   4 ___

Mr B seconded motion. Motion carried with no opposition.   5 ___

Constructed dialogue

Having considered some of the uses of direct and indirect speech forms in written discourse, we will now look at some aspects of speech reports in spoken discourse. Quite a lot of ordinary conversation is devoted to reporting what was said in other conversations. In considering how those reports are presented, it is important to keep in mind that people are not normally able to recall verbatim (exact word-for-word) accounts of what they hear.

The term CONSTRUCTED DIALOGUE is used in recognition of the fact that, on many occasions in English conversation, speakers do not actually present verbatim reports of what they and others have said in previous interactions. Speakers may be using direct speech forms in these reports, but there is a lot of evidence to suggest that they have created or constructed the dialogue they report. On many occasions they also report thoughts or attitudes (that they and others may have had) in a form which looks as if they had given voice, in direct speech, to those thoughts and attitudes during the reported interaction. These direct speech forms are often introduced by a range of QUOTATIVE verbs which, in addition to *say*, include forms of the verbs *to be, to go*, and *to be like*. The 'constructed' aspect of these reports may be most obvious on those occasions when the participants in the dialogue are credited with using direct speech even though they can't talk. In example [21], a woman is describing an occasion when she saw some caterpillars on the back of her friend's shirt. These caterpillars appear to have voices. In example [22], the speaker is describing a visit to a pet store where she had seen two dogs in a small cage.

[21]   she turned around and she had four of them clung to the back of her shirt—they were hanging all over and *I was like*, 'Ahh—what are those?' And I went to brush them off and *they're like*, 'No— don't touch me.'

[22]   They look all weird—*they're like*, 'Oh I'm real worried about my cage—I don't think I get enough room—oh stop biting my ear.' And *the other guy's*, 'Oh I'm always sad I think maybe if I chew on your ear I'll feel better.'

The direct speech forms are introduced, in [21] and [22], by quotative frames containing versions of the verbs *be* and *be like*. We have already had two extracts with examples of *be* as the verb in the quotative frame. In [9], direct speech was introduced by *he was* and in [16] by *you're just*. In [22], the second quotative frame has *the other guy's* before direct speech. The first quotative frame has a version of *be like*, an innovative and rapidly spreading quotative in contemporary American English.

Quotative *be like*

Forms of *be like* have become particularly common for introducing direct speech that conveys a person's attitude. In the second speaker's contribution in [23], there is the appearance of a previous conversation being reported, but the general effect is one in which the reported character's attitude to her dog is being portrayed through her own words. The final quotation is unlikely to have been uttered by the character and seems to summarize the reporting speaker's assessment of the reported character's attitude. It has an evaluative function.

[23]   S   I know a lot of people who just gas their animals because they're inconvenient

   T   Well that's why Wendy—that's why Wendy did it—she was just like—*she was like*, 'I can't take care of this dog. I can't take it with me. It's you know—it was a bad choice. I think I'm gonna put it to sleep.' And *I'm like*, 'Well it's your dog you know. It's your choice.' And I didn't think it was especially bad of her and *she's like*, 'Well if it has—if it's healthy then I know somebody who'll take it but if it's not I'm gonna gas it because it's gonna cost money.' And eh so I mean it was the fact that the dog was inconvenient. *She was just like*, 'This dog's annoying me.'

Versions of *be like* are also often found in the introductory quotative frame when the reporter doesn't actually quote all of a reported speaker's talk, but acts as if the content is totally predictable and consequently doesn't have to be spelled out. Extracts [24], concerning a person who complains a lot, and [25], about someone apologizing a lot, are illustrations of this phenomenon.

[24] Karen does that a lot too—*she's like*, 'every little thing da da da da.'

[25] He started crying and *he's like*, 'I just blah blah blah blah.'

This type of reporting can occur on a much more mundane level when a speaker is talking about a telephone conversation with a friend, as in [26], or in a conversation with a neighbor about an apartment he has for rent [27].

[26] She called me the other night and—eh—*she's like*, 'So hey whatcha doin'?' and *I'm like*, 'Oh, I'm sitting here watchin' TV.'

[27] *He's like*, 'you an LSU student?' *I said*, 'Yes, sir,' cause you know he's an older man and I'm giving him some respect, and *he's like*, 'Know anybody who wants an apartment?' *I was like*, 'Maybe' and *he's like*, 'How about $175 for an efficiency?' and *I was like*, 'Well let me see it.'

In examples like these, it may be that the use of *be like* is an indication that we have to interpret what is being reported in direct speech form as an approximate reconstruction rather than an exact word-for-word account of what was said. It is interesting that, in extract [27], the speaker maintains the use of the PAST TENSE in the quotative frames for her own reported contributions (as background) and the PRESENT TENSE in the frames introducing what was said by the other speaker (as foreground). This example fits a general pattern in English of present tense introducing the speech of authority figures and past tense for non-authority figures in reported interactions.

Quotative *go*

Another common means of introducing reported speech and other expressions is through the use of the verb *go*. In some contexts it is clear that the speaker is not reporting something that was actually said, as in example [28].

[28] I'm too busy making an ass of myself to stop and *go*, 'Hey you're doing something stupid.'

In other examples it is less clear whether some direct speech, as reported in [29], or an interjection, as in [30], was in fact uttered in the circumstances described.

[29]   (The speaker is describing the aimless lives of her friends.) I don't mind when other people do it though—unless they're ignoring things on purpose—if *they're just going*, 'Yeah this is okay.'

[30]   Every once in a while something out of the blue will trigger the thought that I am going to die some day and then *I start to go*, 'Whaaaa!'

When quotative *go* occurs in written reports, it does seem to introduce potential reactions in direct speech form rather than actual quotations. In extract [31], from a magazine article (Sessums 1992: 266), a talk-show host, Jay Leno, is talking about the benefits of having an entertaining guest such as actress Geena Davis. Single quotation marks are used for Leno's speech and double quotation marks are used, following the two occurrences of *go*, to mark the potential reactions of the audience.

[31]   'Whenever Geena's on, she always brings something to the show. It's always a comedy bit ... either a story or an invention. It makes the show more show-and-tell. So if you came from another country and you'd never seen her before and you didn't know who she was, *you'd go*, "Oh, she's funny!" A lot of times, you have movie stars on, and if you'd never heard of them before, *you go*, "Why is this person famous in America?" '

In addition to reporting reactions in this way, speakers and writers can also represent reactions by using direct speech with no obvious introductory marker of quotation. In extract [32], from a magazine article (Frazier 1997: 26), the writer is commenting on people who sound very certain and positive when they are giving a negative response. He describes this reaction as 'the Positive Negative' and creates small imagined interactions to demonstrate its uses.

[32]   The Positive Negative may be adapted to any situation in which the answer is no: 'Will you be back later?' 'I sure won't!' 'Can you give my car a jump?' 'I sure can't!' 'Are you the owner?' 'I'm sure not!'

Examples of direct speech introduced in this way, with no reporting verb at all, have been described as 'zero quotatives'.

Zero quotative

It is not unusual to find direct speech forms reported in contemporary English conversational speech without any quotative frame. Once the identities of the speakers have been established, their speech can often be reported without attribution. These points, where a quotative could occur, are marked by ø in the following transcriptions. Extract [33] is one woman's report (to a friend) of a conversation she had with her mother one Saturday morning.

> [33]   *She's like,* 'So what time did you get in?' We got in at two thirty. ø
> 'Well I got home around a little after one' cause they sleep like the dead—they don't hear us come in anyway and eh so ø 'Did you all have a nice time?' ø 'Yeah.'

In the final line of extract [33], notice that there are no quotative frames such as *My mother asked me* and *I answered* accompanying the lines of dialogue from this reported interaction. The term ZERO QUOTATIVE has been used to describe this type of direct quotation with no quotative frame. One of the problematic aspects of zero quotatives is that there is no attributed speaker indicated. There may sometimes be changes in intonation to indicate a change of speaker. However, if a direct speech form is used in the first person, and no other speaker is indicated, then the quote would normally be attributed to the person speaking. In extract [34], such an attribution would result in a mistaken interpretation. Just before this extract, the two women speakers have been discussing the relationship between Karen and her boyfriend Mark and the fact that Mark says he prays for Karen when they're apart. Zero quotatives are marked by ø in the transcript.

> [34]   S   Are you serious? Who told you that?
> T   Karen
> S   Karen said that he prayed every night?
> T   Uh-hm—prayed for peace—well it's a good line anyway
> S   oh really
> T   ø 'I prayed about you every night.'
> S   ø 'I prayed about you.' ø 'Hey I'll talk to you.'
> T   ø 'Put a ring on me hey oooh I'm yours.'

In extract [34], the last three lines represent constructed dialog in which a conversation between Mark and Karen is created. Notice in the penultimate line that first the male voice speaks and then the female voice responds, yet there are no quotative frames (*he said / she said*) to make those attributions explicit. Making sense of this reported interaction is clearly not dependent on knowing the conventions of marking direct versus indirect speech as presented in most grammar textbooks. The key to understanding in this case is recognizing that a dramatic scenario has been created with characters who have assigned roles and lines of dialogue within the scenario.

A summary of these new quotatives, or constructed dialogue introducers, is presented in Box 10.4.

Summary Box 10.4 **New quotatives in English**

Quotatives	Examples
be	*You're just, ' Well, this is it.'*
	the other guy's, 'Oh I'm always sad'
be like	*I was like, 'Ahh—what are those?'*
	he's like, 'I just blah blah blah …'
go	*they're just going, ' Yeah this is okay.'*
	I start to go, ' Whaaaa!'
zero	*and eh so ø ' Did you all have a good time?*
	ø 'yeah.'

This development of new quotative forms in contemporary spoken English is an ongoing process. As shown in [35], yet another quotative (*be all*) can occasionally be found in spoken American English when a previous language event is being reported.

[35] Sarah was trying to get him to stop doing drugs and *he was all,* 'Hey, that's me—that's me—okay?'

No doubt other forms will emerge in this very open area of the grammar of the contemporary language.

Exercise 10.E

The following transcripts (from tape-recordings) are presented without punctuation. Underline the quotative frames (also marking the position of any zero quotatives with ø). Add punctuation, including quotation marks around what is presented as constructed dialogue (there is only one reporting speaker in each case).

(a) and she was like oh I was just wonderin if you wanted to see a movie or something and I was like umm well really I can't tonight and she—and I said well I'll call you some other time and she's like yeah right and I'm like don't start it

(b) what do I tell them well I was sitting in this bar and this band's playing and I'm just sitting there and my dad's looking at me like yeah right eh mom goes ah see anyone you know there no thank god

---

It is clear from the preceding discussion that direct speech is used for more functions than simply reporting the words that were said. It can be used to make a story more dramatic, even when some of the talking participants are caterpillars and dogs. It can be used to present people as speaking in ways that reveal in their reported words what they are really like or or how they really think (according to the reporter). It can be used to represent attitudes, evaluations, feelings, and reactions, as if they had been expressed. It can be used to present imagined interactions as if they had taken place. It can even be used by speakers jointly to invent conversations that they would find entertaining. There are no doubt other functions to be explored. Most of these uses are not recognized in a grammar of English that simply asks, 'What is direct speech?' They are revealed in a grammar that also asks, 'What is direct speech for?' and goes on to seek explanations in the everyday discourse of English language users.

Discussion topics and projects

1   In the following extract, the writer (Street 1997) has used a number of speech reporting formats. Can you identify all the reported speech formats used and mark where punctuation, especially quotation marks, would make the different spoken elements clearer? (It helps to read it out loud.)

> The time was easy to spend. There were a lot of beaches. There were a lot of beach things to do. I lay on the grass between the palm trees and the banyan trees near the beach. I lay on the mat that I'd just bought, plugged my earphones into the radio and acted as if I went there all the time. I didn't talk first. She was standing beside me. I took the earphones off and sat up. I'm sorry I didn't hear you. She said that my dog had taken her hat. I think I said that I didn't understand. She didn't actually say dog. What she said was more like duck, and she also said had. It was like she was trading close sounds for sounds that should have been there. Why don't you tie him up? Again it was like don't chew, not you. I started to think chew what, but then I got it. I don't have a dog. So whose dog is it? What dog? It was brown and small and you can't have dogs here you know. I don't have a dog. Where you from? The mainland. That would prove it couldn't be my dog. Huh, you a tourist. No, I'm working here. I said that really fast and started to wonder why. Where? At the university. Really fast again. So why you bring your dog here? I don't have a dog. But I had started saying, to be like her, that I didn't have a duck. She turned her head away. She had a small mark at the top of her cheek. She turned and ran off towards the road. She was wearing a black one-piece bathing suit. Mostly women wore bikinis there. She was easy to follow. She went up to a van parked at the edge of the road, with a crowd of people putting beach things in it. She talked to them. I looked away towards the sea. When I looked

back she was coming towards me with a hat on. I'm sorry mister professor, it wasn't your duck. She walked past me.

2   It may be possible to make useful distinctions between the different verbs that are used to report previous talk. Some verbs are always used to summarize (*We* talked *about the problem*); some are mainly used in reporting indirect speech with a *that-* clause (*She* mentioned *that you weren't feeling well*) or with a *to-* infinitive (*He* offered *to help us*); and some are mainly found with direct speech (*What's up?* he shouted).

(a) Using these four categories (or more, if necessary), can you decide how the verbs in the following list are typically used?

answer	communicate	discourage	refer
argue	complain	gossip	remind
blame	congratulate	instruct	tell
call	converse	mention	thank
claim	cry	name	warn

(b) What other elements (e.g. reference to the recipient, prepositions such as *about*, preferred position before or after the reported talk) have to be included in the description of how these verbs are used?

3   In the following extract from the story *Rope* (Porter 1958: 52), there is a continuation of the argument between the couple which was presented earlier as extract [18]. First, try to identify which character, the man or the woman, is the speaker of each of the sentences in the extract. Then, identify those features in the text that are characteristic of indirect speech reports and those that are more typically associated with direct speech. Finally, if this interaction was to be changed into a script for a play, how could the text be rewritten as lines of direct speech dialogue?

It appeared to him that this was going a little far. Just a touch out of bounds, if she didn't mind his saying so. Why the hell had he stayed in town the summer before? To do a half-dozen jobs to get the money he had sent her. That was it. She knew perfectly well they couldn't have done it otherwise. She had agreed with him at the time. And that was the only time so help him he had ever left her to do anything by herself.

Oh, he could tell that to his great-grandmother. She had her notion of what had kept him in town. Considerably more than a notion, if he wanted to know. So, she was going to bring all that up again, was she? Well, she could just think what she pleased. He was tired of explaining. It may have looked funny but he had simply got hooked in, and what could he do? It was impossible to believe she was going to take it seriously. Yes, yes, she knew how it was with a man: if he was left by himself a minute, some woman was certain to kidnap him. And, naturally he couldn't hurt her feelings by refusing!

4   It was suggested in this chapter that the use of direct speech is often not the reported quotation of actual speech. The exact words reported may never have been said. In fact, there may be clues in spoken English discourse that the direct speech being reported was not uttered (at least not exactly in that form).

(a)   Look at the following extracts and try to decide which ones are definitely a genuine quote, which are possibly a genuine quote, and which are definitely not a genuine quote.

(i)   Last week the people in my office were saying, 'You're as thin as a rake. You're not eating enough!'

(ii)   Why didn't someone tell me, 'Okay, it's normal for people to work very hard and get nowhere'?

(iii)   Every time I ask him he says, 'No way, no, no, no, absolutely not!'

(iv)   We'd try to follow his lectures but we'd be saying to each other, 'What is this? What's he talking about?'

(v)   Cathy said, 'Take the first left and go through three traffic lights' or something like that.

(vi)   He's usually whining, 'I'm so tired, I can't do anything.' You know, that kind of stuff.

(vii)   So I figured, 'Who cares?' and just went ahead.

(viii)   She's so arrogant—she's all, 'I'm on top of this, I'm number one, I can do it best, me, me, me!'

(ix)   Kalani was asking about various people, 'Where does so and so live? Is she married?' Things like that.

(x)   We're going up this awful hill and the car's groaning, 'Oh, no, I can't make it, please stop, I'm gonna die.'

(xi)   They're like, 'Well we'd have to like mail it to you and blah blah blah.'

(b)   What evidence would you offer in support of your claim that some examples are not genuine quotes?

(c)   We normally assume that people are responsible for the truth and accuracy of what they say. What explanation would you offer for a speaker reporting as direct speech something that was not a genuine quote? (For help with this question, read Dubois (1989), Chapter 4 of Tannen (1989), Mayes (1990), Overstreet and Yule (1997), or Overstreet (1998).)

Teaching ideas

1 Catching up on their news

A common context for reporting speech is when one person tells another about a recent meeting with one or more people they both know, catching up on their news. A classroom exercise based on this scenario can be created with direct speech quotes from one or two speakers, as exemplified below. The students' task is to report what was said. A photograph of the speaker(s), as shown here, seems to bring this activity to life and encourages students to create their own quotes (often with their own photographs). In this illustration, you have to report to your friend (Mary) what Cathy and John told you (e.g. *Cathy said that she was working in the health clinic*). This can be a spoken or written exercise.

> (Cathy)
> I'm working in the health clinic.
> It's an easy job.
> But I get kinda bored.
> Are you working?

> (John)
> I'm studying German.
> I just started.
> I'll try Chinese next.
> What's up with you?

> (Cathy and John)
> We like our new apartment.
> We don't go out much.
> Where are you living?
> Let's get together sometime.

2 What did she say?

Different scenarios can be created for immediate speech reports where the pronouns have to be changed, but there may be no need for backshifted tenses.

(a) If necessary, provide students with some examples, using the structural frames: *She said that ...* or *She claimed that ...*

For the exercise, each student has to write down one sentence (or more) about themselves. Call on one student (at a time) to read out his or her sentence, then ask another student, 'What did (s)he say?' to elicit an immediate speech report.

If the basic structure is learned quickly, the students can be encouraged to make more entertaining or outrageous claims, as in this sequence: *'I'm going to be rich and famous.' 'What did he say?' 'He said that he's going to be rich and famous.'*

(b) The same basic sequence can be practiced if each student at the back of the group has to write down one numbered statement from a list that is read aloud (by the teacher or another student) to those at the front. After hearing the statement, but before writing it, the student at the back has to ask another at the front for help (*What did (s)he say?*).

3 Didn't you tell me that he was stupid?

Elicit from students (or introduce) some adjectives with opposite meanings (e.g. *clever–stupid, large–small, old–new*). In the exercise, one student has to describe someone or something using one of the adjectives. Then, another student has to report that the opposite had been said before. Two useful reporting structures that can be presented are: *Didn't you tell me that ... ?* or *I thought you said that ...*

Some examples to get started could be:
  (i)   My boss is clever.
 (ii)   English grammar is interesting.
(iii)   This exercise is easy.
 (iv)   I bought an expensive watch.
  (v)   These shoes are old.

4 Telephone

As described by Stephen Thewlis (1993: 437), the game of 'Telephone' organizes students into two or more teams. Student 1 (in each team) has to make a statement to student 2 very quietly. Student 2 then reports to student 3 (*He or she told me that ...*). Student 3 then tells student 4 and so on until the last student in the team receives the message. The final message is compared to the original and the most accurate report wins.

5 News reports

If they have an appropriate proficiency level, students can be encouraged to look closely at the formats for reporting speech used in newspaper and magazine articles. One task would simply be to find speech reports and identify them as summarizing, indirect or direct speech, or even as mixed structures. A follow-up exercise could involve students in creating a report in newspaper format of some recent incident, issue, or event in or around the classroom. They may be able to interview some individuals for newsworthy quotes (as in the next exercise). The following text, from an article on the issue of assisted suicide under consideration by the United States Supreme Court (Reibstein 1997: 36), contains a range of structures and could be used in class.

> Kathryn Tucker, arguing against the Washington law, told the court that the right of terminally ill people to hasten their deaths flowed out of the Constitution's protection of personal autonomy and 'bodily integrity.'

> But even justices who might favor assisted suicide as a matter of policy, like Ruth Bader Ginsburg, Anthony Kennedy and David Souter, seemed to suggest that it was too novel—and its impact too uncertain—for the court to now usurp state legislatures. 'Maybe the court should wait until it could know more', said Souter, who wondered about potential abuses such as coerced suicides. And they seemed troubled by the prospect of spending the rest of their days trying to explain a far-reaching decision. For instance, Ginsburg asked, should non-terminally ill patients be permitted to hasten their deaths? And, Scalia asked, why shouldn't the person who faces 'terrible pain' for 10 years be allowed to choose assisted suicide? 'Surely legislators have a much greater capacity to absorb those kinds of arguments and make those decisions than we do,' said Kennedy.

> Tucker, taking the brunt of the justices' attack, argued that the court needn't worry that permitting assisted suicide would open the door to patients without terminal illnesses. The constitutional right 'ripens', she asserted, only when a patient is terminal. Tucker tried another tack that appeared to get no farther. She suggested the court should intervene because American culture is characterized by a 'denial of death' that freezes the normal political process. Replied Souter, 'That denial simply reflects the way we are.'

6 Interviews

Written reports of personal interviews represent another natural context where reported speech is regularly found. A survey-interview format is described and exemplified in Yule and Gregory (1989). There are in-class and out-of-class versions that can be varied in many ways according to local interests and circumstances.

(a) With a cassette recorder, each student has to interview three (or more) other students on their lifestyle (e.g. favorite foods, TV shows, music) or their opinions (e.g. same-sex marriage, the death penalty). The types of topics and related vocabulary can be discussed beforehand. The interviewer then has to write a report, quoting the other students appropriately, based on the recording. (Oral reports can be used too, of course.)

(b) If possible, there is first a class discussion of a topic area (e.g. *What do people/Americans/students/teachers do with their free time?*) to activate relevant vocabulary and to create some possible interview questions. It also helps to develop an introduction (e.g. *Excuse me, but could you help me with a project for my English class?*). Then, individual students use those questions to do interviews (and record them) with one or more people out of class. Based on the recordings, with appropriate reported speech formats, the interviewer has to create a written (or oral) report. In a later class meeting, individuals can present and compare their findings, even creating a group chart or report.

Note. The recordings of these interviews are a very useful resource for grammar teaching and can be used for reflecting on things said by both the student and the person interviewed. A focus on an individual student's recorded use of the second language, even for a short time, often has a powerful impact on that student's motivation and self-esteem. It may also help the teacher identify areas of the grammar that are being used more and less successfully outside the classroom.

7 Recording the minutes

Another natural context for speech reporting is the written record of what was said by whom during a meeting (i.e. the minutes of a meeting). This type of exercise can take different forms.

(a) For lower proficiency students, a tape-recorded discussion (perhaps based on a script) between the teacher and another person can be created, then played (or provided individually) to the students. Their task is to write down, following an initial example or two, what was said by whom. As a follow-up, the teacher can provide a set of statements (e.g. *The teacher said that students love homework*), each with a 'true/false' choice, to be evaluated on the basis of what was written.

(b) More advanced students can be divided into groups, with a problem-solving or decision-making task. One example: Your group is on a sinking ship near a desert island. You have a list of useful items, but only a small number (e.g. ten) can be taken. Discuss and decide. (See Yule (1997: 71–2) for other decision-making tasks.) One or two members of the group have to record (write down) who said what in the discussion. That written record can then be used to compare the decisions of the different groups.

8 Creating dialog

Recorded casual conversations in English can provide, with teacher support, excellent sources of examples to help students recognize reported (and constructed) dialog. Alternatively, a scriptwriting exercise, where dialog has to be written, represents a more creative exercise.

(a) Casual conversation between young people typically contains reports of other conversations and a range of reporting formats. Identifying those formats and transcribing them is an exercise that would help raise students' awareness of the grammatical structures involved. If it isn't possible to record such conversations, some of the extracts from this chapter (e.g. [21] to [34] and Exercise 10.E) could be presented (without punctuation) as exercises in which students have to indicate where punctuation makes the structure of the dialogue clearer.

(b) The two extended extracts in Discussion topics 1 and 3 of this chapter could be presented to students as a rewriting task. Their task, in groups, is to rewrite the texts in a form that could be used as a script for a play or a TV show.

Further reading

General reference, with examples

Thompson, G. 1994. *Reporting.* Collins Cobuild English Guides 5. London: HarperCollins.
Thomson, A. and A. Martinet. 1986. *A Practical English Grammar.* (4th edn). Chapter 31. Oxford: Oxford University Press.

More theoretical discussions

Clark, H. and R. Gerrig. 1990. 'Quotations as demonstrations.' *Language* 66: 764–805.
Coulmas, F. (ed.) 1986. *Direct and Indirect Speech.* Berlin: Mouton.
Lucy, J. (ed.) 1993. *Reflexive Language.* Cambridge: Cambridge University Press.
Thompson, G. 1996. 'Voices in the text: discourse perspectives on language reports.' *Applied Linguistics* 17: 501–30.

On 'near speaker' forms

Yule, G. 1996. *Pragmatics.* Chapter 2. Oxford: Oxford University Press.

Reporting verbs

Dirven, R., L. Goosens, Y. Putseys, and **E. Vorlat.** 1982. *The Scene of Linguistic Action and Its Perspectivization by Speak, Talk, Say and Tell.* Amsterdam: John Benjamins.

Dixon, R. 1991. *A New Approach to English Grammar, on Semantic Principles.* Chapter 5. Oxford: Clarendon Press.

News reports

Zelizer, B. 1989. ' "Saying" as collective practice: Quoting and differential address in the news.' *Text* 9: 369–88.

Free indirect discourse

Banfield, A. 1982. *Unspeakable Sentences.* Boston: Routledge & Kegan Paul.

Rimmon-Kenan, S. 1983. *Narrative Fiction: Contemporary Poetics.* London: Methuen.

Constructed dialogue

Tannen, D. 1989. *Talking Voices.* Chapter 4. Cambridge: Cambridge University Press.

Direct speech in conversation

Holt, E. 1996. 'Reporting on talk: The use of direct reported speech in conversation.' *Research on Language and Social Interaction* 29: 219–45.

Johnstone, B. 1987. ' "He says …, so I said": Verb tense alternation and narrative depictions of authority in American English.' *Linguistics* 25: 33–52.

Mayes, P. 1990. 'Quotation in spoken English.' *Studies in Language* 14: 325–63.

New quotatives

Ferrara, K. and **B. Bell.** 1995. 'Sociolinguistic variation and discourse function of constructed dialogue introducers: The case of BE + LIKE.' *American Speech* 70: 265–90.

Mathis, T. and **G. Yule.** 1994. 'Zero quotatives.' *Discourse Processes* 18: 63–76.

Romaine, S. and **D. Lange.** 1991. 'The use of *like* as a marker of reported speech and thought: A case of grammaticalization in progress.' *American Speech* 66: 227–79.

Teaching suggestions

Burt, S. 1991. 'Word choice in indirect quotation in Japanese: Some considerations for teaching.' *International Review of Applied Linguistics* 29: 197–212.

Goodell, E. 1987. 'Integrating theory with practice: An alternative approach to reported speech in English.' *TESOL Quarterly* 21: 305–25.

Harman, I. 1990. 'Teaching indirect speech: Deixis points the way.' *ELT Journal* 44: 230–8.

GLOSSARY

ADJECTIVE: A word like *big* or *happy* that provides more information about something as in 'a *big* dog' or 'The man was *happy*'.

AFTER-PREP or AFTER-PREPOSITION: The position of an INDIRECT OBJECT when it follows a PREPOSITION as in 'Give the book to *that student*'.

AFTER-PREPOSITION RELATIVE: A type of RELATIVE CLAUSE in which the relativized element is part of a PREPOSITION PHRASE, as in 'That's the woman *to whom* we talked'.

AFTER-VERB: The position of an INDIRECT OBJECT when it follows the verb, as in 'Give *that student* the book'.

AGENT: The one who performs the action of the VERB, typically expressed as the SUBJECT, as in '*Mary* kicked the ball'. See also THEME.

ANAPHORIC: Referring to someone or something already mentioned, by using a definite NOUN PHRASE (e.g. *the man*) or a PRONOUN (e.g. *it*), as in 'I saw a woman and a man with a small dog. The *man* was carrying *it* carefully'.

ANIMATE: A term used to classify NOUNS identifying living things (e.g. *boy*, *dog*) as opposed to things or ideas (e.g. *table*, *honesty*) which are classified as NON-ANIMATE.

ANTECEDENT: (1) In its most common use, it is the word or phrase used to identify someone or something initially, which 'comes before' an ANAPHORIC expression, as in 'I saw a woman and *a man* with *a small dog*. The man was carrying it carefully.' (2) This term is also used for an initial *if*-clause in a sentence, as in '*If it's sunny*, we'll have a picnic'. See also CONSEQUENT.

ARTICLE: Forms used in NOUN PHRASES before the noun: *the* (DEFINITE ARTICLE), *a*/*an* (INDEFINITE ARTICLE) and *ø* (ZERO ARTICLE), as in 'Where's *the* coffee?'; 'I'd like *a* small coffee'; 'Do you like *ø* coffee?'

ASPECT: There are two types. (1) GRAMMATICAL ASPECT is represented by two forms of the verb: PROGRESSIVE ASPECT, conveying an internal view of an ongoing event, as in 'I am eating', and PERFECT ASPECT, conveying an external view, looking back at an event or state, as in 'I have eaten'. (2) LEXICAL ASPECT is part of the inherent meaning of a word, representing fixed STATES (e.g. 'know') or DYNAMIC situations, such as acts (e.g. 'jump'), activities (e.g. 'swim'), or processes (e.g. 'grow'). See also DURATIVE, PUNCTUAL.

ASPECTUAL VERB: A type of verb that indicates the beginning, continuing, or ending of a situation, such as *start* in 'She *started* smoking'.

BACKGROUND: See INFORMATION STRUCTURE.

BACKSHIFT: The change of forms, such as PRESENT TENSE (e.g. 'I am ill') to PAST TENSE (e.g. 'He said he *was* ill') in INDIRECT speech.

BARE INFINITIVE: See INFINITIVE.

CATAPHORIC: Introducing someone or something, by a definite NOUN PHRASE (e.g. 'the thing') or pronoun (e.g. 'She'), that is more fully identified later, as in '*She* arrived in *the thing*. Maryann had decided to drive her old truck to the wedding'.

CLASSIFYING: Referring to an entity as a member of a class or category, typically with the INDEFINITE ARTICLE, as in 'That's *a dog*, not *a horse*'.

COLLECTIVE NOUN: A kind of noun used to refer to a group as a single unit, as in 'That *crowd* is demonstrating against the *government*'.

COMMITMENT VERB: A type of VERB that indicates some form of commitment to future action, such as *decide* in 'She *decided* to leave'.

COMMON NOUN: See PROPER NOUN.

COMPLEMENT: A phrase or clause following a verb that can be FINITE, as in 'I know *that he is a dancer*', or NON-FINITE, either an INFINITIVE, as in 'He loves *to dance*,' or a GERUND, as in 'He loves *dancing*'.

COMPLEMENT VERB: A verb used in a phrase or clause functioning as a complement, such as *sing* in 'I want to *sing*'.

COMPLEX PREPOSITION: See PREPOSITION.

CONCEPTUAL DISTANCE: The amount of connection or control between one meaning element and another in the interpretation of a situation. There is more conceptual distance between the action of the verb *flew* and the object, *a plane*, in 'He flew in a plane' than in 'He flew a plane'. Conceptual distance is often expressed as LINGUISTIC DISTANCE.

CONCESSIVE CONDITIONAL: A clause beginning with *even if* or *even though* that is presented as contrary to normal expectations, as in 'He plans to drive *even if there is a storm*'.

CONDITIONAL: A type of sentence, typically containing an *if*-clause, that expresses one situation as a condition for the occurrence of another situation, as in '*If it's sunny, we'll have a picnic*'.

CONJUNCTION: A word used to join clauses or words in the same clause, e.g. *and, because, if*.

CONSEQUENT: The MAIN CLAUSE that is used with a ANTECEDENT clause in a CONDITIONAL, as in 'If it's sunny, *we'll have a picnic*'.

CONSTRUCTED DIALOGUE: Reporting thoughts, attitudes, and talk in DIRECT SPEECH as if they were the exact words spoken.

CORE ELEMENT: One of the main parts of an event (AGENT, ACTION, THEME) as expressed by SUBJECT, VERB, and OBJECT, in contrast to PERIPHERAL ELEMENT.

COUNTABLE: An entity treated as one unit (singular) or several units (plural) of its kind, as in *a bag* of *apples*. In contrast an entity is treated as NON-COUNTABLE (or MASS) when it is neither a single unit nor several units of its kind (e.g. *salt, information*).

COUNTABLE CONTEXT: A term used to describe a context in which something, expressed by a NOUN or NOUN PHRASE, is treated as having one or more units, such as *coffee* and *tea* in 'I'd like a *coffee* and two *teas*, please'. In contrast, NON-COUNTABLE CONTEXT describes a context in which something is treated as not having one or more units, such as *coffee* and *tea* in 'I hate *coffee*, but I like *tea*'.

COUNTERFACTUAL CONDITIONAL: A type of sentence, typically with an *if-*clause, expressing something that is not true, or 'contrary to fact', as in '*If we had lived in the 18th century …*'.

DEFINITE ARTICLE: See ARTICLE.

DESCRIPTIVE: An approach to grammar that is based on observed use of forms, and their frequency, in the language, in contrast to PRESCRIPTIVE.

DIRECT OBJECT: The NOUN PHRASE representing the entity directly affected by the action of the VERB, as in 'Mary kicked *the ball*'. It is usually simply called the OBJECT. See INDIRECT OBJECT.

DIRECT SPEECH: A type of reported speech, typically in quotation marks, that represents the exact words used, as in 'She said, "*I'm ill*" '. See INDIRECT SPEECH.

DURATIVE: A type of LEXICAL ASPECT that includes activities ('run', 'write') and processes ('grow', 'harden') that take place over time, in contrast to PUNCTUAL.

DYNAMIC: A type of LEXICAL ASPECT that signals action or change, in contrast to STATIVE.

END-WEIGHT: The tendency to place longer chunks of information at the end of a sentence.

EPISTEMIC MODALITY: The use of MODAL VERBS (e.g. *may, must*) to express what is known, as in deductions or conclusions, such as '*She must be ill*', in contrast to ROOT MODALITY.

EXCEPTIONAL CONDITIONAL: A type of clause introduced by *only if, if only, unless, even if,* or *even though* that indicates some kind of special circumstance.

EXPERIENCER: The one, expressed by a NOUN PHRASE, who is affected by an emotion, as in '*the student* who is bored'.

EXTERNAL NEGATION: See NEGATION.

FACTUAL: Established as being the case, either in the present or the past, in contrast to what has not happened yet. See NON-FACTUAL.

FACTUAL CONDITIONAL: A type of sentence in which one clause, typically introduced by *if*, combines with a MAIN CLAUSE in the same TENSE to express a relationship between two situations as normally being true, as in '*If you heat ice, it melts*'.

FINAL *if*-CLAUSE: A clause introduced by *if* that is placed at the end of a sentence, as in 'I'll try again later *if I have time*'.

FINITE: Any form of a verb that is marked for tense, either past (e.g. *went*) or present (e.g. *goes*), in contrast to NON-FINITE.

FOREGROUND: See INFORMATION STRUCTURE.

FREE INDIRECT DISCOURSE: A form of reporting speech and thought, mostly in narrative, that combines certain elements of DIRECT SPEECH and INDIRECT SPEECH.

FRONTED: Describing a preposition placed at the beginning of a clause, typically before a RELATIVE PRONOUN, as in 'That's the woman *to* whom we talked'. See STRANDED.

FUNCTIONAL DESCRIPTION: Describing what grammatical forms are used for, as when we say that a verb is used to denote actions and states. See STRUCTURAL DESCRIPTION.

GERUND: The *-ing* form of a VERB, used as a NOUN to refer to actions and events, as in 'We like *dancing*'.

GIVEN INFORMATION: Information that the speaker or writer treats as currently known to the listener or reader, usually signaled by the use of DEFINITE ARTICLES and PRONOUNS, in contrast to NEW INFORMATION.

GRAMMATICAL ASPECT: See ASPECT.

GRAMMATICAL PREPOSITION: See PREPOSITION.

GROUNDING: The use of already known information, typically in a RELATIVE CLAUSE, to express what is shared as 'common ground', as in 'The teacher *that I told you about* is leaving'.

HEDGE: A cautious note about how a statement is to be treated, for example, when a CONDITIONAL is added to a request, as in 'It's time to pay, *if you haven't done so already*'.

HISTORICAL PRESENT: The use of PRESENT TENSE in describing past events, typically in stories, as a way of making them more vivid.

HUMAN: A term used to classify nouns identifying people in contrast to all other entities, which are classified as NON-HUMAN.

HYPOTHETICAL CONDITIONAL: A type of sentence with one clause, typically introduced by *if*, expressing a remote possibility (PAST TENSE) that is required before another event (in the MAIN CLAUSE) can occur, as in '*If I was a rich person, I would help homeless people*'.

IDENTIFYING: Referring to an entity as distinct from other members of the same category, typically with the DEFINITE ARTICLE, as in '*The left shoe*, not *the right one*'. See CLASSIFYING.

INDEFINITE ARTICLE: See ARTICLE.

INDIRECT OBJECT: The NOUN PHRASE representing the recipient of something in an act of TRANSFER, as in 'We gave the money to *Cathy*'. See DIRECT OBJECT.

INDIRECT SPEECH: Reported speech that presents what was said in a modified or BACKSHIFTED version rather than the original, as in 'She said that *she was ill*'. See DIRECT SPEECH.

INDIVIDUATION: The process of CLASSIFYING as a distinct single unit, typically via the INDEFINITE ARTICLE, as in 'I'd like *a coffee*, please'.

INFINITIVE: The basic form of the verb, either as the BARE INFINITIVE (e.g. *go*) or the TO-INFINITIVE (e.g. *to go*), as in 'Would you like *to go* with us?'

INFORMATION STRUCTURE: The organization of the message into what is already assumed to be known or GIVEN INFORMATION and what is NEW INFORMATION, or what is BACKGROUND and what is FOREGROUND.

INITIAL *if*-CLAUSE: A clause introduced by *if* that is placed at the beginning of a sentence, as in '*If I have time*, I'll try again later'.

INTERNAL NEGATION: See NEGATION.

LEXICAL ASPECT: See ASPECT.

LEXICAL PREPOSITION: See PREPOSITION.

LINGUISTIC DISTANCE: The amount of language (e.g. number of words, syllables, sounds, or letters) between one linguistic element and another.

MAIN CLAUSE: A clause that is independent of any other in a sentence. In the sentence 'I met an old man who had no teeth', the main clause is 'I met an old man'.

MAIN VERB: The verb which comes first in a verb plus complement structure, such as *like* in 'I *like* to dance'.

MASS: A term in traditional grammar for a noun that is typically used in a NON-COUNTABLE CONTEXT (e.g. *gold, knowledge*).

MODAL VERB: One of a small number of verbs that indicate the speaker's or writer's perspective or attitude about a situation being described. There are SIMPLE MODALS that consist of a single form (e.g. *can, may, must, will*) and PERIPHRASTIC MODALS that consist of two or more forms (e.g. *be able to, be going to, have to*).

NEGATION: Adding a negative element such as *not* or *n't* to the sentence in order to deny the truth of the affirmative form. In EXTERNAL NEGATION, the negative element applies to the whole expression, so that 'You *can't* smoke here' means NOT-permit-smoke. In INTERNAL NEGATION, the negative element applies only to the main verb, so that 'You *can't* be Scottish' means conclude-NOT-be Scottish.

NEGATIVE POLITENESS: Indicating an awareness of another's need to be free from imposition. See POSITIVE POLITENESS.

NEW INFORMATION: Information that the speaker or writer presents as not currently known to the listener or reader. See GIVEN INFORMATION.

NON-ANIMATE: See ANIMATE.

NON-COUNTABLE: See COUNTABLE.

NON-COUNTABLE CONTEXT: See COUNTABLE CONTEXT.

NON-FACTUAL: Not established as being the case, typically applied to future events. See FACTUAL.

NON-FINITE: Forms of the VERB such as the INFINITIVE (e.g. *to go*) or the GERUND (e.g. *going*) that are not marked for TENSE, either PAST or PRESENT, in contrast to FINITE.

NON-HUMAN: See HUMAN.

NON-REMOTE: Not distant from the situation of utterance, signaled by PRESENT TENSE forms, in contrast to REMOTE.

NON-RESTRICTIVE RELATIVE: A type of relative clause that gives extra information, usually separated by commas, as in 'My aunt Jessie, *who lives in Scotland*, still smokes Woodbines'. See RESTRICTIVE.

NON-SEPARABLE: A type of PHRASAL VERB in which the VERB and PARTICLE cannot be separated by an OBJECT, as in 'I *ran into* an old friend'. See SEPARABLE.

NOUN: A word used to refer to people, objects, creatures, places, qualities, and abstract ideas as if they were all things.

NOUN PHRASE: A structure containing a PRONOUN or a NOUN, typically functioning as a SUBJECT or OBJECT, which may also contain an ARTICLE (e.g. *a dog*) or an ADJECTIVE (e.g. *a big dog*) and other modifiers with the noun.

OBJECT: See DIRECT OBJECT.

OBJECT RELATIVE: A type of RELATIVE CLAUSE in which the relativized element is the DIRECT OBJECT, as in 'Isn't that the woman *whom* you met?'

OTHER-DIRECTED: A structure found with COMMITMENT VERBS where the OBJECT is different from the subject, as in '*He* ordered *me* to go'. See SELF-DIRECTED.

PARENTHETICAL CONDITIONAL: A CONCESSIVE CONDITIONAL clause marked off by commas, dashes, or brackets, as in 'Her new boyfriend, *even if he is rich*, is not good for her'.

PARTICLE: An adverb or PREPOSITION used as part of a PHRASAL VERB, as in 'give *in*', 'get *off*', or 'look *up*.'

PAST TENSE: See TENSE.

PERFECT ASPECT: See ASPECT.

PERIPHERAL ELEMENT: A non-central part of an event, such as where, when, or how something happened, often presented in a PREPOSITION PHRASE, as in 'We ate dinner *at five o'clock in the small café*'. See CORE ELEMENT.

PERIPHRASTIC MODAL: See MODAL VERB.

PHRASAL VERB: A VERB plus PARTICLE combination functioning as a single unit of meaning, as in '*get up*', '*go away*' or '*take off*'.

POSITIVE POLITENESS: Indicating similarity and having things in common with another. See NEGATIVE POLITENESS.

POSSESSIVE RELATIVE: A type of RELATIVE CLAUSE introduced by *whose* (or sometimes *of which*), as in 'He's the guy *whose car was stolen*'.

POST-MODIFYING: A phrase or clause that comes after a noun and makes its reference more specific, as in 'the person *who made this mess*'.

PREDICTIVE CONDITIONAL: A type of sentence in which one clause, typically introduced by *if*, expresses a situation as required before a possible future event, expressed in the MAIN CLAUSE, will occur, as in '*If it's sunny, we'll have a picnic*'.

PRE-MODIFYING: A word or phrase that comes before a NOUN and makes its reference more specific, as in 'the *most amazing* woman'.

PREPOSITION: A word used with a NOUN to create a phrase indicating time, place, or other circumstances. SIMPLE PREPOSITIONS are single words. The most common are one-syllable forms called GRAMMATICAL PREPOSITIONS (e.g. *at, in, on*). LEXICAL PREPOSITIONS have two or more syllables and more specific meanings (e.g. *before, behind, below*). COMPLEX PREPOSITIONS consist of two or three words (e.g. *in accordance with, for the sake of*).

PREPOSITION PHRASE: A structure consisting of a preposition and a NOUN PHRASE (e.g. *in the bed, on it*).

PREPOSITIONAL ADVERB: Another term for a PARTICLE.

PRESCRIPTIVE: An approach to grammar that is based on values concerning how the language should be used. See DESCRIPTIVE.

PRESENT TENSE: See TENSE.

PROGRESSIVE ASPECT: See ASPECT.

PRONOUN: A word such as *you, me, it,* or *them* used as a NOUN PHRASE, typically to refer to people or things already identified.

PROPER NOUN: A noun beginning with a capital letter that is typically used as the name of someone or something, e.g. *Anne, Oxford.* All other nouns, without initial capital letters, are called COMMON NOUNS.

PUNCTUAL: A type of lexical aspect that expresses isolated acts at one point in time, as in 'jump', 'kick', or 'smash'. Also called NON-DURATIVE, in contrast to DURATIVE.

QUOTATIVE: A VERB used to introduce a reported utterance, such as *say* or *be like,* as 'He forgot to call and I *was like,* "What's his problem?" '

QUOTATIVE FRAME: A structure with an attributed speaker and a verb of saying, used to introduce reported speech, as in '*He said* he was ill'.

REAL CONDITIONAL: A conditional structure that is used to refer to situations presented as possible or likely, as in '*If it rains, we won't go*'. See FACTUAL CONDITIONAL, PREDICTIVE CONDITIONAL, and UNREAL CONDITIONAL.

RELATIVE ADVERB: Forms such as *when, where,* and *why* used to introduce RELATIVE CLAUSES, as in 'I know the place *where* she stayed'.

RELATIVE CLAUSE: A type of clause that is connected to and gives more information about a noun phrase in another clause. It is often introduced by a RELATIVE PRONOUN, as in 'Did you see the person *who left this package?*'

RELATIVE PRONOUN: One of the forms (*who, whom, whose, which, that*) used to introduce a RELATIVE CLAUSE, as in 'Have you met the woman *who* teaches English?'

REMOTE: Not close to the situation of utterance, either in time or in possibility, typically expressed by PAST TENSE forms, as in 'If that *happened* to me, I *would* be so angry!' See NON-REMOTE.

REPORTING VERB: A verb such as *say* or *claim* that is used to introduce INDIRECT SPEECH, as in 'He *claimed* that he talked to God'.

RESTRICTIVE RELATIVE: The most common type of RELATIVE CLAUSE, used to make the reference of the ANTECEDENT noun phrase more specific, as in 'Isn't she the girl *that you used to like?*' See NON-RESTRICTIVE RELATIVE.

RESUMPTIVE PRONOUN: An extra PRONOUN sometimes found in an OBJECT RELATIVE, as in '*Did you enjoy the film which you saw it?*'

RETROSPECTIVE VIEW: Looking back from a point in time, typically expressed by PERFECT ASPECT, as in 'I *have been* here for a hour'.

ROOT MODALITY: The use of MODAL VERBS (e.g. *may, must*) to express what is socially determined, as in obligations and permissions, for example, 'You *must* keep quiet'. See EPISTEMIC MODALITY.

SELF-DIRECTED: A structure found with COMMITMENT VERBS where the SUBJECT is the same for both the commitment verb and the following INFINITIVE, as in 'He decided to go'. See OTHER-DIRECTED.

SENSORY-PERCEPTION VERB: Any verb that describes an experience of the senses, such as *feel, hear, see, smell.*

SENTENCE: A unit of structure beginning with a capital letter and ending with a period in writing, containing at least a SUBJECT and a VERB.

SEPARABLE: A type of PHRASAL VERB in which the verb and PARTICLE can be separated by an object, as in '*Turn* the light *off*'.

SEPARATION MARKERS: Commas, dashes, or brackets that separate a word, phrase, or clause from other parts of the sentence.

SIMPLE MODAL: See MODAL VERB.

SIMPLE PREPOSITION: See PREPOSITION.

SOURCE: The person or thing that causes an emotion, as in '*The teacher* who is boring'.

STATIVE: A type of LEXICAL ASPECT signaling that a situation is relatively constant over time, as in 'I *know* how to drive', in contrast to DYNAMIC.

STRANDED: A PREPOSITION at the end of a RELATIVE CLAUSE, as in 'He's the person that I talked *to*'. See FRONTED.

STRUCTURAL DESCRIPTION: Describing the forms and arrangements of forms in the language, without reference to meaning or communicative function. See FUNCTIONAL DESCRIPTION.

SUBJECT: A NOUN PHRASE that typically comes before the VERB in basic SENTENCE structure, as in '*He* is crazy' or '*The woman* left already'.

SUBJECT RELATIVE: A type of RELATIVE CLAUSE in which the relativized element is the SUBJECT, as in 'Did you see the man *who was here earlier?*'

SUBJUNCTIVE: A form of the verb sometimes found in a CONDITIONAL IF-CLAUSE describing an event that is known to be impossible (e.g. 'If I *were* you …').

TENSE: A form of the verb which is either PRESENT TENSE, mostly using the basic VERB form and -*s* in third person singular forms, as in 'She *lives* here now', or PAST TENSE, with -*ed* or other variations on the basic verb form, as in 'She *lived* there then'. Past tense is used to indicate that a situation is more REMOTE in some way than a situation represented by present tense.

THEME: The person or thing affected by the action of the VERB, typically expressed by the DIRECT OBJECT, as in 'Mary kicked *the ball*'. See AGENT.

to-INFINITIVE: See INFINITIVE.

TRANSFER: This is the basic meaning expressed by INDIRECT OBJECT constructions, indicating the movement (*sent*) of something (*a letter*) from a source (*the woman*) to a goal (*her lover*), as in 'The woman sent a letter to her lover'.

TRUNCATED FORM: A short form of a structure, as in a CONDITIONAL CLAUSE reduced to '*If so*', '*If you do*', or '*If not*'.

UNGRAMMATICAL (*): Describes a structure that is not acceptable, not generally used, and for which no acceptable context of use can be imagined.

UNREAL CONDITIONAL: A conditional structure that is used to refer to situations presented as extremely unlikely or impossible, as in '*If I had three hands, I could work faster.*' See COUNTERFACTUAL CONDITIONAL, HYPOTHETICAL CONDITIONAL, and REAL CONDITIONAL.

VERB: A word that is the central element of a clause, indicating actions and states, and which can be FINITE (e.g. *wants, wanted*) or NON-FINITE (e.g. *to go*), as in 'He *wants* ice-cream', with one verb, or 'I *wanted to go* to bed', with two verbs.

ZERO ARTICLE: The absence of any ARTICLE (i.e. *a, an, the*) in a NOUN PHRASE, as in 'We go to ø school by ø bus'.

ZERO FORM: The absence of an element in a structure where one is highly predictable, for example, when the SUBJECT is the same for two VERBS in sequence, as in 'They stop and ø chat'.

ZERO QUOTATIVE: The absence of a QUOTATIVE FRAME (e.g. *he said*) in front of a DIRECT SPEECH report, as in 'I got home late last night and he was waiting. ø "Where have you been?" ø "Oh, nowhere special." '

ZERO RELATIVE: A RELATIVE CLAUSE without an initial RELATIVE PRONOUN, as in 'He's the guy ø I talked to'.

BİBLIOGRAPHY

Aarts, F. 1994. 'Relative *who* and *whom*: Prescriptive rules and linguistic reality.' *American Speech* 69: 71–9.

Aitken, R. 1992. *Teaching Tenses.* Walton-on-Thames: Thomas Nelson.

Akatsuka, N. 1985. 'Conditionals and the epistemic scale.' *Language* 61: 625–39.

Akatsuka, N. 1986. 'Conditionals are discourse-bound' in E. Traugott et al. pp. 333–51.

Akiyama, M. and **N. Williams.** 1996. 'Spatial components in the use of count nouns among English speakers and Japanese speakers of English as a second language.' *Language Learning* 46: 217–31.

Alexander, L. 1988. *Longman English Grammar.* London: Longman.

Algeo, J. 1995. 'Having a look at the expanded predicate' in B. Aarts and C. Meyer (eds.): *The Verb in Contemporary English: Theory and Practice.* Cambridge: Cambridge University Press. pp. 203–17.

Allan, K. 1980. 'Nouns and countability.' *Language* 56: 541–67.

Andersen, R. 1991. 'Developmental sequences: The emergence of aspect marking in second language acquisition' in T. Huebner and C. Ferguson (eds.): *Cross-currents in Second Language Acquisition.* Amsterdam: John Benjamins. pp. 305–24.

Asher, J. 1977. *Learning Another Language through Actions.* Los Gatos, Calif.: Sky Oaks Publications.

Azar, B. 1993. *Chartbook. A Reference Grammar.* Englewood Cliffs, NJ: Prentice Hall Regents.

Badalamenti, V. and **C. Henner-Stanchina.** 1993. *Grammar Dimensions.* Book One. Boston, Mass.: Heinle & Heinle.

Bailey, N. 1989. 'Discourse conditioned tense variation: Teacher implications' in: M. Eisenstein (ed.): *The Dynamic Interlanguage.* New York: Plenum Press. pp. 279–95.

Ball, C. 1996. 'A diachronic study of relative markers in spoken and written English.' *Language Variation and Change* 8: 227–58.

Banfield, A. 1982. *Unspeakable Sentences.* Boston, Mass. : Routledge & Kegan Paul.

Bardovi-Harlig, K. and **D. Reynolds.** 1995. 'The role of lexical aspect in the acquisition of tense and grammatical aspect.' *TESOL Quarterly* 29: 107–31.

Barnes, G. 1991. *The International Student's Guide to the American University.* Lincolnwood, Ill.: National Textbook Company.

Batstone, R. 1994. *Grammar.* Oxford: Oxford University Press.

Beardsley, T. 1992. 'Paradise lost?' *Scientific American* 267 (no. 5, November): 18–20.

Bennett, D. 1975. *Spatial and Temporal Uses of English Prepositions.* London: Longman.

Berry, R. 1991. 'Re-articulating the articles.' *ELT Journal* 45: 252–59.

Berry, R. 1993. *Articles.* London: HarperCollins.

Biesenbach-Lucas, S. 1986. 'The use of relative markers in modern American English' in K. Denning, S. Inkelas, F. McNair-Knox and J. Rickford (eds.): *Variation in Language. NWAV-XV at Stanford.* Stanford, Calif.: Stanford University Press. pp. 13–21.

Binnick, R. 1971. 'Will and be going to.' *Papers from the 7th Regional Meeting of the Chicago Linguistic Society.* Chicago: Chicago Linguistic Society. pp. 40–51.

Bley-Vroman, R. and **N. Yoshinaga.** 1992. 'Broad and narrow constraints on the English dative alternation.' *University of Hawai'i Working Papers in ESL* 11: 157–99.

Bolinger, D. 1968. 'Entailment and the meaning of structures.' *Glossa* 2: 119–27.

Bolinger, D. 1971. *The Phrasal Verb in English.* Cambridge, Mass.: Harvard University Press.

Bolinger, D. 1977. *Meaning and Form.* London: Longman.

Bolinger, D. 1979. 'The jingle theory of double -*ing*' in D. Allerton, E. Carney, and D. Holdcroft (eds.): *Function and Context in Linguistics Analysis.* Cambridge: Cambridge University Press. pp. 41–56.

Bolinger, D. 1989. 'Extrinsic possibility and intrinsic potentiality: 7 on MAY and CAN + 1.' *Journal of Pragmatics* 13: 1–23.

Bond, D. (ed.) 1965. *The Spectator.* Oxford: Clarendon Press.

Bowerman, M. 1986. 'First steps in acquiring conditionals' in Traugott et al. (eds.). pp. 285–307.

Brinton, L. 1988. *The Development of English Aspectual Systems.* Cambridge: Cambridge University Press.

Brown, G. and **G. Yule.** 1983a. *Discourse Analysis.* Cambridge: Cambridge University Press.

Brown, G. and **G. Yule.** 1983b. *Teaching the Spoken Language.* Cambridge: Cambridge University Press.

Brown, J. 1988. *Understanding Research in Second Language Learning.* Cambridge: Cambridge University Press.

Brown, P. and **S. Levinson.** 1987. *Politeness.* Cambridge: Cambridge University Press.

Buczowska, E. and **R. Weist.** 1991. 'The effects of formal instruction on the second language acquisition of temporal location.' *Language Learning* 41: 535–54.

Burt, S. 1991. 'Word choice in indirect quotation in Japanese: Some considerations for teaching.' *International Review of Applied Linguistics* 29: 197–212.

Bybee, J. 1985. *Morphology.* Amsterdam: John Benjamins.

Bybee, J. and **S. Fleischman** (eds.). 1995. *Modality in Grammar and Discourse.* Amsterdam: John Benjamins.

Byrnes, J. 1991. 'Acquisition and development of *if* and *because*: Conceptual and linguistic aspects' in S. Gelman and J. Byrnes (eds.): *Perspectives on Language and Thought.* Cambridge: Cambridge University Press. pp. 354–93.

Caputo, P. 1991. 'My last war.' *Esquire* 116 (no. 4, October): 161–66.

Carroll, S. and **M. Swain.** 1993. 'Explicit and implicit negative feedback: An empirical study of the learning of linguistic generalizations.' *Studies in Second Language Acquisition* 15: 357–86.

Celce-Murcia, M. and **S. Hilles.** 1988. *Techniques and Resources in Teaching Grammar.* Oxford: Oxford University Press.

Celce-Murcia, M. and **D. Larsen-Freeman.** 1983. *The Grammar Book.* Rowley, Mass.: Newbury House.

Chalker, S. and **E. Weiner.** 1994. *The Oxford Dictionary of English Grammar.* Oxford: Oxford University Press.

Cheever, J. 1982. *The Stories of John Cheever.* Harmondsworth: Penguin Books.

Chen, P. 1986. 'Discourse and particle movement in English.' *Studies in Language* 10: 79–95.

Chesterman, A. 1991. *On Definiteness.* Cambridge: Cambridge University Press.

Christophersen, P. 1939. *The Articles. A Study of Their Theory and Use in English.* Copenhagen: Munksgaard.

Clark, H. and **R. Gerrig.** 1990. 'Quotations as demonstrations.' *Language* 66: 764–805.

Coates, J. 1983. *The Semantics of the Modal Auxiliaries.* London: Croom Helm.

Collins, P. 1995. 'The indirect object construction in English: An informational approach.' *Linguistics* 33: 35–49.

Comrie, B. 1976. *Aspect.* Cambridge: Cambridge University Press.

Cornell, A. 1985. 'Realistic goals in teaching and learning phrasal verbs.' *International Review of Applied Linguistics* 23: 269–80.

Coulmas, F. (ed.) 1986. *Direct and Indirect Speech.* Berlin: Mouton.

Courtney, R. 1983. *Longman Dictionary of Phrasal Verbs.* London: Longman.

Cowie, A. and **R. Mackin.** 1975. *Oxford Dictionary of Current Idiomatic English. Vol. 1: Verbs with Prepositions and Particles.* Oxford: Oxford University Press.

Craig, R. and **K. Tracy** (eds.). 1983. *Conversational Coherence.* Beverly Hills, Calif.: Sage Publications.

Crowley, M. 1996. 'Nixon unplugged.' *The New Yorker.* July 29, 1996: 42–51.

Dagut, M. and **B. Laufer.** 1985. 'Avoidance of phrasal verbs: A case for contrastive analysis.' *Studies in Second Language Acquisition* 7: 73–79.

Dahl, Ö. 1985. *Tense and Aspect Systems.* Oxford: Blackwell.

DeCarrico, J. 1986. 'Tense, aspect and time in English modality.' *TESOL Quarterly* 20: 665–82.

Declerck, R. 1991. *Tense in English: Its Structure and Use in Discourse.* London: Routledge.

de Haan, P. 1989. *Postmodifying Clauses in the English Noun Phrase.* Amsterdam: Rodopi.

Dirven, R., L. Goosens, Y. Putseys, and **E. Vorlat.** 1982. *The Scene of Linguistic Action and Its Perspectivization by* speak, talk, say *and* tell. Amsterdam: Benjamins.

Dixon, R. 1982. 'The grammar of English phrasal verbs.' *Australian Journal of Linguistics* 2: 1–42.

Dixon, R. 1991. *A New Approach to English Grammar, on Semantic Principles.* Oxford: Clarendon Press.

Dörnyei, Z. and **S. Thurrell.** 1992. *Conversation and Dialogues in Action.* Hemel Hempstead: Prentice Hall.

Doughty, C. 1991. 'Second language instruction does make a difference.' *Studies in Second Language Acquisition* 13: 431–69.

Downing, P. and **P. Locke.** 1992. *A University Course in English Grammar.* Englewood Cliffs, NJ: Prentice Hall.

Dubois, B. 1989. 'Pseudoquotation in current English communication: "Hey, she really didn't say it".' *Language in Society* 18: 343–59.

Duffley, P. 1992. *The English Infinitive.* London: Longman.

Eckman, F., L. Bell, and **D. Nelson.** 1988. 'On the generalization of relative clause instruction in the acquisition of English as a second language.' *Applied Linguistics* 9: 1–11.

Erteschik-Shir, N. 1979. 'Discourse constraints on dative movement' in T. Givon (ed.): *Discourse and Syntax. Syntax and Semantics, Vol. 12.* New York: Academic Press. pp. 441–67.

Ferrara, K. and **B. Bell.** 1995. 'Sociolinguistic variation and discourse function of constructed dialogue introducers: The case of BE + LIKE.' *American Speech* 70: 265–90.

Fleischman, S. 1989. 'Temporal distance: A basic linguistic metaphor.' *Studies in Language* 13: 1–50.

Ford, C. and **S. Thompson.** 1986. 'Conditionals in discourse: A text based approach' in E. Traugott et al. (eds.). pp. 353–72.

Fotos, S. 1994. 'Integrating grammar instruction and communicative language use through grammar consciousness-raising tasks.' *TESOL Quarterly* 28: 323–51.

Fotos, S. and **R. Ellis.** 1991. 'Communicating about grammar: A task-based approach.' *TESOL Quarterly* 25: 605–28.

Fox, B. 1987. 'The noun phrase accessibility hierarchy reinterpreted: Subject primacy or the absolutive hypothesis?' *Language* 63: 856–70.

Fox, B. and **S. Thompson.** 1990. 'A discourse explanation of the grammar of relative clauses in English conversation.' *Language* 66: 297–316.

Frank, M. 1993. *Modern English.* (2nd edn.) Englewood Cliffs, NJ: Prentice-Hall.

Fraser, B. 1976. *The Verb-Particle Combination in English.* New York: Academic Press.

Frawley, W. 1992. *Linguistic Semantics.* Hillsdale, NJ: Lawrence Erlbaum.

Frazier, I. 1997. 'The positive negative.' *Atlantic Monthly* 279 (June): 24–26.

Freed, A. 1979. *The Semantics of English Aspectual Complementation.* Dordrecht: Reidel.

Garcia, C. 1992. *Dreaming in Cuban.* New York: Alfred Knopf.

Gass, S. 1980. 'An investigation of syntactic transfer in adult second language learners' in R. Scarcella and S. Krashen (eds.): *Research in Second Language Acquisition.* Rowley, Mass.: Newbury House. pp. 132–41.

Geisler, C. 1995. *Relative Infinitives in English*. Stockholm: Almqvist & Wiksell.

Gibbs, D. 1990. 'Second language acquisition of the English modal auxiliaries *can, could, may,* and *might.*' *Applied Linguistics* 11: 297–314.

Givon, T. 1984. 'Direct object and dative shifting: Semantic and pragmatic case' in F. Plank (ed.): *Objects.* New York: Academic Press. pp. 151–82.

Givon, T. 1993. *English Grammar.* Amsterdam: John Benjamins.

Goldberg, A. 1992. 'The inherent semantics of argument structure: The case of the English ditransitive construction.' *Cognitive Linguistics* 3: 37–74.

Goodell, E. 1987. 'Integrating theory with practice: An alternative approach to reported speech in English.' *TESOL Quarterly* 21: 305–25.

Green, G. 1974. *Semantics and Syntactic Regularity.* Bloomington, Ind.: Indiana University Press.

Green, P. and **K. Hecht.** 1992. 'Implicit and explicit grammar: an empirical study.' *Applied Linguistics* 13: 168–84.

Groefsema, M. 1995. '*Can, may, must* and *should*: A relevance theoretic account.' *Journal of Linguistics* 31: 53–79.

Gropen, J., S. Pinker, M. Hollander, R. Goldberg, and **R. Wilson.** 1989. 'The learnability and acquisition of the dative alternation in English.' *Language* 65: 203–57.

Gundel, J., N. Hedberg, and **R. Zacharski.** 1993. 'Cognitive status and the form of referring expressions in discourse.' *Language* 56: 515–40.

Guy, G. and **R. Bayley.** 1995. 'On the choice of relative pronouns in English.' *American Speech* 70: 148–62.

Haegeman, L. 1988. 'The categorial status of modals and L2 acquisition' in S. Flynn and W. O'Neil (eds.): *Linguistic Theory and Second Language Acquisition.* Dordrecht: Kluwer. pp. 252–76.

Haegeman, L. 1989. '*Be going to* and *will*: A pragmatic account.' *Journal of Linguistics* 25: 291–317.

Haiman, J. 1978. 'Conditionals are topics.' *Language* 54: 565–89.

Haiman, J. 1980. 'The iconicity of grammar.' *Language* 56: 515–40.

Halliday, M. and **R. Hasan.** 1976. *Cohesion in English.* London: Longman.

Harman, I. 1990. 'Teaching indirect speech: deixis points the way.' *ELT Journal* 44: 230–38.

Hatch, E. and **H. Farhady.** 1982. *Research Design and Statistics.* Rowley, Mass.: Newbury House.

Hawkins, J. 1978. *Definiteness and Indefiniteness.* London: Croom Helm.

Hemingway, E. 1987. *The Complete Short Stories of Ernest Hemingway.* New York: Charles Scribner's Sons.

Herriman, J. and **A. Seppänen.** 1996. 'What is an indirect object?' *English Studies* 77: 484–99.

Herskovitz, A. 1985. 'Semantics and pragmatics of locative expressions.' *Cognitive Science* 9: 341–78.

Hofmann, T. 1993. *Realms of Meaning.* London: Longman.

Holmes, J. 1988. 'Doubt and certainty in ESL textbooks.' *Applied Linguistics* 9: 21–44.

Holt, E. 1996. 'Reporting on talk: The use of direct reported speech in conversation.' *Research on Language and Social Interaction* 29: 219–45.

Hopper, P. 1979. 'Aspect and foregrounding in discourse' in T. Givon (ed.): *Discourse and Syntax. Syntax and Semantics, Vol. 12.* New York: Academic Press. pp. 213–41.

Hopper, P. and **Thompson, S.** 1985. 'The iconicity of the universal categories "noun" and "verb" ' in J. Haiman (ed.): *Iconicity in Syntax.* Amsterdam: John Benjamins. pp. 151–83.

Horowitz, F. 1989. 'ESL and prototype theory: Zero vs. definite article with place names.' *Internaional Review of Appied Linguistics* 27: 81–98.

Horsella, M. and **G. Sinderman.** 1992. 'Aspects of scientific discourse: Conditional argumentation.' *English for Specific Purposes* 11: 129–39.

Huckin, T. and **L. Olsen.** 1991. *Technical Writing and Professional Communication.* (2nd edn.) New York: McGraw-Hill.

Huddleston, R. 1984. *Introduction to the Grammar of English.* Cambridge: Cambridge University Press.

Huddleston, R. 1995. 'The case against a future tense in English.' *Studies in Language* 19: 399–446.

Hudson, R. 1992. 'So-called "double objects" and grammatical relations.' *Language* 68: 251–76.

Hulstijn, J. and **E. Marchena.** 1989. 'Avoidance: Grammatical or semantic causes?' *Studies in Second Language Acquisition* 11: 241–55.

Hurford, J. 1994. *Grammar: A Student's Guide.* Cambridge: Cambridge University Press.

Ijaz, I. 1986. 'Linguistic and cognitive determinants of lexical acquisition in a second language.' *Language Learning* 36: 401–52.

Isaacson, W. 1992. 'Kissinger's Web.' *Vanity Fair* (September): 224–28; 279–87.

Jackson, F. (ed.) 1991. *Conditionals.* Oxford: Oxford University Press.

Jacobs, R. 1995. *English Syntax*. Oxford: Oxford University Press.

James, C. 1981. *Unreliable Memoirs*. London: Picador.

Jespersen, O. 1940. *A Modern English Grammar. Part V*. Copenhagen: Ejnar Munksgaard.

Johansson, C. 1995. *The Relativizers* whose *and* of which *in Present-day English*. Stockholm: Almqvist & Wiksell.

Johnstone, B. 1987. ' "He says ..., so I said": Verb tense alternation and narrative depictions of authority in American English.' *Linguistics* 25: 33–52.

Jolly, J. 1991. *Prepositional Analysis within the Framework of Role and Reference Grammar*. New York: Peter Lang.

Kaluza, H. 1984. 'English verbs with prepositions and particles.' *International Review of Applied Linguistics* 22: 109–13.

Kasper, G. 1992. 'Pragmatic transfer.' *Second Language Research* 8: 203–31.

Kaufman, G. and P. Forestell. 1994. *Hawaii's Humpback Whales*. Aiea, Hawaii: Island Heritage Publishing.

Keenan, E. and B. Comrie. 1977. 'Noun phrase accessibility and universal grammar.' *Linguistic Inquiry* 8: 63–99.

Kenworthy, J. 1987. *Teaching English Pronunciation*. London: Longman.

Kikai, A., M. Schleppegrell, and S. Tagliamonte. 1986. 'The influence of syntactic position on relativization strategies' in K. Denning, S. Inkelas, F. McNair-Knox, and J. Rickford (eds.): *Variation in Language. NWAV-XV at Stanford*. Stanford, Calif.: Stanford University Press. pp. 266–77.

Kirsner, R. and S. Thompson. 1976. 'The role of pragmatic inference in semantics: A study of sensory verb complements in English.' *Glossa* 10: 200–40.

Klein, E. 1994. 'Trump family values.' *Vanity Fair* (March): 122–25; 154–59.

Klein, W. 1992. 'The present perfect puzzle.' *Language* 68: 525–52.

Konig, E. 1986. 'Conditionals, concessive conditionals and concessives: areas of contrast, overlap and neutralization' in E. Traugott et al. (eds.) pp. 229–46.

Lakoff, G. and M. Johnson. 1980. *Metaphors We Live By*. Chicago: University of Chicago Press.

Larsen-Freeman, D. and M. Long. 1991. *An Introduction to Second Language Acquisition Research*. London: Longman.

Laufer, B. and S. Eliasson. 1993. 'What causes avoidance in L2 learning?' *Studies in Second Language Acquisition* 15: 35–48.

Leather, J. and A. James. 1991. 'The acquisition of second language speech.' *Studies in Second Language Acquisition* 13: 305–41.

Le Compagnon, B. 1984. 'Interference and overgeneralization in second language learning: The acquisition of English dative verbs by native speakers of French.' *Language Learning* 34: 39–67.

Leech, G. 1987. *Meaning and the English Verb.* (2nd edn.) London: Longman.

Levinson, S. 1983. *Pragmatics.* Cambridge: Cambridge University Press.

Lewis, M. 1986. *The English Verb.* Hove, England: Language Teaching Publications.

Lindner, S. 1983. *A Lexico-Semantic Analysis of English Verb Particle Constructions with* Out *and* Up. Bloomington, Ind.: Indiana University Linguistics Club.

Lindstromberg, S. 1996. 'Prepositions: meaning and method.' *ELT Journal* 50: 225–36.

Lucy, J. (ed.) 1993. *Reflexive Language.* Cambridge: Cambridge University Press.

Lyons, J. 1977. *Semantics I and II.* Cambridge: Cambridge University Press.

Macdonald, R. 1971. *The Underground Man.* New York: Alfred Knopf.

Mair, C. 1990. *Infinitival Complements in English.* Cambridge: Cambridge University Press.

Marsh, D. 1963. *The Good Housekeeping Cookbook.* New York: Good Housekeeping Book Division.

Master, P. 1990. 'Teaching the English articles as a binary system.' *TESOL Quarterly* 24: 461–78.

Mathis, T. and **G. Yule.** 1994. 'Zero quotatives.' *Discourse Processes* 18: 63–76.

Mayes, P. 1990. 'Quotation in spoken English.' *Studies in Language* 14: 325–63.

Mazurkewich, I. 1984. 'The acquisition of the dative alternation by second language learners and linguistic theory.' *Language Learning* 34: 91–109.

Mazurkewich, I. 1988. 'The acquisition of infinitive and gerund complements by second language learners' in S. Flynn and W. O'Neil (eds.): *Linguistic Theory in Second Language Acquisition.* Dordrecht: Kluwer. pp. 127–43.

McCarthy, C. 1993. *All the Pretty Horses.* New York: Alfred Knopf.

Mead, R. and **W. Henderson.** 1983. 'Conditional form and meaning in economics text.' *The ESP Journal* 2: 139–60.

Mills, D. 1987. 'Infinitival verb complementation: Theory and usage as a basis for pedagogy.' *World Englishes* 6: 227–39.

Mittwoch, A. 1990. 'On the distribution of bare infinitive complements in English.' *Journal of Linguistics* 26: 103–31.

Montaigne, Michel de. 1965. *Michel de Montaigne. Essais. Tome II.* Edited by Pierre Michel. Paris: Editions Gallimard. Livre de Poche.

Nunan, D. 1991. *Language Teaching Methodology.* Englewood Cliffs, NJ: Prentice Hall.

Nunnally, T. 1991. 'The possessive with gerunds: What the handbooks say, and what they should say.' *American Speech* 66: 359–70.

Odlin, T. (ed.) 1994. *Perspectives on Pedagogical Grammar.* Cambridge: Cambridge University Press.

Oppenheimer, A. 1992. *Castro's Final Hour.* New York: Simon & Schuster.

Overstreet, M. 1999. *Whales, Candlelight and Stuff Like That: General Extenders in English Discourse.* Oxford: Oxford University Press.

Overstreet, M. and **G. Yule.** 1997. 'On being inexplicit and stuff in contemporary American English.' *Journal of English Linguistics* 25: 250–58.

Palmer, F. 1988. *The English Verb.* (2nd edn.) London: Longman.

Palmer, F. 1990. *Modality and the English Modals.* (2nd edn.) London: Longman.

Pavesi, M. 1986. 'Markedness, discoursal modes, and relative clause formation in a formal and an informal context.' *Studies in Second Language Acquisition* 8: 38–55.

Perkins, M. 1983. *Modal Expressions in English.* London: Frances Pinter.

Philbin, T. and **S. Ettlinger.** 1988. *The Complete Illustrated Guide to Everything Sold in Hardware Stores.* New York: Macmillan.

Pinker, S. 1989. *Learnability and Cognition.* Cambridge, Mass.: MIT Press.

Porter, K. A. 1958. *Flowering Judas and Other Stories.* New York: Modern Library.

Quirk, R. 1957. 'Relative clauses in educated spoken English.' *English Studies* 38: 97–109.

Quirk, R., S. Greenbaum, G. Leech, and **J. Svartvik.** 1972. *A Grammar of Contemporary English.* London: Longman.

Quirk, R., S. Greenbaum, G. Leech, and **J. Svartvik.** 1985. *A Comprehensive Grammar of the English Language.* London: Longman.

Ransom, E. 1986. *Complementation: Its Meanings and Forms.* Amsterdam: John Benjamins.

Reibstein, L. 1997. 'Whose right is it?' *Newsweek* (January 20, 1997): 36.

Reid, W. 1991. *Verb and Noun Number in English: A Functional Explanation.* London: Longman.

Richards, J. 1985. *The Context of Language Teaching.* Cambridge: Cambridge University Press.

Rickard, T. 1923. *Technical Writing.* (2nd edn.) New York: John Wiley.

Riddle, E. 1986. 'The meaning and discourse function of the past tense in English.' *TESOL Quarterly* 20: 267–86.

Riggenbach, H. and **V. Samuda.** 1993. *Grammar Dimensions.* Book Two. Boston, Mass.: Heinle & Heinle.

Rimmon-Kenan, S. 1983. *Narrative Fiction: Contemporary Poetics.* London: Methuen.

Robison, R. 1995. 'The aspect hypothesis revisited: a cross-sectional study of tense and aspect marking in interlanguage.' *Applied Linguistics* 16: 344–70.

Roeper, T. 1982. 'The role of universals in the acquisition of gerunds' in E. Wanner and L. Gleitman (eds.): *Language Acquisition: The State of the Art.* Cambridge: Cambridge University Press. pp. 267–87.

Romaine, S. and **D. Lange.** 1991. 'The use of *like* as a marker of reported speech and thought: A case of grammaticalization in progress.' *American Speech* 66: 227–79.

Rudanko, J. 1989. *Complementation and Case Grammar.* Albany, NY: SUNY Press.

Rush, G. 1990. *The Dictionary of Criminal Justice.* (2nd edn.) Guilford, Conn.: Dushkin Publishing Group.

Rutherford, W. 1987. *Second Language Grammar: Learning and Teaching.* London: Longman.

Sacks, O. 1986. *The Man Who Mistook His Wife for a Hat.* New York: Summit Books.

Schiffrin, D. 1981. 'Tense variation in narrative.' *Language* 57: 45–62.

Schiffrin, D. 1992. 'Anaphoric *then*: Aspectual, textual, and epistemic meaning.' *Linguistics* 30: 753–92.

Schumann, J. 1980. 'The acquisition of English relative clauses by second language learners' in R. Scarcella and S. Krashen (eds.): *Research in Second Language Acquisition.* Rowley, Mass.: Newbury House. pp. 118–31.

Schumann, J. 1986. 'Locative and directional expressions in basilang speech.' *Language Learning* 36: 277–94.

Schwenter, S. 1994. ' "Hot news" and the grammaticalization of perfects.' *Linguistics* 32: 995–1028.

Scovel, T. 1969. 'Foreign accents, language acquisition and cerebral dominance.' *Language Learning* 19: 245–53.

Scovel, T. 1974. 'I am interesting in English.' *English Language Teaching Journal* 28: 305–12.

Seinfeld, J. 1995. *SeinLanguage.* New York: Bantam Books.

Sessums, K. 1992. 'Geena's Sheen.' *Vanity Fair* (September, 1992): 203–8; 266–72.

Shi, Z. 1990. 'On the inherent aspectual properties of NPs, verbs, sentences and the decomposition of perfectivity and inchoativity.' *Word* 41: 47–67.

Shirahata, T. 1991. 'The acquisition of English infinitive and gerund complements by Japanese EFL learners.' *Annual Review of English Language Education in Japan* 2: 41–50.

Smyth, R., G. Prideaux, and **J. Hogan.** 1979. 'The effect of context on dative position.' *Lingua* 47: 27–42.

Stein, G. 1991. 'The phrasal verb type *to have a look* in modern English.' *International Review of Applied Linguistics* 19: 1–29.

Street, G. 1997. *Life's a Beach.* Unpublished manuscript.

Swales, J. 1990. *Genre Analysis.* Cambridge: Cambridge University Press.

Tanaka, S. 1987. 'The selective use of specific exemplars in second language performance: The case of the dative alternation.' *Language Learning* 37: 63–88.

Tanaka, T. 1990. 'Semantic changes of *can* and *may*: differentiation and implication.' *Journal of Linguistics* 26: 89–123.

Tannen, D. 1986. *That's Not What I Meant!* New York: William Morrow.

Tannen, D. 1989. *Talking Voices.* Cambridge: Cambridge University Press.

Tarone, E. and **B. Parrish.** 1988. 'Task-related variation in interlanguage: The case of articles.' *Language Learning* 38: 21–44.

Tarone, E. and **G. Yule.** 1989. *Focus on the Language Learner.* Oxford: Oxford University Press.

Thewlis, S. 1993. *Grammar Dimensions.* Book Three. Boston, Mass.: Heinle & Heinle.

Thomas, M. 1989. 'The acquisition of English articles by first- and second-language learners.' *Applied Psycholinguistics* 10: 335–55.

Thompson, G. 1994. *Reporting.* London: HarperCollins.

Thompson, G. 1996. 'Voices in the text: discourse perspectives on language reports.' *Applied Linguistics* 17: 501–30.

Thompson, S. and **Y. Koide.** 1987. 'Iconicity and indirect objects in English.' *Journal of Pragmatics* 11: 399–406.

Thomson, A. and **A. Martinet.** 1986. *A Practical English Grammar.* (4th edn.) Oxford: Oxford University Press.

Traugott, E. 1989. 'On the rise of epistemic meanings in English.' *Language* 65: 31–55.

Traugott, E., A. ter Meulen, J. Reilly, and **C. Ferguson.** (eds.) 1986. *On Conditionals.* Cambridge: Cambridge University Press.

Tregidgo, P. 1982. '*Must* and *may*: demand and permission.' *Lingua* 56: 75–92.

Trimble, L. 1985. *English for Science and Technology.* Cambridge: Cambridge University Press.

Ur, P. 1988. *Grammar Practice Activities.* Cambridge: Cambridge University Press.

Vendler, Z. 1967. *Linguistics in Philosophy.* Ithaca, NY: Cornell University Press.

Visser, F. 1963. *An Historical Syntax of the English Language. Part One: Syntactical Units with One Verb.* Leiden: Brill.

Wald, B. 1983. 'Referents and topic within and across discourse units: Observations from current vernacular English' in F. Klein-Andreu (ed.): *Discourse Perspectives on Syntax.* New York: Academic Press. pp. 91–116.

Walton, A. 1991. 'The semantics and pragmatics of CAN.' *Linguistische Berichte* 135: 325–45.

Westney, P. 1994. 'Rules and pedagogical grammar' in T. Odlin (ed.): *Perspectives on Pedagogical Grammar.* Cambridge: Cambridge University Press. pp. 72–96.

Wierzbicka, A. 1982. 'Why can you *Have a Drink* when you can't **Have an Eat?'* *Language* 58: 753–99.

Wierzbicka, A. 1985. 'Oats and wheat: The fallacy of arbitrariness' in J. Haiman (ed.): *Iconicity in Syntax.* Amsterdam: John Benjamins. pp. 311–42.

Wierzbicka, A. 1988. *The Semantics of Grammar.* Amsterdam: John Benjamins.

Williams, T. 1979. *Basic Home Repairs.* San Francisco, Calif.: Ortho Books.

Willis, D. 1991. *Collins COBUILD Student's Grammar.* London: HarperCollins.

Wolfe-Quintero, K. 1993. 'The dative alternation in English.' *University of Hawai'i Working Papers in ESL* 11: 91–120.

Wolfe-Quintero, K. 1998. 'The connection between verbs and argument structures: Native speaker production of the double object dative.' *Applied Psycholinguistics* 19: 225–57.

Wolfson, N. 1982. *CHP: The Conversational Historical Present in American English Narrative.* Dordrecht: Foris.

Yamashita, J. 1994. 'An analysis of relative clauses in the Lancaster/IBM spoken English corpus.' *English Studies* 75: 73–84.

Yaukey, D. 1985. *Demography.* New York: St. Martin's Press.

Yule, G. 1993. 'Vera Hayden's dilemma, or the indirection in direct speech' in M. Eid and G. Iverson (eds.): *Principles and Prediction: The Analysis of Natural Language*. Amsterdam: John Benjamins. pp. 233–42.

Yule, G. 1996. *Pragmatics*. Oxford: Oxford University Press.

Yule, G. 1997. *Referential Communication Tasks*. Hillsdale, NJ: Lawrence Erlbaum.

Yule, G. and **W. Gregory.** 1989. 'Survey interviews for interactive language learning.' *ELT Journal* 43: 142–49.

Yule, G., T. Mathis, and **M. Hopkins.** 1992. 'On reporting what was said.' *ELT Journal* 46: 245–51.

Zelinsky-Wibbelt, C. (ed.)1993. *The Semantics of Prepositions*. Berlin: Mouton de Gruyter.

Zelizer, B. 1989. ' "Saying" as collective practice: Quoting and differential address in the news.' *Text* 9: 369–88.

Ziegeler, D. 1996. 'A synchronic perspective on the grammaticalization of *will* in hypothetical predicates.' *Studies in Language* 20: 411–42.

ANSWERS TO EXERCISES

Chapter 1: Introduction

Exercise 1.A   1 annoying (they), 2 amazed (I), 3 astonished (I),
4 exhausted (teachers), 5 irritated (I), 6 worried (I), 7 interested (they),
8 thrilled (they), 9 boring (film), 10 excited (they), 11 disappointed (I)

Exercise 1.B   1 drank some milk / *drank at some milk,
2 hit the ball / hit at the ball, 3 killed a bug / *killed at a bug,
4 *pointed the picture / pointed at the picture,
5 *smile the baby / smile at the baby, 6 swat a fly / swat at a fly,
7 *yell the students / yell at the students

Exercise 1.C   1 a supermarket, another lady, a little boy, a juice, 2 Yes,
3 the lady (perhaps also 'the bottle'), 4 she, they, I, 5 Yes, 6 which ø took,
7 No, 8 from ø shelf, 9 No, 10 the first lady

Chapter 2: Articles

Exercise 2.A   1 ø (in England), 2 an (an easy thing), 3 the (the teachers),
4 the (the older students), 5 ø (full of energy), 6 a (like a teenager),
7 a (as a typist), 8 the (during the morning), 9 ø (earn money),
10 a (a hard life), 11 an (an important career)

Exercise 2.B   (a) 1 ø, 2 a, 3 ø, 4 ø, 5 a, 6 ø, 7 ø, 8 ø, 9 ø, 10 *the* or *a*

(b) For 3 and 6, you may decide that these are countable contexts for coffee
and sugar and choose *a* instead of ø. For 4, you may decide that home is a
unique referent for the speaker and put *the* instead of ø, creating an
ungrammatical sentence (but you don't want to do that, right?). For 7 and 8,
you may decide that the proper noun rule doesn't work here and use *a* in 7
and *the* in 8 (I would). For 9, you may prefer to use *the*, but this version of the
article machine doesn't seem to recognize definite plurals. For 10, if the
secretary is unique, choose *the*, but if not, choose *a*.

Exercise 2.C   (a) 1 non-countable, 2 non-countable, 3 countable,
4 countable, 5 non-countable, 6 countable, 7 non-countable,
8 non-countable, 9 non-countable, 10 countable

(b) Countable: enemy, England, gang, ticket Non-countable: cash,
equipment, garbage, patience, satisfaction, steel Both: cloth, government,
value Neither: mathematics, scissors

Exercise 2.D   1 a (store), 2 a (shopping cart), 3 a (friend), 4 a (small child), 5 the (small child), 6 a (boy), 7 a (cart), 8 the (woman), 9 the (boy), 10 a (bottle), 11 the (bottle), 12 the (woman), 13 a (mistake)

Exercise 2.E   The original text had: 1 the, 2 the, 3 the, 4 the, 5 the, 6 ø, 7 the, 8 the, 9 the, 10 a, 11 a, 12 the, 13 ø, 14 the, 15 a. (A possible text could have ø in 1 to 9, and in 14.)

Chapter 3: Tense and aspect

Exercise 3.A   1 present, 2 perfect, 3 modal, 4 past, 5 past, 6 progressive, 7 modal, 8 perfect

Exercise 3.B   (a) 1 perfect + progressive + sleep, 2 present + progressive + sleep, 3 present + work, 4 present + perfect + stay, 5 past + stay

(b) 1 have/has fallen, 2 will be talking, 3 was looking, 4 had had, 5 had been waiting

Exercise 3.C   1 Remote, non-factual, 2 Non-remote, non-factual, 3 Remote, factual, 4 Non-remote, non-factual, 5 Remote, factual, 6 Non-remote, factual, 7 Non-remote, non-factual

Exercise 3.D   1 stative, 2 durative, 3 stative, 4 durative, 5 punctual, 6 stative, 7 stative, 8 stative, 9 stative, 10 durative, 11 durative, 12 punctual, 13 punctual 14 durative, 15 stative

Exercise 3.E   1 at that time I looked back at them in an activity viewed internally as in progress, 2 at that time I view us in an activity in progress, 3 at this time I look back at a process viewed internally as in progress, 4 at this time I look back at her in an activity

Chapter 4: Modals

Exercise 4.A   Simple modals: would, should, could, might, can't. Periphrastic modals: are supposed to, be able to, has to, be allowed to, is going to

Exercise 4.B   1 Third person present singular, 2 Emphatic *do*, 3 Question *do*, 4 Progressive, 5 Negative *do*, 6 Perfect, 7 *To* infinitive

Exercise 4.C   1 epistemic necessity, 2 root necessity, 3 epistemic necessity, 4 epistemic possibility, 5 root necessity, 6 root possibility, 7 root possibility

Exercise 4.D   1 animate agent, 2 unexpressed, 3 unexpressed, 4 animate agent, 5 social authority, 6 animate agent, 7 unexpressed, 8 social authority

Exercise 4.E   1 concession, 2 weak possibility, 3 permission, 4 concession, 5 permission, 6 weak possibility, 7 permission, 8 concession

Exercise 4.F   1 conclusion, 2 conclusion, 3 obligation, 4 obligation, 5 conclusion, 6 obligation, 7 conclusion, 8 conclusion

Exercise 4.G   1 intention, 2 prediction, 3 willingness or prediction (or even both), 4 prediction, 5 willingness, 6 intention, 7 willingness, 8 intention, 9 prediction, 10 willingness

Exercise 4.H   1 willingness, 2 prediction, 3 intention, 4 prediction, 5 prediction, 6 intention, 7 willingness, 8 prediction

Exercise 4.I   1 obligation, 2 obligation, 3 probability, 4 probability, 5 obligation, 6 obligation, 7 probability, 8 obligation

Exercise 4.J   1 possible (NOT run), 2 oblige (NOT bet), 3 NOT oblige (listen), 4 oblige (NOT bet), 5 NOT permit (tell), 6 NOT willing (tell), 7 NOT possible (be much good), 8 concede (NOT be the best)

Chapter 5: Conditionals

Exercise 5.A   1 factual, 2 hypothetical, 3 predictive, 4 hypothetical, 5 counterfactual, 6 counterfactual, 7 predictive

Exercise 5.B   (a) 1 typical pattern, 2 typical pattern, 3 predictable consequence, 4 point in a procedure, 5 point in a procedure, 6 real possibility, 7 instruction, 8 instruction

(b) 1 alternative past, 2 imaginary future, 3 imaginary future, 4 alternative past, 5 imaginary future, 6 imaginary future, 7 imaginary future, 8 alternative past

Exercise 5.C
1 if they are provided (contrast); if the listener is told (give example)
2 given this view (restate)
3 If you are currently teaching (list alternatives); If not (list alternatives, plus contrast); If this is not practicable (list alternatives, plus contrast)
4 If language were totally predictable (give example); if I know in advance (restate); If language were totally unpredictable (give example).

Exercise 5.D   (a) 1 If you could … , 2 If you're not too busy … , 3 If it's okay with you
(b) 1 I wonder if you could …, 2 I don't know if you can … or not, 3 I was going to ask if you could …

Chapter 6: Prepositions and particles

Exercise 6.A   1 preposition, 2 preposition, 3 preposition, 4 particle,
5 particle, 6 particle, 7 preposition, 8 preposition, 9 particle, 10 particle,
11 preposition, 12 particle, 13 preposition, 14 particle, 15 preposition,
16 preposition, 17 preposition, 18 preposition, 19 preposition, 20 particle

Exercise 6.B   1 for (grammatical), 2 of (lexical), 3 with(grammatical),
4 for (grammatical), 5 of (grammatical), 6 with (grammatical),
7 to (grammatical), 8 under (lexical), 9 in case of (complex),
10 of (grammatical), 11 during (lexical), 12 at (grammatical)

Exercise 6.C   1 at (point), 2 to (point), 3 onto (surface), 4 up (surface),
5 to (point), 6 into (area), 7 from (point), 8 past (point), 9 across (surface),
10 on (surface), 11 at (point), 12 in (area), 13 out of (area), 14 to (point),
15 along (surface), 16 to (point), 17 on (surface)

Exercise 6.D   1 on (unit), 2 from (point), 3 to (point), 4 in (period),
5 at (point), 6 from (point), 7 to (point), 8 at (point), 9 on (unit),
10 in (period), 11 at (point), 12 at (point), 13 on (unit), 14 on (unit),
15 in (period), 16 in (period), 17 during (period), 18 at (point),
19 in (period), 20 on (unit)

Exercise 6.E   1 emotion, 2 vision, 3 discussion, 4 emotion, 5 vision,
6 discussion, 7 emotion, 8 words

Exercise 6.F   1 type 2, 2 type 3, 3 type 1, 4 type 3, 5 type 4, 6 type 1,
7 type 2, 8 type 4, 9 type 3, 10 type 2, 11 type 1, 12 type 4, 13 type 1,
14 type 3, 15 type 2, 16 type 4

Exercise 6.G   1 increase in visibility, 2 decrease in activity,
3 increase in level, 4 decrease in level, 5 increase in activity,
6 decrease in level, 7 completion, 8 decrease in level, 9 completion,
10 increase in activity

Exercise 6.H   1 unrestrained action, 2 completion, 3 removal,
4 continuation, 5 disconnection, 6 continuation, 7 removal, 8 completion,
9 continuation, 10 disconnection

Exercise 6.I   1 b, 2 a, 3 a, 4 b, 5 b, 6 a, 7 a, 8 a, 9 b, 10 a

Chapter 7: Indirect objects

Exercise 7.A   1 a, 2 a, 3 both, 4 both, 5 a, 6 both, 7 b, 8 a, 9 a, 10 both

Exercise 7.B   1 show, 2 (both), 3 throw, 4 offer, 5 (both),
6 (both), 7 (neither), 8 teach, 9 (both), 10 (both)

Exercise 7.C   (a) 1 one group, 2 (none), 3 anyone, 4 (none), 5 us,
6 a friend, 7 me, 8 (none)
(b) 2 physical, 4 physical, 8 physical

Exercise 7.D   1 (none), 2 denied, 3 (none), 4 (none), 5 (none), 6 refused,
7 (none), 8 forgave

Exercise 7.E   (a) 1 (none), 2 (none), 3 me, 4 your father, 5 us, 6 (none),
7 everyone 8 (none)
(b) 1 museums, 2 dog, 6 hospital, 8 plants

Exercise 7.F   (a) 1 <u>me</u> (some mustard),
2 (letters) <u>everyone in the government</u>,
3 <u>Mrs Weir</u> (an old faded photograph of his son),
4 (a note) <u>one of the guards</u>, 5 <u>you</u> (a car)
(b) 1   1   3   -
    2   -   2   8
    3   3   10   -
    4   -   2   4
    5   1   2   -
The indirect objects which come after the direct objects contain more
syllables.

Chapter 8: Infinitives and gerunds

Exercise 8.A   1 He loved to make (NP V *to*-V),
2 He persuaded his lawyer to include (NP V NP-object *to*-V),
3 Try to revive (V *to*-V), 4 he liked to take … off (NP V *to*-V),
5 People … heard him talking (NP V NP-object V *-ing*),
6 she didn't like his singing (NP V NP-poss V *-ing*),
7 She didn't want to go (NP V *to*-V),
8 He had mentioned retiring (NP V V *-ing*),
9 she had encouraged him to do (NP V NP-obj *to*-V),
10 He didn't stop working (NP V V *-ing*),
11 he decided to hang up (NP V *to*-V)

Exercise 8.B   1 delay (V *-ing*), 2 tempt (*to*-V), 3 implore (*to*-V),
4 challenge (*to*-V), 5 put off (V *-ing*), 6 avoid (V *-ing*), 7 encourage (*to*-V),
8 inspire (*to*-V), 9 proceed (*to*-V), 10 abhor (V *-ing*), 11 dislike (V *-ing*)

Exercise 8.C   1 to see (act), 2 to fly (act), 3 visiting (event), 4 going (event),
5 taking (event), 6 spending (event), 7 to rent (act), 8 being (event),
9 deciding (event)

Exercise 8.D   1 They expect us to come early, 2 I intend to leave tomorrow,
3 She claims to be innocent, 4 He convinced us to stay at home,
5 We chose him to represent us, 6 He longs for her to visit him,

7 They aspire to win, 8 Can you allow us to come in?
9 She's threatening to leave, 10 We swore to get revenge,
11 He taught us to write better

Exercise 8.E   1 being supported (duration), 2 turn (point), 3 run (point),
4 shout (point), 5 laughing (duration), 6 laughing and talking (duration),
7 stumbling (duration), 8 look (point), 9 pulling (duration),
10 standing (duration), 11 taking off (duration)

Chapter 9: Relative clauses

Exercise 9.A   1 that (subject), 2 that (object), 3 ø (object), 4 that (subject),
5 which (object), 6 who (subject), 7 whom (after-prep, fronted),
8 who (subject), 9 ø (after-prep, stranded)

Exercise 9.B   1 that grounds the computer (S–S), 2 that has a socket (S–S),
3 which connects to the power supply (O–S), 4 with which the monitor is
connected to the computer (O–O), 5 which is at the back of the computer
(O–S), 6 to which you can connect the keyboard (O–O), 7 that is used for
the mouse (O–S), 8 that the mouse connects to (S–O), 9 that connects the
mouse to the keyboard (S–S)

Exercise 9.C   1 which always surprises people (NR),
2 who was English (NR), 3 whom he never met (NR),
4 who couldn't leave the country (R),
5 most of which was suddenly in chaos (NR), 6 his mother could do (R),
7 which was a miracle in the circumstances (NR),
8 who had gone on a field trip (NR),
9 who risked their lives in those terrible times (R)

Exercise 9.D   1 where / in which, 2 that / ø, 3 who / that, 4 which,
5 that / which, 6 when / that, 7 who / that, 8 why / that, 9 that / which,
10 whose

Exercise 9.E   1 that she'd just finished (new), 2 she was taking at the
university (new), 3 that had apples instead of eyes (new), 4 that looked like a
banana (new), 5 which was made of white sticks (new), 6 she had painted
(given), 7 you get in lollipops (new), 8 who had a car (new), 9 I had (given)

Chapter 10: Direct and indirect speech

Exercise 10.A   The guard asked Jimmy what he was doing there. Jimmy
said that he worked in that building. The guard asked if he had any
identification. Jimmy said he had left it in his office. The guard asked where
his office was. Jimmy said it was on the fourth floor. He could show him. The
guard said he would go with him.

Exercise 10.B   1 was talking (summary), 2 was describing (summary), 3 was really going on (summary), 4 proposed (indirect), 5 said (direct), 6 say (direct), 7 are actually communicating (indirect), 8 claimed (indirect), 9 exclaimed (direct), 10 whispered (direct)

Exercise 10.C   (a) Why, this country isn't so different from home, Ethel, and these folks are just like us.
(b) use of *this, these, us*; present tenses; direct address form (*Ethel*); exclamation (*Why*)

Exercise 10.D   1 ND (Mr B wants), D (I am going), 2 ND, 3 D, 4 ND, 5 ND

Exercise 10.E   (a) And <u>she was like</u>, 'Oh I was just wonderin' if you wanted to see a movie or something. And <u>I was like</u>, 'Umm, well, really I can't tonight.' And she—and <u>I said</u>, 'Well I'll call you some other time.' And <u>she's like</u>, 'Yeah, right.' And <u>I'm like</u>, 'Don't start it.'

(b) What do I tell them? *ø* 'Well, I was sitting in this bar and this band's playing and I'm just sitting there.' And my dad's looking at me <u>like</u>, 'Yeah, right.' Eh, <u>mom goes</u>, ah, 'See anyone you know there?' *ø* 'No, thank god.'

INDEX